D1318181

DATE		

DISCARD

EUROPE AGAINST POVERTY

POVERTY

The European Poverty Programme 1975–80

Jane Dennett, Edward James,
Graham Room and Philippa Watson

Bedford Square Press | NCVO

First published 1982 by the
BEDFORD SQUARE PRESS of the
National Council for Voluntary Organisations
26 Bedford Square London WC1B 3HU

ISBN 0 7199 1074 9

Photoset by D. P. Media Limited, Hitchin, Hertfordshire
Printed and bound in England by
Robert Hartnoll Limited,
Bodmin, Cornwall

Contents

Note: *Respective contributions are indicated by authors' initials*

Preface

The European Poverty Programme was launched in the early 1970s as part of the attempt to give the European Community a 'human face'. For most of its five-year period, it comprised two main elements: cross-national studies on specific aspects of poverty and a wide range of locally-based action projects.

During the final two years of the Programme, two additional activities were initiated by the European Commission, the body responsible for the Programme. First, a newly established research unit at the University of Kent, ESPOIR (European Social Policy Observation, Information and Research), was engaged to undertake a systematic evaluation of the cross-national studies, the action projects and the Programme as a whole; secondly, a series of reports was commissioned dealing with the extent of poverty in the different member states and the effectiveness of national policies in alleviating and eliminating poverty. The ESPOIR report and these national reports have since been used by the European Commission in preparing its own final report to the Council of Ministers and European Parliament, submitted in December 1981. On the basis of the Commission's report, the Council and Parliament will decide what further action should be taken.

This book is a revised and condensed version of the ESPOIR report and provides a unique account of the first such cross-European Programme. It aims to bring the individual studies and projects involved in the Programme to the attention of a wider audience; to illuminate the different social, economic and political contexts of poverty within which these projects and studies were undertaken in the different member states; to assess the value of this sort of cross-national collaborative programme; and to point the way to more vigorous anti-poverty policies at the European level. Last but not least, it offers lessons in regard to the problems, both methodological and practical, of evaluating such a cross-national programme of action and research.

We wish to record our appreciation of the co-operation we have been given by the staff of the European Commission and the other participants in the Programme. The names and addresses of those responsible for the studies and projects are given at the end of this book, so that readers may make direct contact with them in search of further information.

It is far from certain that a further Poverty Programme will be launched, even though the need for a co-ordinated Community-wide attack on poverty is, if anything, even more pressing now than it was when the Programme was launched. The year 1981 saw the beginning of a major debate within the European Community over its expenditure priorities. It seems likely that social and regional policies will in the future be given greater weight. The entry of Greece and, in due course, of Spain and Portugal will add further to the pressures for more energetic social policies at the Community level, including measures to combat poverty in its various forms. The European Poverty Programme demonstrates the potential value of co-ordinated action to combat poverty throughout the Community; whether or not the various participants in these debates will attend to its lessons remains to be seen. We offer this book as a contribution to these deliberations.

Chapters 1 and 14 have previously appeared as articles in *International Social Work* and *Community Development Journal*. We are grateful to *International Social Work* and Oxford University Press for permission to reproduce them.

ESPOIR is now based at the University of Bath. Copies of the full ESPOIR report may be obtained from there or from the European Commission (DGV, 200 rue de la Loi, 1049 BRUSSELS, Belgium).

Jane Dennett is a research assistant at the University of Kent

Edward James is Reports Secretary to the Occupational Pensions Board

Graham Room is a lecturer in sociology at the University of Bath

Philippa Watson is a research worker at the Free University of Brussels

PART I

Introduction

1
From Paris to ESCAP[1]

Paris: October 1972. The leaders of the nations of the European Community and those about to join it have met to consider their future. After twenty years of immense economic achievement and an impressive expansion of social provisions, they look forward to even higher rates of growth and social progress. In their communiqué, the national leaders pledge themselves to channel more resources towards the social field, building a Community with a 'human face':

> The Heads of State or Heads of Government emphasised that they attached as much importance to vigorous action in the social field as to the achievement of Economic and Monetary Union . . . they invited the Institutions of the Community, after consulting labour and management, to draw up, between now and 1st January 1974, a programme of action providing for concrete measures and the corresponding resources.

The Social Action Programme (SAP) had been conceived.

As the politicians and their entourages dispersed, a score of mothers from poor families were taking their children to the pre-school run by Aide à Toute Détresse at Noisy-le-Grand, on the outskirts of the city, where Abbé Pierre's encampment for the homeless had recently stood. Other mothers were setting out to work from another suburb of another city, Croydon in London, knowing that there was nobody to care for their children when they came home from school, for they belonged to fatherless families. On the coast of Donegal, other women were getting ready for a less financially rewarding day's work, knitting heavy Aran sweaters for the middleman to collect from their homes. In Stuttgart, dozens of vagrants were being put out from their public shelters with no homes, families or work to attend to that day. The common thread that was to link their lives was a proposal that appeared in the programme commissioned that day by the national leaders: 'to implement in co-operation with the Member States specific measures to combat poverty by drawing up pilot schemes'.[2]

(1.1)   GENESIS

Several groups, notably Aide à Toute Détresse, had long been trying to interest the European Commission in anti-poverty projects, but the successful initiative for the European Programme of Pilot Schemes to Combat Poverty came from the Irish government, who gave it its cumbersome title. Soon after joining the Community, Ireland had elected a Fine Gael-Labour coalition government to succeed sixteen years of Fianna Fáil rule. In Dublin a new social policy was being put together at the same time that the Social Action Programme was being drawn up in Brussels. The programme of pilot schemes proposed from the Labour Party looked promising as a timely and dramatic gesture. It seemed to be easy to launch, relatively cheap and could demonstrate a commitment to fighting poverty in general, without tying the coalition to any line of policy in particular.[3]

The government's sincerity was not in question, but it takes more time to gather political support for specific long-term policies than it does to launch an unspecified range of experimental schemes. As one of the programme's originators put it:

> The whole programme was seen both as in initiative and also as a form of holding operation – one that kept doors open, kept subjects under discussion, and that would enable progress to be made as feasible.

These words would have been equally appropriate for the programme emerging at European level.

The Irish Programme was conceived with the possibilities of a wider European enterprise in mind. The proposal had much of the same appeal for the European Commission as it had for the Irish. It could show the 'human face' of Europe without specific policy commitments and within budgetary limits acceptable to the Council of Ministers. At the same time it was a foot in the door, a precedent for Commission activity in this field which might lead to a more ambitious anti-poverty policy. The entire SAP was part of a long institutional tussle between the Commission (the European bureaucracy) and the Council of Ministers (representing the member governments) to develop a stronger social policy. Hitherto the Commission's progress had been limited; a break-through seemed to be imminent.

By October 1973 the Irish proposals had found their way into the first draft of the SAP:

> Quite apart from the measures proposed in this programme to deal with particular aspects and causes of poverty, the Commission recognises

that there will still remain problems of *chronic poverty* which are unacceptable in an advanced society. There is in the Community a neglected minority of chronically poor, such as the 'unemployable' and their families, families on exceptionally low incomes or fatherless families. Because they are unable in many cases to help themselves or to respond to the help being offered to them, these groups find themselves trapped in an almost inescapable cycle of poverty. The rehabilitation of these people and their families is primarily the responsibility of the Member States. However, the Commission believes that it can help the Member States to identify the problems and methods of solution through pilot studies and experiments involving, among others, social workers, psychiatrists and vocational guidance experts.[4]

Both Ireland and the Commission at this stage saw the pilot schemes as tackling a residual problem of 'hard-core' poverty while other measures attacked the broader issues of economic and social welfare. However, by the following year the Irish Advisory Committee on Pilot Schemes to Combat Poverty was seeing itself in a more pioneering role, not a mopping up operation at the rear of the great social advance but more a spearhead for social change:

> It is fundamental to the philosophy of the programme that poverty in Irish society should be recognised as largely a result of inequality and its eventual elimination will involve long-term structural reform. Such reform must require the redistribution of resources and power in society, implying basic changes in the socio-economic and political systems.
>
> It is necessary to emphasise that poverty itself cannot be eliminated by a small number of experimental schemes. Each pilot scheme will be implemented because of its potential for bringing about change either in structures, services or attitudes. The programme as a whole is to be seen as part of the overall social policy of the country and the EEC.[5]

In time, the Commission's statements were to adhere more to the Irish line, partly due to the arrival of the new British and Irish staff but also because its thinking on poverty had had more time to evolve. In late 1973 this was still new territory for the bureaucracy.

(1.2) GESTATION

In January 1974 a resolution of the Council of Ministers expressed 'the political will to adopt the measures necessary' to carry out nine priority actions from the SAP, including the programme of pilot schemes.

The Commission had less than a year to present specific proposals, had no experience with anti-poverty projects and with the current pressure on the size of the bureaucracy (an internal review in 1973 had proposed to cut the Social Affairs Directorate-General)[6] had little possibility of bringing in outside expertise on a full-time basis. A working party of ten consultants was, however, assembled and during the first half of the year helped draw up a consultative document with fifteen 'illustrative' projects.[7] This was approved at the Commission's first 'Action Against Poverty' seminar in Brussels in June, bringing together sixty experts (including one unemployed miner) from government and non-government agencies.

The first objective set out in the paper was 'a balanced range of approaches'. For this a four-fold typology was developed: area-based community action projects, projects for special categories of poor people, 'specific interventions' for poor people and 'improving service delivery and organisation'. The Commission later merged the last two under the title 'improving social services'. The paper did not suggest an ideal mix.

The second objective was a strong research component in each project 'that permits a clear evaluation of its operation and enables conclusions to be drawn from its experience'. Considering the difficulties experienced in America and Britain in evaluating social programmes, this seems a rather naive aspiration.

The paper also called for basic research into the 'dimensions and nature of poverty', foreseeing the cross-national studies which later accompanied the action-research projects. As an example the paper outlined a comparative analysis of poverty and social security.

Objective three was regional balance. Although the Commission succeeded in involving all the Member States, not without difficulty, the hopes for an urban-rural balance were not realised. A balance of participating organisations was also recommended with an invitation to the non-government sector. This was well received at the seminar in which a prominent role had been allotted to the International Conference on Social Welfare.

A page was given over to 'Comparability of Projects'. This envisaged a degree of cohesion which the programme never achieved. It was chastening for the ESPOIR evaluators (see p. 11), who reported on the programme in 1980 to see most of their recommendations already set out in 1974. The 1974 text speaks of the exchange of ideas, applicability of experience across frontiers, matching comparable projects in different countries and even gives a sample cross-national welfare rights project similar to that proposed in 1980 by a group of German and UK projects.

In conclusion, the paper presented four criteria for selecting schemes: innovation; participation of 'the population concerned'; 'future potential' (that is experience which could be generalised, assimilated into the structures of services and guide future policy); and finally:

> Every project must be planned so as to provide for regular reporting, analysis and evaluation. This presupposes a clear definition of objectives, means and methods. Arrangements should be made with both governmental and non-governmental organisations of local, national and Community level to ensure collection and dissemination of the findings and to promote discussion of their relevance for policy.

Whatever the Commission's other failures they were not failures of imagination.

(1.3) BIRTH

A proposed administrative and financial structure for the programme was submitted to the Council in January 1975, but no Council Decision was taken until 22 July. There were two difficulties: one constitutional and the other political.

The Treaty of Rome requires the Commission to undertake studies in the social field (Article 118) and there is a long history of such research. In 1975 the Commission merely sent a 'communication' on the programme to the Council, implying that specific authorisation was unnecessary. The Council demurred, seeing the programme as an activity not provided for in the Treaty and requiring sanction under the exceptional clause (Article 235). Action under this clause requires the unanimous consent of the Council. The Commission's legal service was still contesting the Council's interpretation in 1980, but in 1975 the Commission finally compromised by seeking Council consent 'at the request of the Parliament'. The European Parliament, while warmly supporting the programme, had urged that it should be enshrined in 'a stronger legal form'.

The political problem arose from the programme's ill-fortune in being conceived just before the oil crisis. The message of the October 1973 guide-lines for the SAP had been that economic growth was no longer enough. The growth ran out that very week in the sands of Sinai.

The social policy envisaged by the Community in 1973 had been to fill in gaps as social legislation progressed in the Member States, 'setting minimum standards capable of being regularly improved'. Proposals to extend social security coverage and link benefits to an 'increasing standard of living' seemed reasonable at the time; within two years they were considered too unrealistic for detailed propositions to be submitted to the Council. Against this background the pilot schemes, once seen as a non-contentious mopping up of hardcore poverty, now found themselves in the firing line, not leading the advance but fighting a rearguard action.

It is more surprising that the Council still supported the pilot schemes in January 1974 than that it had grown sceptical by 1975. Germany in particular wanted to set an example of retrenchment. In the 1974 resolution the Council had committed itself to some form of programme, but on German insistence this was now limited to two years.

The text of the Council Decision includes a definition of poverty with a clear line of descent from Professor Townsend:

- persons beset by poverty: individuals or families whose resources are so small as to exclude them from the minimum acceptable way of life of the Member State in which they live.
- resources: goods, cash income, plus services from public and private sources.

Only three criteria for the choice of schemes appeared in the decision: that projects be 'planned and carried out as far as possible with the participation of those concerned' (echoes of 'maximum feasible participation' in the American War on Poverty); that they 'test out new methods to help the poor'; and that they were relevant to more than one Member State. Provision was also made for studies 'to improve understanding of the nature, causes, scope and mechanics of poverty in the Community'.

The decision set out only the bare bones of the programme. It left the choice of projects to the Commission, which in theory could have imposed further criteria or specified certain major themes. In 1976 the Commission attempted an action programme 'From Education to Working Life',[8] on these lines. Pressure of events in 1975 made such a course difficult for the Commission with the anti-poverty programme. Firstly, the Member States insisted that they alone could nominate projects, apart from cross-national studies. Secondly, the 2.5 million units of account agreed for the first year had to be committed by the end of 1975. This did not permit lengthy negotiations on submissions; rather there was a problem that the money would be unspent, leaving the programme to exist in name alone.[9] In the circumstances the Commission gave priority to getting responses from all the Member States and signing contracts before the deadline.[10] In the Commission's own words, looking back from 1979:

> Over the first two years of its life the urgent problems for the programme were birth and survival . . . the Commission had to get into business quickly in a new field, translating the political will of the Community into rapid and effective practical activity. . . . The Commission's foremost concern now must be to weld together a coherent programme that is much more than a set of separate projects with a certain element of common funding.[11]

Behind these brave words is the recognition that the programme might not unfairly be described as a hotch-potch.

As in the Social Fund, support for 'schemes' was shared 50-50 between the Commission and national sources. Matching funds did not have to be provided by governments, although almost all were. There was no restriction on the types of organisation to be supported and a wide range of non-government agencies participated. The cross-national studies, as we have noted, could be financed 100 per cent by the Commission and did not depend on a submission from Member States.

The system of accountability to national governments also mirrored the Social Fund, with an advisory group of representatives of the nine governments and the two sides of industry plus seven independent experts. The group had no formal constitution to emphasise the impermanence of the programme. It was to be consulted 'on all matters of importance', which in practice meant all but the most minor decisions. Its main function has always been to comment on Commission proposals – in effect legitimating them. Its only major contribution to Commission policy was the eight-nation study on poverty, mentioned later in this chapter.

(1.4) SURVIVAL

The first twenty-one schemes and studies were approved by the
Commission in November 1975 and contracts were signed the following month, just in time to save the 1975 budgetary allocation. The
twenty-one contracts covered about sixty separate actions including
those among the groups at Noisy-le-Grand, Croydon, West Donegal
and Stuttgart mentioned in our opening paragraph.

The programme had only a two-year expectation of life, but it
developed its own will to survive. Thanks in part to pressure from the
German projects on their own government a Commission proposal to
extend the programme was agreed by the Council in December 1977.
Approval came very much at the eleventh hour; for the first week in
December 1977 the programme was operating without any legal
basis. The Commission had tried to abolish the time limit on the
programme entirely, but again the Council handed out only an
instalment of life, to November 1980. The Commission was, however, able to launch a few more action projects, in Naples, Belfast,
London and Bavaria, and four more cross-national studies. There was
also enough money to commission eight national reports on poverty
and policies to combat it. Similar reports had been requested from the
national governments for the June 1974 seminar, but as the governments had been given only three months to prepare them and no extra
funds, the results were naturally rather summary. This time a research
team funded 100 per cent by the Commission was set up in each
country (although Luxembourg shared a team with Belgium), with
almost two years to complete its task.

The price of survival and growth was an evaluation report – 'as soon
as the Programme has been completed and not later than 30 June
1981 the Commission shall submit a report giving an assessment of
the results obtained'. Since the Commission has no internal evaluation unit and there were only five administrative staff of all grades
allocated to the programme (only one of whom was exclusively
engaged on it), there was no alternative but to contract out the work.
A similar arrangement had already been made by the Research and
Education Directorate-General for the pilot schemes on Education to
Working Life.

The research group was brought together specifically for the evaluation. Named ESPOIR (European Social Policy Observation, Information and Research), it had five members with its head office at the

University of Kent in Canterbury, UK. Although based at the university, it was an independent non-profit organisation financed entirely by contracts.

The Commission had been thinking about evaluation since before the start of the programme, as evidenced by the 1974 Working Party Report. A consultation at Illinois in April 1975 had been on this theme. An attempt was made in 1976–77 to use the independent experts on the Advisory Group as an evaluation team. Each expert visited several projects and the reports were submitted to the second Action Against Poverty seminar at Chantilly in September 1977. This was the programme's first general meeting of project leaders. The exercise gave several experts their first direct contact with projects and the project leaders seemed appreciative. For many it was their first 'European' visitor. As an evaluation exercise it was not very highly rated, and the group decided not to repeat it.

The activity of the ESPOIR team in 1979–80 inevitably increased contact between projects. The team visited almost every project and all the parent organisations, as well as providing the documentation for two project workers' meetings in Brussels and the third Action Against Poverty seminar at Brussels in April 1980. It also held its own colloquium for study leaders in Luxembourg in July 1980.

The strongest manifestation of the European dimension was, para-doxically, promoted by the imminent demise of the programme. Towards the end of 1979 the fourteen British projects came together spontaneously to support the Commission's proposals to the Council for an 'interim programme' for the years 1981–2, i.e. to cover the interim before the hoped-for Council Decision based on the 1981 evaluation report could be implemented.

Representatives of several Irish and Continental projects were invited to the British meeting, out of which sprang ESCAP (European Social and Community Action Programme). ESCAP held several meetings in the course of 1980, including an exhibition and press conference at Strasbourg during the European Parliament's debate on the interim programme. In June 1980, however, the Council turned down the proposition.

At the time of writing, therefore, we are uncertain whether this brief history is a progress report or an obituary. We have set it out to explain how the European Programme came to be as it was, which in turn explains some of the difficulties in evaluating it and the limitations on what can be learnt from the experiment. The history is essential to an understanding of how far the programme met its objectives and our recommendations on future Community policies in combating poverty.

Notes

1 Written by Edward James.

2 Social Action Programme, Bulletin of the European Communities Supplement 2/74.

3 The Labour Party's interest in pilot schemes dates from the Kilkenny Conference on poverty in 1971 at which was presented Séamus O'Cinnéide's paper which estimated that over 25 per cent of the Irish population was in poverty. The whole 'rediscovery of poverty' and the enthusiasm for pilot schemes was of course part of a movement which had already run through most of the other nations of the English speaking world, starting with Ford Foundation's work in the 'grey areas' of several US cities in the early 1960s.

4 Social Action Programme, Bulletin of the European Communities Supplement 4/73.

5 Statement reproduced in 'Combat Poverty, an introduction to the workings of the National Committee on Pilot Schemes to Combat Poverty', May 1975.

6 For an analysis of the Commission's internal staffing problems in 1973 see H. Michelmann, *Organisational Effectiveness in a Multinational Bureaucracy*, Saxon House, 1976.

7 The working party consisted of Mr Brown (Ireland) who had the greatest claim to being the originator of the Programme, Dr Friis (Denmark), Mr Lenze (Germany), Mr Leblanc (Belgium), Mme Laureáut (France), Prof Schaber (Luxembourg), Mr van Ijzeren (Netherlands), Mr Sinfield (UK), Mme de Vos van Steenwijk (Independent, ATD) and Mr d'Acunto (Italy), chaired by Mr Crijns of the Commission.

8 This was certainly the opinion of a group of veterans of the US War on Poverty who discussed the issue at a small seminar at the University of Illinois convened by one of the Commission officials in April 1975: 'Do not say the programs will be "evaluated". Rather say their impact will be documented, their distinctive approaches will be described and disseminated, and the positive results will be reported. Also, new insights about barriers to reducing poverty will be reported and explained.'

9 Spending the allocated funds is a serious problem in all the Commission's main financial intervention programmes apart from agricultural

price support. In 1976–7–8 the Agriculture Guidance Fund, the Social Fund and the Regional Fund each spent less than 50 per cent of the allocation.

[10] This compares with the War on Poverty approach in the USA which began as a free-for-all of local initiatives and was progressively brought under tight guidelines, preference being given to schemes conforming to models put out from Washington, derogatively known as 'canned programmes'. (E. James, *America Against Poverty*, Routledge and Kegan Paul, 1970)

The Irish Programme attempted a more considered approach, spending much of its first two years in recruiting its own corps of community workers and research officers and studying which districts in the Republic warranted an intervention. The organisation was soon under pressure to spend its funds more quickly and produce results. By 1978 the main emphasis had switched to grant aiding other bodies resulting in rapid expansion of activities to the detriment of any clear design.

[11] 'Europe Against Poverty, Second Report of the European Programme of Pilot Schemes and Studies to Combat Poverty', Commission of the European Communities, Brussels 17.10.79, p. 114.

2
The Approach to Evaluation[1]

(2.1) INTRODUCTION

Within the European Community's programme of pilot schemes and studies to combat poverty, the ESPOIR unit was charged with undertaking 'an evaluation of the individual projects and studies and of the programme as a whole'.[2] Although the very idea of a 'pilot' programme suggested that the results would be evaluated, our evaluation exercise was compressed into the final two years of the programme.

Evaluation is a form of research. It is also, however, a form of action – an intrusion into the existing pattern of relationships among the various participants in the programme. The theoretical principles on which it is based, the obstacles it faces and the methods it demands must be understood as those which arise in a process of action-research. These are the issues to which this chapter is addressed.

(2.2) THEORETICAL FOUNDATIONS

The evaluation of social policies has come into prominence during the last decade in particular, especially in the USA. There is a burgeoning literature and a growing number of social evaluation agencies.

The dominant approach in this literature relies on policy-makers specifying their objectives in operational terms and making clear the costs they attach to inputs and side-effects. It also relies on those policy-makers sticking resolutely to their objectives, rather than changing direction in mid-stream. Much of the evaluation literature focuses on the problems which arise when these conditions are not met.

Here is an approach which might be termed *evaluation-from-above-and-outside*. The evaluator claims a privileged and neutral language and vantage point which can largely disregard the perceptions held by the actors involved. Observable outcomes are the principal datum, rather than the historical and subjectively meaningful processes of action which lead to those outcomes.

Nevertheless, those who have undertaken the evaluation of action-research programmes elsewhere have pointed to the inappropriateness of this approach. For example, the goals pursued tend to change over time, as projects are reoriented to cope with changing situations and to take account of what has been learnt. So too, goals tend continually to be contested by the various actors involved, so that the evaluation report must make clear from whose standpoint the evaluation is being made.[3]

Within the ranks of the contributors to the literature on evaluation, a second approach is also however in evidence which is more attuned to these difficulties. Here evaluation is akin to the activity of the historian. It deals with the diverse perceptions, goals and actions of the various actors involved; it looks at processes of meaningful action rather than merely at outcomes; it recognises the exploratory character of action-research and aims to provide an interpretive history of that exploration; and instead of claiming some privileged and neutral vantage point, the evaluator is involved in a continuing conversation and dialogue with the actors themselves.

Here the evaluator's dependence upon the actors involved is explicitly recognised and affirmed as a normal feature of social policy evaluation. In effect, evaluation becomes a process of *collective self-evaluation* by those actors themselves, with the evaluator acting as a resource and facilitating agent. Instead of evaluation from above and outside, we have *evaluation from below and within*.

This second approach or paradigm was also more suited than its rival to two further features of our evaluation exercise. First, the Poverty Programme was conceived and launched in the early 1970s, in a context of continuing economic growth. Today, in contrast, recession and unemployment are the context for social policy priorities. Should our evaluation be carried out with respect to the goals of today or those of the early 1970s? The dominant paradigm in the evaluation literature makes the *original* goals the criteria for evaluation. Only in this way, it is held, can policies be subjected to scientific evaluation. In consequence, however, these evaluation reports often suffer from being out of date and of little relevance to the policy-makers who receive them. In contrast, if evaluation is seen as the writing of interpretive history, it is today's concerns that provide the criteria for interpreting and evaluating the experience of the past; the past informs the policy-maker in his present situation as he seeks to design the future. In our evaluation we have attended, therefore, not only to the original goals but also to the emerging priorities of the 1980s. So too, by recording the changing goals of individual projects we try to reveal how they have responded to their changing political context and have, indeed, themselves attempted creatively to shape this wider policy agenda.

Secondly, an evaluation must involve judgements of success and failure. Yet many of these judgements cannot finally be made until we know the responses of the European Commission and the national governments to the programme. The impact of the projects' activities will depend in part on national and Community decisions. Evaluation does not produce closed, definitive judgements; instead, it poses questions for policy-makers, the answers to which affect how successful or otherwise the programme can be judged to have been.

Theoretical considerations and the experience of our predecessors encouraged us therefore to promote a process of collective self-evaluation among the various participants in the programme. This did not preclude criticism of the work which had been undertaken by the action projects and the studies. Nor did it give participants in the programme a right to veto any part of the evaluation report which they did not like. Nor, finally, did it mean that ESPOIR was reduced to a largely reactive role, assembling its report out of parts provided by the projects and in line with a blueprint which they dictated. What it did mean was that ESPOIR's report would develop through a process of continuing consultation with the projects, individually and collectively, and that the authoritativeness of the report would spring not only from ESPOIR's status as the Commission's official evaluator, but also from the validation which the projects and studies were prepared to grant the report as an authentic account and synthesis of their experiences and findings.

(2.3)   EXTERNAL EVALUATION AND INTERNAL SELF-EVALUATION

The individual action projects have themselves carried out internal self-evaluation (albeit with varying degrees of rigour) in order to illuminate the continuing process of action. These endeavours have included methods for assessing particular services which projects have developed (e.g. day centres) and particular techniques (e.g. group-work). They involve considerations not only of technical effectiveness, but also of the extent to which the poor themselves have participated and developed autonomous and self-sustaining forms of mutual aid and collective action. They include seminars, as part of training programmes for project staff; but they also include exercises in cost-benefit analysis of the innovations which have been developed, for presentation to government and other funding agencies. They include technical reports which take up major methodological and theoretical questions in the practical application of the social sciences; they also, however, include films which enable a much wider audience to gain an appreciation of the work done.

There have, moreover, been various forms of inter-project evaluation in different parts of the European Programme. In the United Kingdom, the Area Resource Centres have collaborated in a joint evaluation exercise funded by the programme sponsors, as also have the Family Day Centres. The Irish projects were involved in a similar form of collaboration from the start. The French government has sponsored various inter-project meetings concerned with evaluation. The German projects have met quarterly since 1977 in Frankfurt (although in their case, the original impetus for these meetings was a *political* crisis, the impending termination of the European Programme).

The ESPOIR evaluation has drawn heavily upon the products of this internal and inter-project evaluation. At the same time, as outsiders we have sought critically to confront the projects with the strategies, experiences and findings of projects elsewhere in the programme (and indeed outside it), in order to provoke the project workers into more critical self-reflection and self-justification, and in order to expose the different contexts and constraints which they variously faced and the different assumptions with which they operated.

What, then, were the questions upon which our evaluation of the individual projects has concentrated? The Council Decision required that the action projects should test and develop new methods for combating poverty, in co-operation with the disadvantaged themselves and in ways which were of potential interest to the Community as a whole. In Part II of this report, where we assess the individual projects, we have therefore tended to focus upon three principal issues:

   (i) the context within which the project was established and the 'problem' which it was set up to address;

  (ii) the core strategy it has developed and the obstacles it has encountered;

 (iii) its significance as a pilot project within the European Programme:

     (a) in successfully pioneering innovations which can engage longer-term support from the disadvantaged themselves and from non-Community funders;

     (b) in demonstrating the relevance of these strategies to projects elsewhere in the Community, including those working in very different contexts and facing very different obstacles, etc.;

     (c) in producing 'concrete information' of relevance to wider policy-making at national and European levels.

This has not, however, meant that our reports on the individual projects follow precisely the same format; on the contrary, the organisation of these reports has often had to be adapted in order to highlight the distinctive ways in which different projects work including, for example, the relationship which they have forged between action and research. Finally, we have sought to emphasise that the different goals of the various actors involved in the work of a project mean that the evaluation made of the project's work is inevitably contentious.

(2.4)   OBSTACLES TO THE EVALUATION EXERCISE

From the start, the ESPOIR team worked under certain constraints which prevent our findings being as authoritative or definitive as we might have wished. These constraints arose in part from the nature of the programme itself and in part from the characteristics of the evaluation exercise with which we were charged.

(2.4.1)   The Questions were Ill-defined

The ESPOIR contract required the evaluation report to deal with 'the individual schemes (i.e. action-research projects) and studies and the programme as a whole'.[4] The Council Decision of July 1975 implied certain criteria for evaluation of the programme and its elements. Nevertheless, from the start it was difficult to decide more specifically the questions to be raised and the methods by which these questions might be answered.

No questions can be asked in a void: they must be oriented to some goal or purpose. For the internal evaluators working within an individual project the goal is clear: to illuminate the continuing process of action. In contrast, at the level of the programme as a whole, there has been no well-defined process of action by reference to which our questions could be selected. On the one hand, it was only during the final year of the programme that the various project and study workers began, haltingly, to work together, at least in working to forge a follow-up programme. On the other hand, neither the Commission nor the Council has as yet indicated how the present programme of pilot schemes and studies might lead on to a coherent European policy to combat poverty.[5]

(2.4.2)   The Evaluation Exercise was launched too late and would finish too early

The evaluation exercise began later than half-way through the programme.[6] Our late entry has meant that our evaluation has had to be largely retrospective and has had to rely on the evaluation, monitoring and research which had already been carried out by those in the projects, the studies and the Commission. The evaluation methodology and our working relationships with the projects have had, moreover, to be developed at the same time as we collected the data upon which our report is based.

The evaluation exercise was to be completed by November 1980, the same time as the individual projects and studies themselves terminated. Only in the case of the cross-national studies which were launched in 1975 and the Danish project (which ended prematurely) would it be possible for ESPOIR to make a retrospective assessment of their achievements and impact. The other cross-national studies would be producing their detailed results too late for consideration in our report save as an afterthought. Similarly, not until very late in the programme would some of the activities which the action projects launched reach maturity and the form in which they might survive under alternative sponsorship be decided; the ESPOIR report had therefore necessarily to focus on the distinctive strategies which the individual projects developed rather than upon their lasting impact. However, by indicating what was the potential value of each element in the present programme the ESPOIR report might, we hoped, help to inform the decision over how the fruits of the programme could be harvested and provide the seed corn for future programmes.

(2.4.3)   The Vacuum of Communication

A major question in the evaluation of the individual pilot projects is the relevance of their innovatory strategies to projects elsewhere. The programme itself provides the most obvious testing ground on which to assess this potential relevance. However, in order for this assessment to be at all rigorous, at least two conditions should have held. First, the programme should have been coherently designed, with a systematic selection of projects having comparable target groups and/or working methods and/or organisational structures and/or socio-economic environments. Secondly, and at least as important, there should have been extensive cross-fertilisation and exchange of experiences among these projects, with strategies developed in one being applied and adapted elsewhere. In this way, the various projects within the European Programme could have collectively assessed the mutual relevance of the methods and strategies which they have individually developed. Unfortunately, however, these two conditions have held to only a very limited extent and our assessment of the more general relevance of any given strategy often cannot therefore be more than impressionistic.

We wanted also to assess the more general implications of the studies' and the action-research projects' work, first as contributions to an improved understanding of poverty and, secondly, in terms of the recommendations for policy which follow from their findings. Again, however, in order to elucidate these implications at all rigorously it would have been necessary for the various participants in the programme to have been drawn together at a European level, not only in plenary discussions but also in working groups on specific topics. It would have been necessary for them to consult with local, national and European policy-makers and with experts familiar with a broader range of research findings. In practice, however, few such encounters have occurred; our assessment of these more general implications of the studies' and projects' work is again, therefore, inevitably tentative.

It is because of this partial vacuum of communication within the programme that we were ourselves eager to assist in the various cross-programme contacts which did take place during 1979–80 – those organised by the Commission and others organised by programme participants. We also sponsored a variety of meetings ourselves and attempted to facilitate communication among the various participants in the programme. This was costly on our resources; it tended to involve us in *animation* of the programme rather than merely in detached analysis; but such activities were a necessary pre-condition for any systematic evaluation of the programme as a whole.

(2.4.4)   ESPOIR's Political and Scientific Legitimacy was Fragile

ESPOIR was set up under the auspices of the European Commission but without prior consultation with the action-research projects and the cross-national studies which were to be evaluated. Initially, at least, we were viewed by many of the programme participants with caution or even suspicion: partly because the ESPOIR team had yet to establish their scientific credibility as evaluators; partly because the ESPOIR evaluation might be in rivalry with existing evaluation systems within the programme; partly because of uncertainties regarding the criteria and goals of the evaluation exercise and the use to which its fruits would be put;[7] and partly because of the extra workload (in terms of the preparation of reports etc.) which the evaluation exercise might impose upon them. For reasons already given it was vital for us to overcome this caution and to enlist the active co-operation of all the projects.

From the start, therefore, the evaluation exercise was complicated by the *diplomatic* task which had to be undertaken simultaneously. Stated negatively, this consisted in allaying the fears of some projects and their 'internal' evaluators; more positively, it consisted in demonstrating that the ESPOIR exercise might be useful not merely to the Commission but also to the projects themselves.[8]

(2.5)   PROGRESS OF THE EVALUATION EXERCISE

Over the period of the evaluation exercise we used a variety of methods – and avoided others – to obtain the data we needed to produce this report. These methods were chosen by reference not only to the questions we had selected but also in view of the obstacles which we faced.

(i) Before the start of our work we had drafted a schema for evaluation of the individual action projects. One of the first decisions we faced was the use to which this should be put. The reports which projects had previously been sending to the Commission varied greatly in their form and detail. If a common schema were circulated to all projects it could result in more standardised reports being sent to ESPOIR, assisting our efforts to compare projects' work. Nevertheless, for several related reasons we decided against this course of action.

Early in the European Programme, action projects had been provided with a schema for reporting. This claimed to provide 'a framework for reporting rather than a rigid questionnaire', so that 'creative and descriptive reports' would be encouraged. In the event, however, the projects had used this schema to only a limited and decreasing extent. We suspected that this under-utilisation would have occurred with any standard schema – including the new one we had drafted – because of the lack of opportunity which it gives projects to offer a creative account of the distinctive innovations they have individually pioneered. A great deal of the information sought by the new schema was in any case already being provided, but in formats distinctive to the various projects. To ask them to forsake their preferred frameworks and to adopt the common schema would have risked inhibiting them in their accounts; and might also have reduced their willingness to co-operate, because of the extra workload involved.

We therefore decided to use our own schema, not as a framework for reporting by the projects but simply as a checklist for the researchers in ESPOIR, as they visited and corresponded with the projects. In some cases, the schema was handed over, as a guide to the issues we hoped their reports would cover; in others, it served simply to alert the ESPOIR evaluator to particular gaps in existing, but otherwise adequate, reports. The schema also helped the different members of the ESPOIR team to co-ordinate their investigations and to ensure some uniformity in the compilation of their reports.

(ii) Two of the members of the ESPOIR team[9] had previously been involved in the programme and were therefore already familiar with much of the work being done. Nevertheless, we undertook an extensive series of visits to the projects and studies. Most of the projects readily furnished us with their research findings and some of them even modified their own research priorities in the light of our needs. Some projects have themselves commissioned external evaluation reports which they have made available to us.

In the case of the Danish project, which terminated prematurely, we sponsored a follow-up study of its impact by the former project leader.

(iii) On the basis of our visits and the documentation gathered we drafted our reports on the individual projects and studies which are included in Part II. As far as time has allowed, these reports were discussed in detail with the projects concerned — partly in order to ensure their factual accuracy, but also to provoke collaborative reflection on the interpretations which the reports contain.

Nevertheless, the relationship which we built up with project workers was always somewhat ambivalent: we were in one sense collaborators but, at the same time, the ESPOIR report offered interpretations and judgements of projects' work which could be fateful for their futures.

(iv) We presented papers at various meetings of project workers — some organised by the Commission, others by the projects and some, finally, by ourselves. Some of these meetings were concerned specifically with evaluation of activities undertaken in the present programme. Others were concerned more with the planning of possible future activities, but these also involved participants in assessing, if only implicitly, the work carried out so far.

(2.6) AN EVALUATION OF EVALUATION

An evaluation exercise involves continuous reflection upon the appropriateness of the questions which are being asked and the reliability of the information which is being gathered. It also, however, prompts reflection upon itself — a retrospective evaluation of the evaluation exercise.

We set out to promote a process of 'collective self-evaluation', involving a 'conversation' among all the participants in the European Programme. This attempt, while it appeared theoretically and methodologically sound, was also ambitious. The obstacles which it faced were formidable. In the event it was at best a partial success, at worst a mere aspiration. Nevertheless, precisely because we pursued this ambitious goal, the evaluation exercise was itself a process of learning and of action-research; it offers lessons on which the evaluation systems to be used in future poverty programmes may usefully build.

(i) The ESPOIR team intruded upon existing 'conversations' already going on in different parts of the programme: in other words, various groups of projects were already engaged in forms of collective self-evaluation, involving the various project workers and, very often, some central facilitator. As seen earlier in this chapter, ESPOIR was established without preparatory consultation with these existing evaluation networks, but we were heavily dependent upon their co-operation for the production of our own report. They provided us with models of evaluation strategies from which we were able to learn valuable lessons, they furnished us with data and they acted as forums in which we could discuss our own preliminary findings.

The first question which is, therefore, posed by the programme concerns the relationship which should obtain between the various evaluation systems in future programmes. It may be, for example, that instead of carrying out the evaluation of the programme as a whole by means of a central but relatively isolated agency, what is needed is a decentralised network of researchers and evaluators, albeit with some central facilitating agency. It might be possible to arrange for rotating membership of this central agency, so that researchers within individual projects are able to spend periods collaborating with the central evaluation team.

(ii) The programme demonstrates that the achievements of individual projects will be stunted if they work in isolation. For their *full* value to be realised there must be intense and sustained collaboration among them, so that they can exchange ideas and experiences. What therefore is needed is an effective system of communication among the various participants in future programmes, keeping them in touch with each other but also with a variety of outside specialists and consultants, upon whose skills they may wish from time to time to draw.

As has been repeatedly argued in this chapter, such a system of communication is also a pre-condition for a thorough evaluation of any programme as a whole. It provides the evaluator with a forum in which he can confront the various participants collectively, rather than having to rely upon visits to them individually. It also allows him to bring into this forum independent experts capable of subjecting the work which is going on to still more critical scrutiny. Finally, a well-developed communications system enables the rapidly changing and diverse experiences of the various participants in the programme to be shared, adapted and disseminated, in ways which allow the evaluator to assess more precisely the conditions under which specific strategies are of value.[10]

(iii) There seem nevertheless to be certain inherent tensions between the idea of a 'conversation' and the task of evaluation. The goals of our evaluation exercise were defined in advance by the European Commission. The purpose of the conversation which we promoted was 'closed'; and, in so far as the Commission would be making judgements on the different projects, there was an incentive for them to concentrate upon emphasising their successes and achievements. In contrast, a 'conversation' properly involves mutually valuable communication among the various participants in the programme, serving their various interests: an 'open' system of communication whose goals are various and continually changing and which involves the participants in disclosing their difficulties and limitations, in an attempt to learn from each other.

It is hardly surprising, therefore, that projects are generally ambivalent towards external evaluators. To judge by the experience not only of ESPOIR but also of the external evaluators who have been concerned with particular groups of projects in the programme, the external evaluator is seen principally as an agent of political control and scrutiny acting in the interests of the funding bodies. Admittedly, such exercises in external evaluation generally offer opportunities for projects to exchange ideas and experiences and this provides a positive inducement for them to co-operate in the evaluation; indeed, the external evaluator will often in consequence present the exercise in this facilitative role. Nevertheless, it is only because of the monopoly in the valued means of inter-project communication which these external evaluators enjoy, by virtue of the resources (financial, manpower and information) at their disposal, that they are able to offer this inducement; and they do so at constant risk of creating resentment among project workers over the lack of communication channels under their own control.

This suggests that, although the evaluation of future programmes requires as a pre-condition an effective communications system, the two exercises cannot after all be wholly integrated. Instead, an 'open' communications system would need first to be established; this could then be used, *inter alia*, by anyone (the Commission, project workers, etc.) wishing to pose specific or 'closed' evaluation questions.

Nevertheless, these tensions between evaluation and communication are potentially creative. No conversation is devoid of criticism, conflict and divergent interests. What remains to be done, however, is to specify in more concrete terms how this creative tension between communication and evaluation can most fruitfully be managed in future Poverty Programmes.

Notes

[1] Written by Graham Room.
Over the last two years I have greatly benefited from discussions of methodology with S. Burgess (Craigmillar), L. Carrino (Giugliano), G. Cimino (Dublin), J. Cowan (London Voluntary Service Council), R. Lees and M. Mayo (UK Area Resource Centres), Phyllis Willmott (Institute of Community Studies) and various of the German project workers.

[2] ESPOIR contract of 22.12.78, Article 1.

[3] P. Marris and M. Rein, *Dilemmas of Social Reform*, Penguin, 1972.

[4] The Commission excluded from our remit the eight national reports on poverty and anti-poverty policies in the Member States. The initial remit for these reports was that they should provide background material to help in assessing the results of the action projects and the cross-national studies. In practice, however, the contact which the reporters have had with other elements of the programme (including ESPOIR) has been largely informal and has depended upon initiatives taken by the reporters and the project workers themselves.

[5] As emphasised by Edward James in Chapter 1, the programme was launched more as a symbolic expression of a broad European commitment than as a systematic prelude to a coherent policy.

[6] Indeed, not until 22.12.78 was the contract with ESPOIR signed, with the Commission expecting staff to be in post and starting work on 1.1.79.

[7] These uncertainties were of particular concern to those projects, such as the Irish, which feared that their domestic political support was insecure and could be further damaged by any criticisms which ESPOIR might make.

[8] Thus, for example, at the April 1980 seminar and elsewhere, projects have voiced the hope that ESPOIR would act as a communication system among the projects, rather than merely writing a report for the Commission.

[9] Edward James and Philippa Watson.

[10] As was emphasised earlier in this chapter, the specific objectives and strategies which action-research projects use tend continually to change, as circumstances change and lessons are learned. A well-developed communications system allows this process of continuous innovation to draw upon lessons developed elsewhere in the programme. For the evaluator, it means that although the projects may be shifting away from their original goals and blurring the original design of the programme as a whole, these shifts at the level of the individual project, precisely because they draw upon experiences throughout the programme, can reveal more (rather than less) systematically and rigorously the value and relevance of the different strategies which are being developed.

Part II

The Individual Projects and Studies

3
Benelux and Denmark[1]

(3.1) INTRODUCTION

Belgium, the Netherlands and Denmark each contributed one action project to the European Programme. All three are dealt with in this one chapter, but this is more for convenience than because of basic similarities among the projects or among the social, economic and political contexts in which they have been working.

In both the Netherlands and Denmark, poverty has been insignificant as an issue of public debate, certainly in comparison with Britain. It is hardly surprising, therefore, that in both countries the projects were very small; and indeed, in the Netherlands the project was sponsored by a French-based international organisation, Aide à Toute Détresse. The Belgian situation is less far removed from the British: not least, the deepening recession has exposed the similar weakness of the antiquated industrial structures of the two countries. The Belgian project, based in Brussels itself, has been a community action project using strategies similar to those which have been developed in Britain to tackle common problems of inner-city deprivation.

(3.2) THE MAROLLES PROJECT[2]

(3.2.1) Origins

The origins of the Marolles project go back to thirty years ago when a group of Christian Democrats decided to take steps to improve the living conditions of the area's inhabitants. However, the immediate roots of the current project spring from the setting up of the Marolles General Action Committee by Jacques van der Biest following the 'Battle of the Marolles' in 1969, which succeeded in obtaining the withdrawal of eviction notices served on the residents of the Marolles to clear the area for an extension of the Palais de Justice. These events showed that the survival of the area depended upon the solidarity of the inhabitants which in turn relied upon the fostering of a community spirit and a common identity. The MGAC determined to increase residents' involvement in the life of the area by creating grass-roots groups through the medium of which the people could express and realise their needs. More importantly still, the MGAC decided to encourage the participation of the Marolliens in administrative decisions which directly affected them.

(3.2.2) The Environment

The Marolles district is situated in the heart of Brussels and has a population of approximately 12,000. The general level of *economic activity* is low. About one third of the population is permanently unemployed and dependent upon a variety of welfare benefits. Another third is intermittently employed; when unemployed, this group derives support from unemployment benefits and 'moonlighting'. The rest of the Marolliens, mainly Belgian traders of long standing, are in regular employment. The *immigrant population*, whose right to enter and stay in Belgium depends upon their remaining economically active, is mainly Moroccan and Spanish. Although traditionally hostile to one another both groups live peacefully in the Marolles; being immigrants they have the common problem of integration into society.

(3.2.3) Problems of the Marolles

The inhabitants of the Marolles suffer from constant insecurity, because of the authorities' intention to redevelop the area. The MGAC believes that renovation is necessary in order to create a healthier and more comfortable environment for the residents; but any changes should be made in a manner designed to preserve the characteristics and life-style of the neighbourhood.

The Marolliens all suffer from *social exclusion* or *marginalisation*. This is due to lack of the education and training which are necessary to participate in the normal economic life of the city. Deprived of the opportunity to earn a decent living, the Marolliens are forced to live in sub-standard housing and are denied the right to enjoy the same quality of life as their fellow citizens. The marginalisation in turn affects their children. There is evidence of *transmitted deprivation* in the area due to the inability of children, because of the deprived environment, to follow normal schooling.

(3.2.4) The Project

The project has eight main programmes operating independently of one another, but co-ordinated by the MGAC. A research team from the Centre de Sociologie Urbaine et Rurale of the University of Louvain is responsible for research and evaluation.

The Marolles Development Association tries to create jobs in the area by setting up production units suitable for a workforce which is largely unstable, unaccustomed to fixed working hours and has little or no training. The Arabic-Islamic Information and Reception Centre (Caria) and the Belgo-Spanish Mutual Aid Association cater for the needs of the immigrant population, helping it to integrate into Belgian society whilst at the same time maintaining contact with the country and culture of origin. The Information Group circulates news and information about the area to residents. 'Symbol' attempts to cultivate a common sense of identity among the Marolliens. The Marolles Workshop is concerned with adapting the skills of deprived adolescents who have had poor schooling to the demands of modern urban society. The Marolles Legal Advice Centre provides advice and help to those with legal problems. The District Preservation Group is concerned with the physical environment.

Diverse though the activities of the project may be, they have a common aim: the elimination of poverty by self-help. The project encourages people to improve the quality of their lives. It does not impose a lifestyle, rather it provides the means by which the population can express and satisfy its own needs and requirements.

The novelty of the project lies in its reversal of the normal pattern of social work in inner-city areas. Instead of helping citizens to cope with the exigencies of modern urban life and to adapt their modus vivendi accordingly, the project aims at moulding the environment to suit the needs and values of the inhabitants. The project is trying to create a village atmosphere which would give the Marolles a certain amount of autonomy.

The project believes in equality of treatment for the poor and the non-poor in the provision of services and it believes that services should be provided on a non-categorical basis. Action should be encouraged and services provided on an integrated basis. This avoids the stigmatisation of the poor and leads to concerted action on the part of the entire population of a deprived area to improve their quality of life.

(3.2.5) Conclusions

The Marolles General Action Committee from its own experiences and from discussions with other members of the European Poverty Programme concludes that integrated or global, universal action is necessary to combat poverty. Secondly, the MGAC is of the opinion that action-research is necessary to overcome poverty. To determine the direction of the practical activities of a project, it is essential to determine the basic aims of the action and to subject these to constant assessment. Likewise, research on poverty is useless unless it takes cognisance of workers in it engaged in action.

Finally, the MGAC is firmly convinced that poverty within the European Economic Community can be overcome only by action on a European level. The project workers, through contacts with other action-research projects, have concluded that the problems they encounter in the Marolles are not peculiar to Brussels or Belgium but are, in fact, common to all inner-city communities. Consequently, they feel that there should be a Community solution to what is essentially a Community problem. This solution should be formulated on a European level and should result from a sharing of the ideas and experiences of all the Member States.

(3.3) COMMUNITY DEVELOPMENT WITH THE 'FOURTH WORLD' IN BREDA, THE NETHERLANDS[3]

This is one of six projects in the European Programme run by Aide à Toute Détresse (ATD). In Breda, a small town near the Belgian border, ATD is trying to gain recognition for the rights and needs of the 'Fourth World' or sub-proletariat (see Section 4.3) by the public authorities, fellow citizens and private institutions in order to enable the Fourth World to play a full part in the life of the community.

The project is operated by a team of workers living with the Fourth World. This has led to a heightened awareness and understanding by the project team of the problems of the target population and it has helped to increase the confidence of the Fourth World in the project team.

One of the primary objectives of the project is to enable the Fourth World to express its own identity and to determine its own lifestyle. The team has made strenuous efforts to encourage the Fourth World to take the initiative in determining the activities of the project.

These are varied and numerous, ranging from activities for specific groups of the population (children, old people) to activities for the Fourth World as a whole (Fourth World evenings, summer holidays on a farm). A monthly newspaper reports on these activities, encourages the further participation of the Fourth World and reflects their views.

The main achievement of the project has been to take a group of isolated families from the lowest levels of society in Breda and create among them not only a network of mutual aid and recreational activities but a sense of common identity. After a hesitant start the municipal authorities have responded to the project sufficiently to provide the area with a social centre and to increase expenditure on leisure facilities. To this extent the Fourth World are not isolated among themselves or totally excluded from the decision-making structure of their locality.

(3.4)   THE COPENHAGEN PROJECT[4]

Like the Stuttgart project, to be discussed in Chapter 5, the Danish project has been working with vagrants. The sponsors of the project have been the Institute of Applied Social Research and Kofoeds Skole, a private voluntary welfare organisation which has been concerned for the last half-century with this group of people.

The project set out to develop a three-stage programme for integrating vagrants into the community: a programme which would be applied to successive cohorts of about a dozen participants each. First, each cohort would be carefully selected from among the users of Kofoeds Skole's hostel facilities. Secondly, there would be a phase of community living with the project workers themselves in order to restore the vagrants' social confidence and competence. Thirdly, they would be assisted in relocating themselves in normal housing and jobs.

During the crucial three month co-living phase with the first cohort, the project workers lived communally with them: structuring their day and week in a way which could encourage their personal stabilisation and organisation of their time; joining in small ·group activities on an equal basis, with rotating tasks; and involving the clients themselves in decisions over the continuing development of the communal life. The project workers recorded significant improvements in patterns of participation in communal life by the former vagrants; the conventional relationship between social worker and client was progressively transformed from one of 'treatment' to one in which the professional workers were resources or tools, available to the men in their dealings with official agents; a co-operative furniture renovation business started which continued during the follow-up phase.

Nevertheless, it had proved impossible to find premises in Copenhagen itself for the crucial co-living phase; it had instead been located in a country house far from the city. In consequence, it was difficult for the project workers to keep contact with Kofoeds Skole and with the Institute which had been charged with evaluating the experiment and assessing its worthiness for continuing support by the sponsors. It also increased the difficulty of the transition to the follow-up phase, when the former vagrants were to be rehoused in Copenhagen.

By 1978, the commitment which Kofoeds Skole was able to offer the project had declined relative to other claims on its resources, and the project was prematurely terminated. Nevertheless, during the closing months of its life, it succeeded in securing flats in Copenhagen for all those vagrants who had participated; they were also less dependent upon social assistance, having been enabled to claim various pensions or to obtain employment.[5]

The Copenhagen project dealt with the same target group as the Stuttgart project, to be discussed in Chapter 5. The Stuttgart project has largely rejected the 'socio-pedagogic' focus upon 'vagrants' of the Copenhagen project and has instead focused upon remodelling the wider institutions which prevent, ameliorate or cause unemployment or homelessness more generally. However, this difference springs in part from the different institutional contexts in which the different projects were working: the Stuttgart project was set up as the 'research and development' arm of established agencies dealing with vagrants, whereas the Copenhagen project worked largely outside official and charitable agencies of this sort, including Kofoeds Skole. To this extent the two projects offer alternative and perhaps complementary, rather than contradictory, models for working with the single homeless who have descended into a life of vagrancy.

Notes

[1] Sections (3.1) and (3.4) have been written by Graham Room; Sections (3.2) and (3.3) by Philippa Watson.

[2] Philippa Watson acknowledges the assistance she has received in particular from Jacques van der Biest, leader of the Marolles project.

[3] Philippa Watson acknowledges the assistance of ATD Netherlands and the international ATD Federation in the preparation of this section.

[4] Graham Room is grateful to George Mortag, the former leader of the Danish project, for his help with an early draft of this section.

[5] A follow-up study conducted in 1980 suggested that these improvements had largely endured, as also had their reintegration into Danish society.

4
France[1]

(4.1) NATIONAL BACKGROUND

The booming metropolis from which the national leaders issued their 1972 Paris communiqué which launched the Social Action Programme was the main centre of growth for a nation experiencing the most hectic phase of economic expansion in its history. In the late 1960s the French growth rate had been the highest in the European Community and second only to Japan in the whole world. France had also recently experienced a rapid growth in population and was still in the throes of massive social changes, with big shifts of population between regions and occupations. The long-standing decline of the rural population had accelerated in the post-war period, while the larger towns, above all Paris, were faced with an influx of migrants which they had great difficulty in absorbing.

The projects selected by the French government for the European Programme of Pilot Schemes to Combat Poverty reflect the concerns of this period. Four projects were run by the private organisation, Aide à Toute Détresse (ATD), which originated in the shanty towns or *bidonvilles* which had mushroomed around Paris and other large towns in the early sixties. Although not primarily concerned with housing problems, all four projects dealt mainly with families living in emergency accommodation which has now replaced the bidonvilles. Three projects focused on pre-school activities with young children, two in the Parisian region and one on the Mediterranean coast, while the fourth was a more general community action venture in Reims, a manufacturing town in the North-East. Another set of projects was run by the federation of housing associations named PACT. These were at three centres, all in areas of relative or absolute decline: Roubaix, an old textile town on the Belgian border; Guémené, a decayed agricultural centre in Brittany; and Orange, a picturesque medieval town in the South. All three dealt with various aspects of the housing problem, which in these areas was principally a problem of decay and obsolescence. In contrast four projects launched late in the life of the programme as part of the Habitat and Vie Sociale Programme (HVS) were sited in areas of new housing put up in the previous ten years at Strasbourg, Metz, Dieppe and Le Havre respectively. These were in the so-called *grands ensembles*, large estates of subsidised dwellings, which are now plagued by a variety of social problems. The final French project, while it had obvious links with the housing problem in Paris, was directed at a reform of the child care services in France. It was based on the Montparnasse district of the capital.

A noteworthy feature of the French projects was the degree of interest shown by the central government in their inception and progress. The four HVS projects in the European Programme were part of a national programme of over fifty projects, in which the central government subsidised local initiatives. The PACT project in Brittany was initiated in response to a government invitation to the federation to submit a project in this region. The child care project in Paris was part of a wider experiment promoted by the central government to pioneer a new system of co-ordinating child care services. All this is in the centralist tradition of French government, although the participant style of central government intervention is comparatively new. This degree of central government involvement holds out the promise that the experience of the projects will be taken into account in developing future policy at national level.

The work of the projects, especially the ATD projects, has also helped to keep alive concern for poverty in France during the depression years since the European Programme was launched. Neither the right nor left-wing parties could afford to neglect the issue of poverty and as a consequence the prospects for further action in this field seem better than in most other member states.

(4.2)   CHILDREN OF MONTPARNASSE

The 14th Arrondissement of Paris is one of the more affluent districts of one of the world's richest cities, but it contains within it extremes of poverty and wealth. A large number of families, many of them headed by immigrant workers, live in overcrowded, sub-standard housing. From these families come most of the children who are taken into public care.

About thirty years ago a group of doctors and psychiatrists in the big public hospital which serves the district came together to study the problems of children in public care and the project which was eventually to take its place in the European Programme derived directly from their observations. They concluded that the traditional practice of sending children to large institutions often a long way from Paris simply condemned them to re-live the poverty of their parents, by handicapping them psychologically and educationally and stigmatising them socially. They set up an organisation named COPES (Centre d'Orientation Psychologique et Sociale) devoted to promoting new methods of public care and assisting families to overcome difficulties in caring for their children at home.

A number of public agencies in France are concerned with child care. There are at least five separate relevant agencies in the 14th Arrondissement, which until 1975 worked largely independently of each other, each addressing itself to a different aspect of the problem (e.g. poverty, mental health, physical well-being and school performance). From 1969 onwards it became government policy to promote the co-ordination of child care services through the creation of Unified Children's Centres, which meant basically the appointment of a co-ordinating officer at *département* level. In 1975 an experiment was launched in the 14th Arrondissement by the Paris prefecture to co-ordinate services at a more local level. COPES was employed as consultants to this project, which aimed not only at rationalising the administration, but more importantly, at developing new methods of preventive care based on more comprehensive forms of service. COPES already had a project which had been adopted for the European Programme, and this was now subsumed in the larger design.

There were two main branches of COPES' activities, on the one hand education and training and on the other direct work with families. The education and training activities were directed at workers at all levels in the child care services. Probably the most important activity took place in the study groups for field workers drawn from all the relevant agencies, which were set up in 1977 throughout the Arrondissement. Their main concern was to consider a document drawn up by COPES listing the warning signs which indicated when a child was at risk in a family, the social service agencies concerned and the appropriate action. This document was not well received by all the workers, some of whom distrusted what they saw as an attempt to 'psychiatrise' social work and invade individual liberty and privacy. After three years of discussion and dispute the document was re-issued in a revised form[2] and numerous copies have been distributed in Paris and elsewhere.

Training courses for all types of social service personnel were also run by COPES to promote its concepts of 'medico-psycho-social prevention' not only in Paris but throughout France. Particular use was made of film material, some of it based on casework in the 14th Arrondissement.

In the field of direct service the principal achievement was to eliminate the 'export' of deprived children from the district, except occasionally where this appeared to be in the child's interests. To accommodate this change twenty-two local foster parents were recruited, there was an expansion of supervised child minding facilities and the number of short-term admissions to care was reduced in favour of supervision at home. This policy was facilitated by extending the traditional role of the mother and infant welfare service in recruiting, training and supervising child minders to cover similar activities with foster parents who accepted children placed by the public assistance authorities. This was a significant breach of inter-agency frontiers. The work was entrusted to five area-based inter-professional teams, in one of which COPES participated directly. In 1977 COPES formed an agency to take over a local *halte garderie* (a day nursery taking children for occasional short spells, e.g. while the mother is shopping) which was reorganised to take some children on a more regular basis, whose mothers were in part-time employment. The local tenants' association was closely involved in running the garderie and it was hoped that they would eventually take it over completely. It did not, however, prove possible to find an adequate financial basis for the association to do this and, after a threatened closure, the establishment was finally taken over by the mother and infant welfare service.

The original COPES proposal to the Commission had envisaged the creation of what in Britain would be called a family group home. This was not finally set up until late 1979 and then it survived for only five months. It was closed for lack of space and personnel. COPES considered, however, that they had demonstrated the utility of this form of care.

It is evident that the project was not without its difficulties and setbacks. It has nonetheless assisted in pioneering methods of care which were new in its Parisian setting, although now well established in some other countries. It was one of the few projects in the European

Programme which was a pilot project in the full sense of being intended for replication in other areas. Replication in other parts of Paris is already in progress.

(4.3)   ENCOUNTERS WITH THE FOURTH WORLD

The movement Aide à Toute Détresse-Quart Monde has its own perception of poverty and its own techniques for combating it, which deserve a brief mention before describing the movement's four French projects. These remarks are also relevant to the movement's two other projects in the European Programme, in the Netherlands and the UK.

ATD was founded in 1956 in the bidonville at Noisy-le-Grand, near Paris. The bidonville had originated three years earlier as a tented camp for homeless families, but by 1956 it consisted mainly of Nissen huts, known colloquially as 'igloos'. ATD's central activity was a pre-school, which along with two others elsewhere was eventually to form part of the European Programme. The mud and degradation of those early years had a profound influence on the philosophy and structure of ATD.[3]

In 1980 there were thirty-four ATD projects in France, financed about 50 per cent by grants from public authorities and 50 per cent from the movement's own resources. Between them the projects mobilised about 240 full time 'volunteers'. The ethic of the volunteers was that as far as possible they lived among the people they served and shared their standard of living, being paid the state minimum wage. Most of them were young people who had committed themselves to the work for three years or more. In 1967 ATD became the focus for a federation of six organisations, the other members being in Belgium, Germany, the Netherlands, the UK and the USA. The international headquarters was in the Parisian suburb of Pierrelaye.

The basic thesis of ATD is that there is a sub-proletariat in all industrial nations amounting to about 2 per cent of the population. ATD terms this group the Fourth World ('Quart Monde') to emphasise its exclusion from the wider society. It is part of the ATD analysis that there is a strong inter-generational permanence in the Fourth World. The movement concentrates on these 'poorest of the poor', trying on the one hand to motivate them to struggle for their own advancement and on the other hand to open up the wider society to accept them. The latter activity involves recruiting 'allies' to assist the movement, trying to influence administrative and political structures at all levels from the President of the Republic to local nursery school teachers, and producing a constant stream of propaganda and research.

(4.3.1)   Work with Young Children

Three of the four ATD projects in France which were included in the European Programme centred around work with children up to six years old. They formed an integrated scheme in that there were six staff at Pierrelaye who serviced all three projects, but each project had its own staff, a distinctive setting and a different range of activities. The general title for all three was 'community development based on early childhood', emphasising the role of the work with children as a starting point for a wider community involvement.

Two of the projects were sited in the Parisian suburbs, at Noisy-le-Grand and Herblay, in *cités de promotion*. A cité de promotion is a small housing estate intended as short-term accommodation for families who would otherwise be homeless. The Noisy cité is the successor to the camp where ATD was born. In both cités the number of families declined during the course of the programme. In Herblay this was partly due to a decision to empty the entire cité in 1979, rehouse the residents and renovate the dwellings. The cité had not been fully reoccupied by the close of the European Programme. This radical action was designed to overcome the tendency of the cités to 'silt up' with families whom the publicly sponsored housing associations were reluctant to accommodate.

In both cités there was also a sharp decline in the number of young children, with the changing structure of the families passing through. This was partly due to increasing family limitation, but also the younger age of the parents. The homeless families coming in during the 1970s were no longer migrants from the countryside, as in earlier years, but young families from the surrounding suburbs who had often never known a home of their own or a regular income, apart from social benefits. This changing nature of poverty was also noted in the Roubaix project described later in this chapter. By 1980 the cité at Noisy had only 62 children under age six (100 in 1976) and the cité at Herblay 15 (45 in 1976).

The third project near Toulon was in a *cité de transit*, which in theory was intended only as temporary housing but was now overdue for demolition. The declining population here resulted mainly from the destruction of several blocks of dwellings by accidental fires. The families were mainly North African and Gypsy, with a tendency for the Gypsy element to increase as more of the North Africans moved into normal housing.

The threefold objective of the projects was to improve the development of young children, especially in verbal skills, prepare them for later school life and to promote community solidarity in a struggle for a better future for its children.

ATD ran pre-schools at both Noisy and Herblay. They were originally intended for children aged three to four, but with the falling enrolment more younger children were admitted, so that eventually they catered for children from eighteen months old. The smaller numbers also enabled the teachers to give more individual attention, including work with children in their own homes. The Toulon pre-school was closed down before the European Programme started, to encourage the parents to use the state nursery school which had opened in the area. The Noisy and Herblay schools also ran 'green classes' in the summer in the Jura mountains, until the declining average age of the children made residential classes impracticable.

The pre-school staff endeavoured successfully to persuade the parents to send their children to the state nursery schools serving their localities when the children reached four years of age. As a reinforcement to the nursery school work the ATD teams ran a series of after-hours cultural activities for three to six year olds, partly on special premises, but also out-of-doors and in individual homes. The emphasis was on encouraging reading, as well as music and craft work. The pre-school team in Toulon, being the only ATD personnel on the site, were also involved extensively with other children.

All the teams were closely involved with the staff of the local nursery schools, and at Toulon participated in classroom activities. Noisy and Herblay gave particular attention to health education and at Noisy infant welfare consultations were held at the pre-school. A great deal of effort was directed to involving parents at every level, besides running activities directed specifically to the parents, such as film shows and attendance at rallies.

The whole activity was accompanied by ATD's typically lavish attention to collecting participant observation data and preparing profiles and case studies. A large number of different psychological tests were administered in an attempt to measure the children's intellectual progress. An account of some of this work and ATD's teaching methods was published during the course of the programme.[4]

The children's progress proved difficult to measure, in part because of the continuous dispersal of the families into other accommodation, often at a distance. ATD's clearest achievement was to get almost every family to send its children to the pre-school and then to the nursery schools, with good attendance records. The children almost all settled easily into the nursery schools, but after a few months they began to fall behind the children from less disadvantaged backgrounds.

The lessons ATD draws from its experience are the importance of sustained support beyond the pre-school years, the importance of early language development and the need for parental involvement. Detailed proposals have been submitted to the Ministry of Education for improving pre-school work with disadvantaged groups. On a wider plane ATD has used its experience in the cités to submit proposals to the government for new policies in income maintenance and housing, to give families the stable base on which their children can make consistent progress.

(4.3.2) Champagne and Poverty

The fourth ATD project was at Reims, the principal town of the Champagne region of NE France, with a population of about 200,000. Besides being a centre for the wine trade it is an important manufacturing town, which has suffered disproportionately from the unemployment of recent years.

ATD has been working in Reims since the late 1960s, when a local group set up a pre-school in the bidonville on the outskirts. With the demolition of the bidonville ATD's volunteers followed its inhabitants into the four cités de promotion where most of them were rehoused. In 1974 ATD proposed the town to the European Commission as the site for an experiment in 'comprehensive and concerted action' to help the Fourth World.

The action was comprehensive and concerted in the sense that it tried to reach beyond the cités de promotion to contact the extreme poor dispersed throughout the urban area. It also covered a multiplicity of activities in different fields, including not only direct work with poor people but also attempts to influence the range of administrative agencies which served and regulated them, and to shape public opinion at large. The objective was to break down the social isolation of the sub-proletariat and ultimately create a more open and caring society.

Work with the Fourth World: activities with adults
The basic strength of the project was the presence of the ATD volunteers in the cités de promotion and the web of informal contacts they built up with their neighbours. From this flowed group activities such as street festivals and the improvement of open spaces, as well as individual support for families in difficulties. Although the project subsequently involved a number of families from outside the cités, the cités remained its main source of support.

The first step towards city-wide activities was the series of fortnightly 'Fourth World Evenings' held at Fourth World House, a former youth hostel near the city centre, from 1977 onwards. These were discussion meetings ranging over topics such as employment, family life, children, and immigration. About 200 families participated at some time or another, with an attendance averaging thirty in 1978–9. It was through the Fourth World evenings that ATD recruited participants for the movement's regional and national rallies. One hundred and twenty Rémois attended ATD's twentieth anniversary celebrations in Paris in 1977 and 1,200 came to the local festival in 1979 to mark the International Year of the Child.

The movement issued a newspaper, *Solidarity*, which kept up a regular publication although it never had many written contributions from the Fourth World.

By 1979 the project workers felt able to bring together a group of activists ('militants') whom they hoped would eventually become the recognised spokesmen for the Fourth World. The militants took a leading role in the ATD campaign to improve the family allowance system (which includes a large range of means-tested supplements) and in organising the adult literacy groups known as 'Challenge Clubs', launched in October 1979. The clubs had thirty-one students at the end of the project.

ATD looked to the militants to carry the project to its fulfilment, which necessarily lies well in the future. By the end of 1980 the militants numbered only ten and they were still relatively inexperienced.

Activities with young people and children

The ATD team ran a youth club from 1972 to 1976, to provide leisure activities for young people from Fourth World families. In 1976 this was discontinued in favour of small discussion groups in each of the cités focused on the theme of vocational training. From these emerged in 1979 the 'Knowledge Clubs', which varied from forty to seventy participants. These were organised around a series of talks by guest speakers introducing the members to different aspects of the world of skilled employment. They also included current affairs discussions on issues such as the Vietnamese refugees. Alongside these were literacy groups and craft workshops. The latter made simple furniture and some group projects such as a bus shelter. In the project's final year the team succeeded in persuading a public agency to run two five-month pre-vocational training courses for seventeen trainees.

The work with children had less emphasis in Reims than work with young people and adults. It consisted mainly of out-of-school cultural activities for primary school pupils (*pivots culturelles*) and a branch of the ATD children's club, Tapori.

Work with social service agencies

The project had been originally conceived primarily as an attempt to influence the established social services agencies in the fields of health, education, housing and so on to introduce innovations which would open up their services to the extreme poor. This promised to be more effective than conducting small-scale experimental schemes under private auspices which the established agencies were likely to ignore. The availability of other public funds for specific activities to some extent shifted the emphasis of the project towards direct service with poor families, but even here the accent was on stimulating a demand, e.g. for vocational training, which ATD then tried to persuade the authorities to satisfy.

The experience of trying to influence the 'institutions' was frustrating. Several of the projects proposed by ATD received scant attention; others made considerable headway but foundered at different stages in the process of planning and implementation. A school project in the cité de transit probably would have been launched but for a fire in the cité which led to most of the residents being relocated. The only solid achievement was the running of two pre-vocational training courses by a national educational agency in 1980, which may become a regular activity.

The project team has had for the most part to content themselves with drawing a number of negative lessons from this work.

Influencing public opinion

As in all ATD projects a corps of 'allies' was built up composed of individuals willing to give unpaid assistance to the project and, hopefully, to influence the milieu in which they lived and worked in favour of the Fourth World. By 1980 the project had about ninety allies. Unfortunately few were drawn from working-class backgrounds, giving few possibilities for entrée into, for instance, the Trade Union movement.

Research

Much of the research activity of the team was devoted to the short-term needs of the project. However, several long-term pieces of work were carried out and published, notably a study of 2,000 poor families receiving less than the minimum wage from social benefits,[5] and a month-by-month analysis of the income of forty poor families over thirty months.[6] A follow-up study of a group of families rehoused from the bidonville in 1969 was being written up at the end of the project.

The project leaders freely admit that overall progress has been very limited, but they have been working with a very depressed minority of the poor and a set of public agencies oppressed by growing economic difficulties in the wider society. What had been a relatively prosperous town in 1973 had developed an exceptionally high level of unemployment by 1980. The Communist municipality which replaced the right-wing parties in 1977 tolerated ATD as a social work service but distrusted its attempt to influence public agencies. But, if nothing else, ATD has given the Fourth World a name which is used in discussing social issues well outside ATD circles, and hence given the group an identity and a visibility it hitherto lacked.

(4.4)   HOUSING FOR SPECIAL GROUPS

PACT (Programme d'Amelioration, Construction et Transformation d'Habitat) is a housing association movement which began in Lyons just before the Second World War, aimed at renovating old housing for the use of socially disadvantaged groups. There are now 150 autonomous local associations affiliated to a national federation. A regional structure was inserted in the 1960s. There were three PACT projects in the European Programme, on the Belgian frontier (Roubaix), in Brittany (Guéméné-sur-Scorff), and in the extreme South (Orange).

(4.4.1) The Homeless and the Hard-to-House

Roubaix is one of the oldest industrial towns in France, which grew up around the nineteenth-century textile industry. Most of the long, brick-terrace houses are now worn and obsolete. The local PACT association (CAL-Roubaix) was set up in 1954 to make temporary improvements in such housing, pending its demolition. Much of it is, however, still in use, saved first by the housing shortage and later by a policy of definitive restoration. In the course of rehousing families from these dwellings CAL-Roubaix developed a form of housing management/ social work known as 'personalised management'.

In 1962 CAL put up a hostel for homeless families, rebuilt in 1972, primarily to avoid the children of these families being taken into care. Part of the project included in the European Programme consisted of a pre-school for the hostel. The other component was a more intensive version of personalised management based on a *cité de promotion*, completed by a sister housing association in 1977.

Homeless families

In 1973 CAL carried out a detailed study of the families using its hostel. Since then they have observed similar changes to those noted in the ATD cités at Noisy and Herblay. The large families of former years which arrived in Roubaix from the adjacent rural and mining areas to seek work have been replaced by younger, smaller families who have grown up in Roubaix and whose menfolk have far more difficulty in finding employment. Few of them have ever had a home of their own. In 1973 the textile industry was already faltering, kept alive on cheap migrant labour. Today the last textile mill has become an industrial museum. With little prospect of regular employment the families in the hostel have little chance of permanent accommodation except through CAL, which eventually rehouses about half of them.

The pre-school is more informal than the ATD schools at Noisy and Herblay and has a far higher turnover of pupils. It must be admitted that the classrooms are dark and drab compared with most schools. The hostel itself is very overcrowded and more spacious premises are urgently needed, although the 1972 approach of renovating a group of ordinary dwellings in the neighbourhood was probably wise, avoiding too institutional an appearance to the hostel.

Given the cramped conditions at the hostel the pre-school has been a great help, both in widening the range of social and physical experiences for children who would otherwise spend most of their time in their hostel bed-sitting rooms, and in giving the parents some respite. The school has a similar mix of informal play, formal language and psycho-motor activities and outside visits to the ATD pre-schools, by which it is consciously influenced.

The Cité de Promotion Familiale

CAL was anxious to create a special pool of housing for families which would otherwise be hard to accommodate, meaning in the main exceptionally large families with low incomes. It was not attracted to the cité approach of creating a segregated ghetto for 'social cases', but it proved to be easier to obtain cheap government loans for such a project, so a cité was built. Also, loans being more easily available to build housing for immigrants, half the dwellings in the cité were allotted to immigrant (mainly North African) families. Since these formed a very small proportion of families in the CAL hostel, the cité was not as effective as it might have been in relieving the worst problems of homelessness, although a third of the cité families were drawn from the hostel. Nor was there much chance of families being rehoused from the cité until their children had grown up.

The cité was completed in 1977 and in 1979 it housed twenty-five families, with a total of 180 children. The European Community's funds provided the social component of the project, consisting of a community worker attached to the cité and a special training project for teenagers.

The community worker at first lived in the cité, but had moved out by 1980. He felt he was just as effective this way, and he had freed another house for occupation by a homeless family. He had been very busy helping families settle into their new homes, both individually and collectively. The most persistent difficulty was debts arising from the high central-heating charges, and some progress was made in educating residents to handle their heating systems more economically. Another major problem was education. At first the children were scattered in ten different schools and it took some time to press the education service to set up a local primary school. Contacts with schools were still considered unsatisfactory in 1980. The cité children were in general about three years behind the average in school attainment.

A number of community activities were organised, including several very successful summer camps for children. By the end of the project some mothers were organising their own minibus outings. The peak of community activity had, however, been in the first eighteen months of the cité's existence. Once the initial difficulties had been overcome the level of community participation declined significantly.

Part of the European money went to a special pre-vocational training project, run by a national organisation with links with the trade union movement. The trainees were all teenage boys, many of North African origin, some of them from outside the cité. A lengthy report was prepared on the 1979 course, giving a detailed account of the trainees' experience in learning to handle money, organise a trip to Paris, and so on. The hobbies exercise resulted in the setting up of a TV studio and the making of a film on delinquency. The report will be of interest to everybody concerned with the training of young people from disadvantaged backgrounds, particularly from minority groups (several youths had linguistic handicaps).

The pre-school was clearly particularly useful in the context of the homeless families hostel and the social component of the cité project proved its worth in helping families settle into a strange environment, and to some extent modify the environment (e.g. obtaining the creation of a new school). The training project is a valuable addition to the body of experience on pre-vocational training built up elsewhere in the programme.

(4.4.2) Housing for the Elderly

Guéméné-sur-Scorff is in the agricultural heartland of Brittany, in an area from which young people have been migrating to more prosperous areas of France for over a century. Guéméné canton now has only half the population it had in 1900. The town and surrounding villages thus have a high proportion of elderly people, most of whom live in old housing, some of which lacks even such basic amenities as running water.

The Guéméné project is based on the thesis that many elderly people in the area are forced into residential care because they are no longer able to cope in the old, cold, damp and inconvenient houses in which they live. Faced by a Ministry of Health policy of limiting residential care to persons who need invalid care, the regional organisation of PACT launched a 'programmed action' to improve the conditions of elderly people living in their own homes. A programmed action concerts the activities of a varity of different services, in this case in the fields of housing, social services and community organisation.

One element of the project was the creation of several small *foyers de soleil*, that is grouped dwellings with common services. These are widespread in France. The originality of the Guémené project lay in creating very small foyers to meet the needs of thinly populated areas, using buildings converted from other uses. In Guémené itself the foyer was a former hotel which was converted into twelve flats, with a warden, a social area, a laundry room and a room for medical consultations. In two nearby villages there were foyers in former schools, with a total of ten flats.

The work on this aspect of the project progressed very slowly, mainly due to difficulties in raising finance. The Guémené foyer was not occupied until April 1980. The cost was far higher than anticipated, obliging the project to build more apartments of smaller size, to keep down rents. It also proved too expensive to install lifts, so that some upper-floor apartments had to be let to young couples.

Alongside this activity was a house improvement programme which eventually renovated about 230 houses for elderly people in Guémené and the surrounding villages and 100 houses in Guémené for the population in general (the latter was under a separate set of government loans). Again progress was slow, partly because the local construction industry was not geared to this type of work, and partly because of a reluctance by many elderly people to suffer the disturbance involved. Indeed some were judged to be too frail to be disturbed. The programme was limited to minor works – installing water, toilet, heating and kitchen facilities, insulation and flooring, etc – which although of enormous benefit to the residents meant that the worst dwellings could not be improved.

On the social services side, a home help service was established for the first time in the area and was in operation throughout the canton by the end of the project. There were difficulties in getting the service accepted by some elderly people, and some houses had to await improvement before the home helps could hope to keep them clean. A laundry service was also installed, using washing machines in the foyers or at the local old people's clubs.

The old people's clubs were the final element in the project. By its close every community in the canton possessed a club, set up with the help of an organiser paid by one of the social security agencies. The clubs performed an important role in the project, helping to identify priority cases for each of the project's activities, winning acceptance for the services on offer, and helping in certain aspects of the project design, for example, planning the layout of the foyers.

The project is a good example of a social planning exercise, even though it took longer to get going than was anticipated and it had to be modified in detail. The project was focused on a defined problem which had been explored by several preparatory studies, not detailed in this summary. It co-ordinated the resources of many different agencies to bring about practical improvements in the lives of several hundred elderly people in the district. What we do not yet know is if it actually reduced the need for residential care, and we may never know as the number of residential places is likely to be reduced in any event.

(4.4.3) New Life for an Ancient Town

Orange is a small town (2,500) on the lower reaches of the river Rhône. Once an independent principality, it has given its name to the royal house of the Netherlands and indirectly to the Protestant community in Northern Ireland. Today many of the small houses in the mediaeval part of the town are worn and lacking in modern amenities, providing cheap accommodation for the elderly and immigrant workers. The project proposed to the European Programme envisaged a comprehensive renovation of the old town, co-ordinated by the local PACT association, for the benefit of its poorer residents.

The major part of the project was not even started during the life of the European Programme. Not until the final year did the municipality fully commit itself to the proposal, and even then there were still delays in mobilising the finance and securing the agreement of the other agencies involved. It is a good example of how difficult it can be to run a social planning exercise without political authority. Most of the European Community's financial support went on sustaining the process of planning and lobbying – 'laying seige to the municipality' in the words of the 1978 project report.

Apart from preparing plans and studies in support of its main proposals the PACT team occupied itself with a scattered programme of housing improvements. About 170 dwellings in the area were improved, with indoor toilets, running water, central heating and so on. A redundant public building was converted into a hostel for twelve immigrant families.

(4.5) THE URBAN DESERT

We have already referred to the massive shift of population in France in the 1950s and '60s. One of its consequences was a severe housing shortage in the more prosperous urban areas, of which the bidonvilles were the most dramatic manifestations. Most migrants did, however, find permanent accommodation, thanks to a housing programme of heroic proportions.

Much of the new housing was in big estates known as *grands ensembles* on the outskirts of existing towns. Although mostly only between ten and twenty years old, many of these estates are now considered to be badly in need of renovation and improvement and the lack of community life is widely deplored.

The improvement of the grands ensembles was established as a priority action in the seventh National Plan and an inter-ministerial working party was set up to implement it in 1977. The resulting programme was based on the Model Cities programme in America in the 1960s. It relied upon local authorities to take the initiative in proposing comprehensive schemes for government subsidy. Schemes were expected to include a significant social component, co-ordinate the work of a range of agencies and involve the participation of the residents of the ensembles in both planning and execution. This programme, named Habitat et Vie Sociale (Housing and Social Life), is part of a trend away from the technocratic centralism which has been the tradition of government in France since Napoleon.

By June 1980 forty-eight HVS projects were under way and a further eighteen submissions were awaiting approval. Four projects were proposed for inclusion in the European Programme by the government and accepted by the Commission in April 1978. For reasons which are not clear the contract with the Commission was not signed until September 1979 and no progress reports had been received in Brussels by the end of the programme. One project team declared emphatically in June 1980 that they no longer regarded themselves as part of the European Programme. For the sake of completeness, however, we list the four projects. The experience is a warning against including ambitious projects which have not yet passed the planning stage in a programme which has only two years to run (not that the HVS projects suffered but they were unable to contribute any useful experience to the European Programme).

The largest HVS project in the European Programme was in a huge housing complex near Strasbourg. The Community funds were intended for the support of a group of architectural and town planning consultants working for the *collectif*, a local residents' group which the town council recognised as spokesmen of the ensemble. The project was notable for the sharp conflicts between the collectif and the council.

The second largest project was in an isolated estate near Metz. This estate also had an active residents' association which took a leading part in the project, but in this case relations with the town council were close and cordial. The other two projects were at Le Havre and Dieppe, where residents' organisations played a smaller role.

All four projects envisaged extensive physical renovation of the estate dwellings, the most radical being at Le Havre. A range of social service and community activities were included in each project, such as the *centre social éclaté* (literally the splintered social service centre) at Le Havre, which involves having facilities for recreational activities, playgroups, medical consultations and so on dispersed in small premises throughout the estate. In some projects empty storage space in blocks of flats was put to use in this way. Most of the Community funds were earmarked for community work teams, engaged on 'socio-educational' activities.

(4.6) CONCLUSION

The French projects in the European Programme were mainly social planning exercises, which is not surprising given the French experience in social planning acquired through the series of national plans since 1946. Some projects, like COPES, succeeded because they were backed by the political authority in the district. Others, like the ATD project in Reims and the PACT projects in Guéméné and Orange, attempted co-ordination from a base outside government and the statutory agencies. In Guéméné this was ultimately successful; less progress was made in Reims and hardly any in Orange. ATD's success in Reims lay largely in the area of community action work directly with poor people.

There was some attempt to co-ordinate the work of various French projects in the European Programme through a government committee set up in early 1980. Certainly the national government took more interest in the programme in France than in most other Member States, and the issue of poverty has remained live in France in a way it has not done elsewhere.

Notes

[1] Written by Edward James.

[2] 'Document C, Early Medico-Psycho-Social Prevention', revised and supplemented edition 1979, published by COPES, 23 rue Lalande, 75014 Paris. English translation included in ESPOIR report to the Commission of the European Communities, November 1980 (annexe to Chapter 6, Volume III).

[3] De la Gorce, F, *La Gaffe de Dieu*, Editions Science et Service, Pierrelaye, 1978. This is an autobiographical account of the experience of a young Belgian volunteer in the early days of the ATD movement at Noisy-le-Grand.

[4] De Vos van Steenwyk, A, *Il fera beau . . . le jour ou le sous-proletariat sera entendu*, Editions Science et Service, Pierrelaye, 1977.

[5] *Les familles pauvres d'une ville moyenne*, Economie et Statistiques, No 105, November 1978.

[6] *Familles pauvres à Reims: de l'argent pour vivre*, ATD, Pierrelaye, 1980.

5
Germany[1]

(5.1) INTRODUCTION

Of all the countries in the European Community, it has been the Federal Republic of Germany that has most obviously enjoyed continuing economic growth and prosperity during the post-war period. During the 1950s and 1960s, the result was steadily rising levels of real wages coupled with falling unemployment after the dislocations of the immediate post-war period. During the same period there has also been sustained expansion of Germany's social security programmes, with major reforms of pensions, for example, in 1957 and 1972.

The experience of this period led most commentators and opinion-leaders to assume that poverty was a diminishing social problem, compared with the austerities of the 1940s. It was, at most, restricted to various marginal groups (*Randgruppen*) of the population: social casualties requiring individual assistance to make use of social opportunities or, alternatively, feckless individuals who were unwilling to take responsibility for themselves and their children. Public interest in the extent of poverty has been far more limited in Germany during the post-war period than, for example, in Britain; and the British network of poverty lobbies finds no real counterpart in the Federal Republic.

During the late 1960s and 1970s, however, social research and political debate have paid increasing attention to the extent and significance of poverty in West German society. Among social theorists and researchers, the resurgence of 'critical theory' in the late 1960s prompted attention to the marginal groups who stood outside the mainsteam of a society based on acquisitive individualism and the achievement principle. The advent of Social Democratic-led governments following 1969 prompted generally more critical attitudes towards the social costs of the 'economic miracle' and also gave an impetus to applied social research designed to assist social planning. From the political right, the persistence of poverty was paraded to demonstrate that the self-interested bargaining groups of the modern welfare state – most notably the trade unions – are socially irresponsible in their neglect of the weakest.

The pensions reforms already noted have undoubtedly lifted the majority of pensioners from the threat of poverty. Like other social benefits, however, the level of payment is heavily dependent upon the work and earnings career of the person concerned and those with an interrupted record or low pay tend to be neglected. Only in the 1970s has a minimum pension been introduced and this also has been dependent on a substantial record of employment. A wide range of other benefits, although in the main generous by international standards, are similarly graduated according to employment and earnings careers. In consequence, women, those in casual employment and immigrant guest workers (*Gastarbeiter*) have been relatively unprotected. Moreover, at least until the 1970s, transfer payments to families have been neglected relative to support for the elderly and relative to some other countries of the European Community, most notably France. Finally, successive reforms of the Federal Social Assistance Law (BSHG) have increasingly emphasised the *right* to social assistance for those unprotected by social insurance, etc. and have prompted attention not only to the increasing numbers of people dependent upon social assistance but also the 'hidden poverty' of those who, although eligible, do not claim.

By the mid-1970s, therefore, when the European Programme was launched, the agenda of political and academic contention and debate centred on certain key issues. These included: (a) the recruitment of the *Randgruppen* – the marginal groups of paupers traditionally identified by the poor law – and their social and political significance; (b) the 'new poor' who were becoming dependent upon social assistance and the inadequacies which their increasing numbers suggested in the new social legislation; (c) the extent and significance of 'hidden poverty'; (d) the likely impact of slower economic growth and public expenditure restrictions upon the extent and significance of poverty in Germany's consumer-oriented society.

It would be misleading to suggest that the three (later four) German projects were jointly established as a systematic exploration of this agenda. Nevertheless, the span of their interests overlaps with it to a considerable extent. The Duisburg and Stuttgart projects are concerned with two of the traditional *Randgruppen* – the homeless (*Obdachlosen*) and vagrants (*Nichtsesshaften*) respectively. The Cologne project confronts some of the 'new poor' – the growing numbers of social assistance recipients recruited from wider sections of the population and the significant 'hidden poverty' which national studies have revealed. Finally, the Amberg project was established to deal with immigrants – albeit a colony of political refugees from the 1940s, rather than any community of more recent and temporary *Gastarbeiter*. Together, therefore, these projects address many of the key questions defined by the emerging German debate of the 1970s, and they provide up-to-date insights into the impact of the current recession on patterns and rates of deprivation.

More than most other projects in the programme, the German projects have been continually and self-consciously concerned with the methodological problems of action-research. They distinguish themselves, on the one hand, from conventional academic research studies, such as the cross-national studies in the present programme and the national reports; on the other hand, they distinguish themselves from the routinised and relatively unreflective agencies of conventional social provision. As action-research projects, each of them aims to provide a new understanding of the specific problems of poverty with which they are confronted and to demonstrate innovatory methods for combating those problems. As pilot projects, they aim not only to produce credible results in their local contexts, but also to provide strategies relevant to projects elsewhere and to feed into social policy-making and debate at regional, national and European levels. In each of the sections which follow, therefore, the work of the project concerned is examined in terms of the new understanding of poverty which it provides and the innovatory methods which have been developed, before assessing the *pilot* significance of the project's work.

(5.2) THE COLOGNE PROJECT – POVERTY AND SOCIAL ASSISTANCE[2]

(5.2.1) Introduction

The Cologne project has attempted to evaluate the system of social assistance in terms of its accessibility and effectiveness. The long-term dependence of many social assistance recipients contradicts the intention of the Federal Social Assistance Law (BSHG) to assist a speedy return to independence; while the apparently large 'Dunkelziffer' indicates that in practice perhaps as few as a half (or even less) of those eligible actually receive assistance. The Cologne team have been working in two areas of the city: Zollstock, a mature area with a high proportion of old people attracted to the area during the inter-war period, and Chorweiler, a high-rise estate containing many one-parent families and large families. The team set out to illuminate the extent of hidden poverty and to develop new methods for promoting self-sufficiency among social assistance dependents. Finally, it hoped to make proposals for the reorganisation of the social assistance system.

(5.2.2)   Poverty and Social Assistance in Cologne

The project began by carrying out various surveys in the two areas and analysing the records held by local social assistance offices. The findings from these conventional research enquiries have been combined with the results obtained through evaluation of the project's subsequent experiments in action, in order to build up a picture of poverty in the two areas. In both areas women are over-represented, especially among the poor. In Zollstock, the numbers of elderly residents and the relative longevity of women means that there are a large number of elderly women living alone and dependent upon low pensions (whether on their own account or as widows). In Chorweiler, the many one-parent families are predominantly headed by women, who are either confined to home, relying largely on means-tested assistance, or else dependent on employment which is generally unskilled, low-paid, and intermittent.

Many of these households are therefore dependent indefinitely upon social assistance. The BSHG of 1961 lays down a broad framework for the administration of social assistance. Within this, individual administrative districts issue regulations which determine how benefits are to be provided, but a considerable area of discretion remains, particularly regarding the provision of special non-recurrent grants for specific additional needs. The Cologne researchers have investigated how this provision works in practice. The local officials who administer social assistance have typically received a general administrative training, but few of them are able to master the complexity and detail of the relevant statutes and administrative regulations. Furthermore, few have received any preparation for providing personal help to claimants; and they tend to hold negative stereotypes of certain categories of clients (especially the unemployed).[3] In consequence, the project workers suggest, these officials are unlikely to exercise their discretionary powers in a way which is sensitive to clients' needs and which ensures they receive the benefits to which they are entitled; and the personal help which these officials offer is unlikely to be such as to assist claimants in returning to an independent life. It is therefore unsurprising that about a half of the people questioned by the project are in 'hidden poverty'; that is, although apparently eligible for social assistance, they are not receiving it. They lack information regarding their eligibility for claiming their benefits; they are reluctant to reveal their personal financial circumstances and to become dependent upon the discretionary powers of the officials concerned. The reluctance seems to be especially marked among the elderly, who also fear the pressures which the officials may bring to bear upon their immediate relatives and the consequent threat to their kinship ties. Finally, the same fear and ignorance tend to restrict the capacity of claimants to contest the benefits awarded to them.

In the inner-city area of Zollstock, the project has also monitored the activities of voluntary organisations which cater for the elderly. Those who participate in these activities incur financial costs, for example subscriptions, which deter those who are less well off. At the same time these activities tend to presuppose and to enforce passivity on the part of their elderly participants, and thereby to reinforce their dependence, rather than promoting self-help. Those who supervise these activities tend to be untrained and to be ignorant of the various social services and social assistance benefits upon which the elderly poor might call. In their dependence-generating effects, therefore, these voluntary organisations are not unlike the official providers of social assistance.

Finally, it appears that the poor in both areas are isolated socially, lacking any well developed networks of social support. Financial poverty tends to limit people's ability to maintain social contacts and to participate in a consumption-oriented society. Deprived of such social contacts, the elderly poor in Zollstock have, in particular, come passively to accept their lot in life; however, this resignation and withdrawal commonly serve then to confirm the staff of the social assistance offices and of voluntary organisations in their perception of the elderly poor as deficient and incapable of self-direction.

(5.2.3)   Innovations through Action-Research

Over a period of three years the project has tried to promote various forms of self-help and mutual aid among the disadvantaged of the two areas, in the belief that only by enabling them collectively to develop their understanding, skills and strategies, can they reap the social benefits to which they are entitled and avoid long-term dependence on social assistance. This practical work in the field of social assistance has little legacy on which to build in Cologne, or even more generally in Germany as a whole; unlike some of the projects in the programme, the Cologne project had to begin from scratch. The surveys already mentioned provided the researchers with their first contact with the people concerned. Progress proved very different, however, in the two areas.

It seems likely that many of the isolated elderly people living in Zollstock are among the 'hidden poor' who do not claim benefits to which they are entitled. The project set out to provide them with information about benefits and to assist them in developing mutual aid and self-help through collective organisation. From the start however, there were problems in even reaching these people, in part because of their suspicion of unknown intruders. Even those who were contacted could not be forged into self-sustaining groups. While, therefore, this work was innovatory in seeking out the passive and isolated elderly poor and seeking to activate them, the time and resources available were too limited to have any lasting impact.

In Chorweiler, the project sought to create new networks of mutual aid among social assistance recipients and, at the same time, to make local assistance offices more accessible. Largely in consequence of these efforts, a Social Assistance Action Group was established in 1976 (consisting mostly of women); this aimed to assist members in claiming benefits and, in the long term, to simplify and raise the level of benefits. More generally, it became a focus of mutual aid and leisure activities for claimants, enabling them to develop a more positive self-image in opposition to the stigmatised identity imposed on them by members of the wider society.

From early in the life of this new Social Assistance Action Group, its activities began to extend beyond the confines of the Chorweiler estate. The group's efforts to confront and combat the negative images which social assistance recipients commonly suffer led it to engage in various forms of publicity work in the city and the region as a whole; the result, however, was that individuals and groups in that wider area came also to seek the advice and support which the group provided to those dependent on social assistance. During the later phase of the project's life, therefore, the Social Assistance Action Group was engaged in building a regional federation of similar groups, which it co-ordinated by means of such instruments as a regular newsletter. One of the main aims of this new federation has been to secure recognition from the political authorities of its right to be consulted as an acknowledged expert on social assistance legislation and implementation. There have been demonstrations in Bonn and the Family Ministry and elsewhere. (Nevertheless, this increasing concern with activities at a regional and federal level has meant that the action group has been severely limited in its capacity to embrace and support new members within Chorweiler itself.)

The project has attempted an enabling role in regard to the individual members of the Chorweiler population, the Social Assistance Action Group, and the regional federation: by providing technical information on social assistance benefits; by stimulating the action group in the development of its overall strategy; and by providing documentation and information for use in the political argumentation in which the federation is now engaged. Nevertheless, the project has restricted its attention throughout to social assistance, rather than widening its concern to other arms of social policy as many of the community development projects in the programme have done.[4]

(5.2.4) The Implications for Social Policy

From this programme of action-research, two main conclusions emerge of relevance to wider social policy debates. First, the so-called new poverty is not confined to marginal groups of the population or to individuals in need of short-term emergency assistance. German pensions, although generous for most of the population, leave those with an incomplete record of social insurance contributions below the official poverty line, where they are reluctant to resort to social assistance. Low levels of child benefit, and low rates of pay for women's work, leave many one-parent families similarly vulnerable to poverty. Unless these wider inadequacies in pensions, benefits and female employment opportunities can be tackled, the most that can be done is to increase the accessibility of social assistance and the sensitivity to individual needs with which it is administered. Secondly, the project's work reveals that an important factor which determines the way benefits are administered is the knowledgeability and persistence of the individual claimant; and this in turn is strongly dependent upon the patterns of mutual aid and collective organisation which exist amongst social assistance recipients. Traditionally, and still in general to this day, such patterns of mutual aid have been very limited, as also has the right of the poor to participate in discussions over the content and administration of social assistance. To improve the levels and accessibility of benefits is not, therefore, enough; what is also needed is the promotion of self-help organisations such as the Social Assistance Action Group as an effective instrument of self-help and political participation for the poor.

(5.3)   THE DUISBURG-ESSEN PROJECT: HOUSING THE HOMELESS[5]

(5.3.1)   Introduction

In the Federal Republic, local authorities have a responsibility for housing the homeless in emergency accommodation. In practice, they give priority to families. At the start of the European Programme, more than three-quarters of a million people were *Obdachlosen* in Germany as a whole. The emergency accommodation they occupy tends to be perceived by the municipal authorities and population at large as 'social problem areas': areas, that is, of multiple deprivation likely to be transmitted intergenerationally and fertile breeding grounds of social delinquency.

Since early in the 1970s, the Arbeiterwohlfahrt (AW), a nation-wide social welfare organisation loosely linked to the Social Democratic party, had been supporting social work projects within these areas in such cities as Duisburg and Essen. The European project involved collaboration between the existing AW teams and the team of researchers from the Frankfurt-based Institut für Sozialarbeit und Sozialpädagogik (ISS). The European project team has continued the work in the areas of emergency accommodation but has also concerned itself with the wider context of social planning in the two cities, engaging the cities' social policy-makers in negotiation for reform.

(5.3.2) Obdachlosigkeit: Genesis and Persistence

Duisburg and Essen are situated in the Ruhrgebiet, the traditional industrial heartland of Germany. The region's growth and economic prosperity were founded on the coal and steel industries, which also helped to make the region the heartland of Germany's trade unions. In recent years, however, this foundation has begun to crumble: the coal and steel industries are stagnating, new industries are being established in less congested areas elsewhere, and unemployment is above the national average. The region is losing population, with those who stay behind disproportionately concentrated among the elderly, immigrant workers and large families, all of whom tend to be especially dependent on social services. With the erosion of the local tax base, however, resources available for such expenditure by local authorities tend to fall. The research undertaken by the project suggests that many of those in the unskilled and low-paid sector of the labour force, particularly those with large families, continually face difficulty in meeting the rising level of rents, and are in danger of falling into debt and into rent arrears. These are also the members of the labour force who are most at risk of becoming unemployed; and as unemployment has risen over recent years, evictions, principally on account of rent arrears, have also risen significantly. Also at risk are one-parent families and migrants from the east and from the countryside.[6] All of these groups tend to have an incomplete record of social insurance contributions and to be especially dependent therefore on social assistance when unemployed; and they are all over-represented among the homeless.

They are then offered emergency accommodation as *Obdachlosen*, a specific socio-legal category inherited from the poor law. Here they lack the normal rights of housing tenancy and they tend to become segregated – legally, residentially and socially – from the rest of society. They become trapped in these settlements by their inability to compete in the labour market, the discrimination which they encounter from the official decision-makers, and their isolation from networks of informal community support.

Excluded in these ways, therefore, the Obdachlosen tend progressively (i) to lose any sense of the wider social, political and economic context in which they live, becoming parochial in their horizons and interests; (ii) to become resentful and apathetic vis-à-vis the formal institutions of the wider society and to lose the knowledge and skills which are required in order to locate and manipulate them; (iii) to lose contact with wider networks of social support, discipline and control; (iv) to develop patterns of behaviour which are 'irresponsible' as judged by the wider society; and (v) to lose their self-esteem and sense of personal efficacy, to suffer psychological disturbance, and in the case of children, to suffer cognitive and linguistic handicaps. Each aspect of this response tends then to be perceived by officials and by society at large as a pathology, along with the unemployment, poor school performances and ill-health of the Obdachlosen, which serves to justify their continuing supervision and segregation.

(5.3.3) The Programme of Action-Research

The project has worked in three major directions. First, the ISS team has acted as a centre for co-ordination, planning and training of the AW teams. This training work has in itself been an innovation, in as much as traditional social work training, virtually monopolised by the large welfare organisations, has been largely divorced from day-to-day fieldwork.

Secondly, the project has begun the reintegration of the Obdachlosen as full members of society. It insists that the distinctive behaviour patterns attributed to the Obdachlosen, rather than justifying their supervised segregation in settlements, are instead a symptom of the pressures to which they are subject; the assistance that the project therefore offers focuses on the reintegration of the Obdachlosen into employment and normal housing, coupled with measures to remedy their educational backwardness and help in claiming social assistance and other benefits. At the same time, however, instead of treating the Obdachlosen in isolation, the project insists that the problems which they face are common to those of the lower working class; accordingly, it has attempted to develop services which can be of assistance to disadvantaged neighbourhoods as a whole, at the same time serving to bring together different groups of the disadvantaged and to dispel the discrimination which the Obdachlosen experience from their immediate neighbours. This neighbourhood work is a distinctive innovation, at least in Germany, where social work and other official services for the disadvantaged have traditionally tended to reinforce stigmatisation by focusing on specific and segregated categories of individuals.

Such neighbourhood work is, however, to some extent an alternative to the strategy which the Arbeiterwohlfahrt had developed prior

to the European Programme, of building city-wide associations of the
Obdachlosen alone. Nevertheless, it has been a slow and difficult
process to win the trust and to sustain the interest and motivation of
the Obdachlosen; and the project has been forced to recognise the
difficulty of developing in collaboration with the Obdachlosen any
long-term general strategy for combating deprivation.

Thirdly, the project has engaged local policy-makers in negotiation over long-term policy changes; again, these efforts to combine
social work with reforms of the wider social infrastructure represent a
break with German tradition. These discussions have focused on the
inaccessibility and poor co-ordination of the services ostensibly
intended to assist the Obdachlosen, together with their tendency to
reinforce deprivation because they deal exclusively with this group.
These negotiations have also dealt with the possibilities of resettling
the Obdachlosen in normal housing, and ensuring adequate follow-
up services for reintegrating them into the community. However, the
municipal authorities have in general tended to demand evidence of
the 'good behaviour' of the Obdachlosen *before* transferring them to
normal housing, ignoring the pressures which lead Obdachlosen to
behave 'irresponsibly' in their existing settlements. More generally
still, the cities' financial situation has been at least partly responsible
for the official reluctance to accept these reforms.

(5.3.4)   The Implications for Social Policy

The project points to the injustice suffered by the Obdachlosen and
the inadequacy this suggests in the existing welfare state provisions.
It is those least able to survive in the labour and housing markets who
become segregated and supervised as morally and intellectually
inferior human beings; the social provisions ostensibly designed to
prevent and/or ameliorate distress and deprivation, tend instead to
perpetuate them; and social planning tends predominantly to reflect
the interests of the more advantaged sectors of the population, who
have the political knowledge and resources to ensure their participation in policy-making. The project has, like the other German
projects (especially Cologne and Stuttgart) begun to build a poverty
lobby to articulate these grievances in the political arena. However,
since more advantaged groups (with the possible exception of the
Trade Unions) have apparently little interest in problems of poverty,
this is bound to be a difficult and uncertain task.

(5.4)   THE STUTTGART-TÜBINGEN PROJECT: VAGRANCY AND SOCIAL INJUSTICE[7]

(5.4.1)   Introduction

In Western Europe, vagabonds for centuries have been counted among the poorest of the poor. At the same time, however, they have been popularly perceived as incompetent, feckless and potentially disruptive, leading a sub-human existence on the margins of society. Traditionally, therefore, the public assistance which they have been offered has been provided in hostels and asylums under strict discipline and regulation. Within Germany, successive reforms in the Federal Social Assistance Law – most recently, that of 1974 – have strengthened the social right of the citizen to such assistance as he may need in order to participate as a full member of society: but as yet these reforms seem to have had only a very limited impact upon the pattern of aid offered to vagrants.

The Stuttgart-Tübingen project is sponsored by the University of Tübingen, the Verein für Soziale Heimstätten (the Evangelical Church's Association of Social Welfare Hostels); and it has co-operated closely with various local hostels dealing with vagrants in Baden-Württemberg, for whom it has acted as a sort of 'research and development' unit. The project team have developed an analysis of vagrancy and poverty which fundamentally challenges the traditional diagnosis; they have at the same time developed new provisions for vagrants, as well as recommendations for much wider institutional, administrative and policy changes.

(5.4.2)   Vagrancy and Poverty in Germany

In Germany, as in other member states of the European Community, the current recession has seen increasing unemployment. This has been concentrated particularly among older workers with obsolete skills, women, unqualified young people, and the handicapped. These are predominantly those categories of the population who are already relatively disadvantaged in terms of job security, social insurance, levels of income, and degree of union organisation. Unemployment among these groups is, moreover, tending increasingly to be long-term. The victims easily lose their accommodation also, and without job or home, domestic breakdown is frequent. For the menfolk, especially those lacking social support, vagrancy is then commonly their fate.[8] During the 1970s, the numbers of first-time vagrants mounted dramatically, to reach 70,000 or more in West Germany as a whole.

Among the rising numbers of social assistance recipients in recent years, the proportion of long-term unemployed has increased significantly. In practice — contrary to the Federal Social Assistance Law — social assistance beyond a few days is often provided only to those of fixed address; those without accommodation are compelled to move elsewhere, in order to obtain assistance for a few days from some other office, and their rootlessness is thus reinforced. Often, moreover, social assistance for the unemployed is in practice also denied, unless the recipient, if able-bodied, is actively seeking employment; however, the official labour exchanges, eager to preserve their credibility with employers, are often reluctant to send vagrants to available vacancies. In short, then, these forms of official intervention in the labour market, instead of protecting and compensating those categories of population who, precipitated from the labour market, bear the burden of long-term unemployment in the present recession, instead ignore them or even reinforce the processes whereby they are excluded from the labour market and ultimately from society.

For those who are thus forced to live a life of vagrancy, a segregated form of existence in residential hostels is all that remains. The societal processes whereby vagrancy arises are thereby still further obscured and attention is focused on the supposed individual failings of the residents. This 'assistance' serves to reinforce the distrust, resignation and loss of self-esteem felt by the vagrant and his social isolation; and in practice, the hostel managers tend to give prime attention to the orderliness of the hostel, rather than reintegrating the vagrant into society.

The project workers therefore conclude that vagrancy is fundamentally a problem of social injustice. Vagrancy arises in the first place because the social costs of economic change, in particular of recession, are imposed disproportionately upon the unskilled and unorganised, who typically have least resources to survive such costs and whose work and domestic worlds are put at risk. Vagrancy persists because the official agencies designed ostensibly to assist their reintegration, in practice operate in such a manner as to erect major barriers to vagrants and to other persons low in public esteem. Finally, by offering assistance only in institutions segregated from normal accommodation, work, income and social contact, the hostels which cater for vagrants are essentially coercive. By pointing to this injustice the project workers expose the inadequacies of the reformed Social Assistance Law of 1974, which declared the right of the citizen to such assistance as may be necessary in order to overcome the hindrances which he faces to full participation in society.

(5.4.3)   The Programme of Action-Research

At the level of understanding, the project redefines the problem of vagrancy as a problem of poverty among the single homeless. At the level of *action*, the project has therefore developed innovations which should be seen, not so much in terms of effective rehabilitation of a well defined marginal group of the population, but more in terms of securing the social rights of homeless and unemployed people as laid down in the Federal Social Assistance Law.

The project's work has developed in three main directions. First, the project has attempted reforms within conventional residential provision; most obviously, by establishing small self-governing groups of residents capable of developing the emotional strength and moral self-direction required for an independent, self-sufficient existence in the wider society. Nevertheless, the continuing lack of opportunity which the vagrant faces, for reintegration into housing and employment outside the hostel, puts in question the value of these reforms; and the injustice of these barriers is still further highlighted.

Secondly, therefore, the project has moved outside the hostel in order to establish new agencies capable of assisting the single homeless and unemployed in general to secure adequate housing, financial support and employment opportunities.[9] The project has itself begun to sponsor various housing and job creation projects. These forms of non-coercive assistance have also provided the project workers with a base for entering into contact with the street tramps (*Stadtstreicher*) who refuse the assistance offered by traditional hostels and are particularly subject to harassment by police and public authorities, on account of their intrusion into public places.[10] This second focus of the project's work has also led it to seek more active co-operation with local and private agencies operating in the housing and employment fields, and into publicity campaigns to counter hostility towards vagrants. Nevertheless, during the present recession and housing shortage, even these forms of assistance are often insufficient to reintegrate the homeless and unemployed people with whom the project is concerned.

Thirdly, the project has increasingly been involved in political lobbying and social planning. It has helped to establish federations of those undertaking similar innovations elsewhere in Germany: as a means of disseminating ideas, of undertaking nationwide research and of exerting collective political pressure for reform. It has fed to government at regional and federal level its evaluation of existing measures for assisting vagrants, and recommendations for wider social policy changes on the basis of the innovations which have been developed: most obviously, in respect of the administration of social assistance and access to the employment and housing markets.

(5.5)   AMBERG – AM BERGSTEIG[11]

(5.5.1)   Introduction

Few of the projects in the European Programme have been specifically concerned with immigrants, despite their obvious interest for Community policies. One of the exceptions is the Amberg project in north-east Bavaria, added to the programme in 1978, and working on a federal housing estate on the outskirts of the town peopled mainly by people of foreign origin. These are not, however, recent immigrants; they are mainly displaced persons of the war-time years, particularly Poles, who found themselves in southern Germany following the end of hostilities.

The project involves workers from the University of Erlangen-Nürnberg in co-operation with the Social Services Department (Sozialamt) of Amberg and a variety of local government and charitable organisations. At the level of research it has attempted to understand how the Bergsteig estate has become stigmatised by the rest of Amberg, as a 'multi-problem' neighbourhood; at the level of action, it has attempted to improve living conditions on the estate, and to integrate the Bergsteigers into Amberg without losing their ethnic and cultural distinctiveness.

(5.5.2)   The Analysis of Deprivation in the Bergsteig

Immediately following the war, displaced persons became the responsibility of the occupying powers and subsequently of the federal government. The Bergsteig estate was developed to house some of those from south Germany. This federal plan, however, did nothing to ameliorate the extremely bad living conditions of the native Germans of Amberg; and the weakness of the local economy, in a generally underdeveloped area of Germany, meant that the foreigners concentrated on the estate appeared as a potential threat to the employment prospects of natives. These were particularly unfavourable conditions for integration of these foreigners into Amberg, and from the start the estate has been socially segregated and an object of resentment.

Continuing segregation over the post-war period has limited the employment and educational opportunities for the Bergsteigers; the better qualified residents have tended to move away, leaving behind the unskilled. Many of the residents are dependent in the long term upon social assistance. Stigmatised as a 'problem' area, the estate has been used as a dumping ground for other groups of disreputable and stigmatised families, gypsies, etc. The estate attracts disproportionate police attention and hostility in the local media. The conclusion must be, therefore, that any effective measures to counter the patterns of multiple deprivation on the estate must deal with the distinctive social and political relationship which has developed between Amberg and the Bergsteig since the last war.

(5.5.3) Action against Deprivation in the Bergsteig

The project's activities have been addressed to all three aspects of the deprivation which the Bergsteig suffers: poverty, their ethnic marginality, and the stigmatisation which they suffer from their fellow Ambergers. An advice centre offers information on social assistance, housing allowances, and the other social benefits upon which the Bergsteigers are especially dependent. Extra classes are provided for local school children; school leavers are assisted in obtaining employment and accommodation. The project has helped to promote the vitality of local sports clubs, etc. as a focus for the Bergsteigers' collective self-esteem, and as a vehicle for modifying the negative image of the Bergsteig which outsiders hold. Finally, the project has established a liaison committee which brings together the local authority and representatives of the Bergsteigers, for consultation on the policies which impinge upon the estate. Through this committee, the project's research workers have also fed to higher levels of government proposals regarding naturalisation procedures for immigrants in general.

Nevertheless, given the very limited time and resources at the disposal of the project, only limited achievements have been possible. The conservatism of the local political establishment means that changes in the wider policies which impinge upon the estate are unlikely. The project set out to promote 'plural integration', involving the recognition and encouragement of different ethnic cultures; in practice, however, the educational system is so rigid that no major change in the curriculum of local schools, in order to give equal worth to the various ethnic cultures, is feasible. Consequently, the project has increasingly tended to concentrate upon assimilation of the Bergsteigers into the German host society, with reduced emphasis on 'plural integration'.

(5.5.4) The Implications for Social Policy

The project's work has a potential relevance to the European Community's responsibility for the education and integration of migrant workers. The project demonstrates that the problems of ethnic ghettos must be understood in terms of their historical origin and political position in society as a whole. Ethnic segregation is typically the legacy of conquest, colonisation or migration, often associated with violence. One legacy of these disruptions is the fossilised stereotypes whereby members of the host society justify their segregation from the newcomers. It follows, therefore, that policies at national or European level which treat ethnic segregation as a matter of cultural pluralism alone, neglecting to understand these divisions in terms of this political history, are likely to be ineffective.[12]

(5.6) CONCLUSION

Many of the people with whom the projects are working, particularly in Duisburg, Stuttgart and Amberg, display the accepted symptoms of *Randgruppen* (marginal groups): over many years they live a segregated and even isolated existence; they give their children little support and encouragement to seek educational success; and among themselves they are often quarrelsome, disorderly and mutually denigrating. Some suffer the continuing effects of war-time dislocation and post-war expulsion from the East – dislocations which were, however, once and for all. It would be possible, therefore, to draw together certain of these findings in support of the dominant post-war view that poverty is a diminishing social problem confined largely to displaced minorities and that the most urgent policy task is to rescue the younger generation from the dangers of inherited deprivation.

Such a conclusion would be highly selective, however, and would certainly not correspond to that which the projects themselves draw. Instead, individually and jointly, the German projects point out how, over the last five years, economic austerity, increasing unemployment and rising rents have highlighted the insecurities with which certain vulnerable categories of the population have continually to contend: immigrant workers, women, the handicapped and the unqualified in particular. Jettisoned from the labour market, they tend also to be vulnerable to homelessness; inadequately covered by social insurance, they become dependent upon social assistance and the discretionary powers of the officials concerned; prevented by their reduced financial means from participation in many conventional social activities, they become isolated and tend to lose the skills and information necessary to live independently in an urban-bureaucratic society. They are the new recruits to the ranks of the poor and face the prospect of long-term and demeaning dependence on social assistance. Unemployment, housing and social assistance have therefore provided some of the most obvious fields in which the German projects have sought jointly to articulate their critique of existing social policies.

The innovations which the projects have developed, though various, provide the material for this critique. First, the German projects contest the *segregation* of the poor – still more of particular categories of the poor – in official provision. Ambulante Hilfe (ambulant aid) in Stuttgart and neighbourhood work in Duisburg provide models of attempts to tackle poverty within a non-segregating framework. Secondly, the projects contest *the assumption that poverty can be tackled independently* of policies in the labour market, housing market, etc. The Stuttgart project has worked increasingly with the Ministry of Labour; the Duisburg team has given increasing attention to negotiations with the city's social planners in regard to housing and social infrastructure; the Amberg project has collaborated with local political leaders in pointing to the folly of concentrating refugees in economically weak areas such as north-east Bavaria. Thirdly, the projects contest *the wider assumptions of public opinion* which constrain what policy-makers are willing and able to do. All of the projects have developed programmes of public education: Cologne, for example, has made extensive use of the mass media, while Amberg has, *inter alia*, used the sporting achievements of the Bergsteigers in an attempt to dissolve public prejudice.

Fourthly and finally, the German projects contest the *exclusion* of the poor from participation in policy-making and administration and the monopoly of organised expertise which social policy-makers and officials enjoy vis-à-vis their clients. They argue that this reinforces the dependence of the poor and thereby undermines the intentions of social legislators. Instead, all four German projects demonstrate how new forms of collective organisation and mutual aid among the poor themselves can significantly improve the effectiveness of official agencies, in promoting their clients' independence. The Amberg team, for example, supports the Bergsteig-Amberg liaison committee as a forum for such participation, while the Cologne project has devoted much of its energies to securing the right of welfare rights self-help groups to be consulted at local, regional and federal levels in the administration of social assistance. Indeed, one of the principal questions which the experience of the German projects now presents to social policy-makers who may wish to learn from their pilot experience is: by what means can such self-help networks be promoted on a grander scale as the legitimate and effective partner of official social agencies? It is here, perhaps, that lessons are offered not only from the German projects but also from those in some of the other participating Member States: for example, the area resource centres in the United Kingdom.[13]

Notes

[1] Written by Graham Room. I am grateful to Roger Lawson for his helpful comments. The opening paragraphs draw heavily upon his chapter 'Poverty and Inequality in West Germany', in V. George and R. Lawson (eds.), *Poverty and Inequality in Common Market Countries*, Routledge and Kegan Paul, 1980.

[2] I am especially grateful to Helmut Hartmann and Maria Kröger for their assistance with earlier drafts of this section.

[3] These stereotypes persist partly because of the resentment felt by these officials at their own low status in the eyes of their colleagues in other departments.

[4] See, for example, the British community development projects: Chapter 8 below, Sections (8.5) to (8.7).

[5] I am especially grateful to Ursel Becher, the leader of the Duisburg project, for her assistance with earlier drafts of this section.

[6] These are migrants who enjoy German citizenship rights; other immigrants who become homeless are less likely to have their families with them and more likely to be sent back to their place of origin.

[7] I am especially grateful to Bernd Rothenberger for his comments on previous drafts.

[8] Women and children will generally be received into emergency accommodation by the local authority, to become *Obdachlosen*: see Section (5.3) above, on the work of the Duisburg project.

[9] More than 80 per cent of the men dealt with are no longer vagrants, the project claims, and many of the able-bodied have found jobs. The costs of this 'ambulant aid' are significantly lower than those of institutional aid.

[10] During the late 1970s, the German municipalities began to adopt a much harsher policy towards the increasing nmbers of street tramps; much of the project's work has been concerned with reversing this trend.

[11] I am especially grateful to Günther Ruopp for his assistance with earlier drafts of this section.

[12] The classic treatment of these problems is provided by Max Weber: see, for example, his chapter on ethnic groups (*Economy and Society*, Part II, Chapter 5).

[13] See Section (8.5) below.

6
Ireland[1]

(6.1) A MIRROR FOR EUROPE

We have entitled this first section of our chapter on the Irish projects
'A Mirror for Europe' because the Irish National Programme was a
microcosm of the European Programme, with twenty-six constituent
projects, as many as in all the rest of the Community. Its national
co-ordinating body, the Irish National Committee for Pilot Schemes
to Combat Poverty ('Combat Poverty') made a serious attempt to run
a coherent programme. Its successes and failures convey important
lessons for any European Programme which may try for greater
coherence than the 1975–80 venture achieved.

The salien features of the Irish background can be sketched very
briefly. Although a small nation which is poorer than any other
Member State except Greece, Ireland encompasses important regional
disparities. The East and South of the country, particularly Dublin
and Cork, prospered during the 1960s and still maintain a degree of
economic growth, while the thinly populated West and North-West
remain backward. In consequence the latter areas continue to lose
population through migration, although the migrants now seldom go
overseas, while one of the principal social problems of the cities is the
chronic housing shortage. Dublin also exhibits features of inner-city
decay, similar to Belfast and the older cities of Britain and Germany.

The Irish National Programme, and indirectly the European Programme, was as we noted in Chapter 1, born of a change of government in Ireland in 1973. The new coalition government seized upon
the idea of a nationwide set of pilot schemes as a new initiative in
social policy. Overall responsibility was vested in a twenty-five strong
committee of government officials and independent members under
an independent chairman. This proved an unwieldy body, particularly once it had assumed executive responsibilities, and it was
frequently divided in its counsels. The main problems, however,
arose from friction between the committee and its professional staff,
exacerbated by recurrent financial crises caused by cuts in public
spending. The first director was dismissed in 1977 and the second

resigned in 1978. Yet the programme survived and had a creditable array of projects at its close in 1980. Regretfully several had only recently been established.

The two most striking features of the Irish Programme's history are that it took a long time to get projects established in the field and that when they emerged they bore little resemblance to the project designs submitted to the Commission in 1974. Although the committee was set up in 1974 it was not until 1977 that its project teams began to create the local structures that marked the true beginning of their work. This delay was in part because, unlike other Member States, Ireland did not proffer the Commission a group of off-the-peg projects but tried to tailor a programme to meet an overall policy objective. Unfortunately one of the attractions of pilot schemes to politicians is that they appear to be cheap and easy to implement, and there is frequent pressure on the organisers to start activities in the field earlier than they would wish, with fewer resources than they would like and to produce prompt 'results'. To some extent the Irish Programme yielded to these pressures and gradually turned away from the time-consuming task of starting up its own projects, to subsidising those run by other organisations. In its last two years a lot of its resources were passed on to other agencies with no clear pattern to its largesse.

A contributory factor to the delay in building up activities in the field was the extreme shortage of experienced community workers in the country. The first project teams consisted mainly of pairs of young, inexperienced workers thrown into unfamiliar settings. An advantage of the later 'contracted-out' projects was that they were operated by agencies already established or with antecedents in the areas or with the groups they served.

The initial project submissions to Brussels envisaged a balance between community development and social planning activities. The first director, appointed only three weeks before the submissions were made, was, however, a devotee of the community development approach and successfully swung the emphasis of the programme in this direction. His successors followed the same path, seeking, as they saw it, to prevent poverty by stimulating co-operative endeavour in poor communities rather than to alleviate it through the delivery of improved services. By 1980 the social planning component of the directly run projects had dwindled to two small research studies, on supplementary welfare allowances and social service councils, while all six field projects were intended as community development ventures. The three rural projects were called community action projects, but Combat Poverty does not seem to have distinguished in its terminology between community development and community action and all three were very development-oriented. The three urban projects were eventually styled urban resource centres, and to some extent they tended towards the Area Resource Centre model developed in Britain. A more militant, community action mode of thought was evident in these projects. Some of the contracted-out projects closely resembled these directly run area-based projects, but others were focused on particular problem groups or particular issues, such as battered women or legal aid.

One of the disadvantages of the Irish National Programme from the point of view of Brussels was that relations with the Community were handled almost exclusively through the central office in Dublin and there was hardly any direct contact, even in writing, between the Commission and the field projects. New projects came and went, the structure and balance of the programme changed and the Commission learned of this only through the often belated annual reports from the central team. Co-ordination at the national level need not exclude co-ordination at European level, but if there is ever to be a better co-ordinated European Programme the central body at the European level (and the Commission may choose to delegate this task) will need to be much better informed of what is happening at project level, than was the Commission in the case of Ireland.

(6.2)   RURAL PROJECTS

Six of the Irish projects were rural community development ventures, five in remote locations on the west coast and the sixth on the Northern Ireland border. Arising out of these projects were three actions at national level, which are also mentioned in this section.

Three projects, all on the west coast, were directly run by Combat Poverty, at West Donegal, West Connemara and Beara. All were in thinly populated areas where the inhabitants live largely by fishing and agriculture, with some craft activities and tourism. A spin-off from the West Donegal project was a project on the island of Arranmore, which eventually assumed contracted-out status. This was the only example of a directly run activity becoming an autonomous project run by the people it served. Another contracted-out project was set up on the isolated Erris peninsula in 1978, managed by a group sponsored by the local retail co-operative society and the development committee, following an initiative from Combat Poverty. The initiative for the project in North Leitrim, an inland area on the border, came from a local development federation which applied to Combat Poverty for a grant. In both these last two instances the management committee was dominated by local business interests whose objectives did not always coincide with those of Combat Poverty or the projects' professional staff.

All six local projects conformed closely to what we describe in Chapter 12 as the area community development model, defined by the UN in 1955 as 'a process designed to create conditions of economic and social progress for the whole community with its active participation and the fullest possible reliance on community initiative'.[2] The process of building up 'community capacity' through co-operative relationships and structures thus took precedence over the achievement of specific tasks. In two instances, however, project teams became involved with conflict strategies, more in line with what we term area community action, when they championed the cause of certain disadvantaged groups. In West Connemara 'users' groups' were formed which had some success in pressing the statutory authorities to provide electricity, water and mains drainage to several remote and scattered settlements. In Beara the project workers supported an unsuccessful bid to abolish private fishing rights in the local estuary, a move which later involved Combat Poverty in supporting the National Salmon and Inshore Fishermen's Association (NSIFA).

(6.2.1)   **Co-operatives**

Five projects supported producers' co-operatives, while the Arranmore project was an all-purpose community co-operative.

The idea of a community co-operative had been mooted before Combat Poverty came to the island, but its establishment owed a great deal to the West Donegal team's first research officer who spent most of her time canvassing every household on the island and helping to draw up the application for the co-operative's £15,000 starting capital. The co-op was a considerable success in its first year (1978), setting up a stone-crushing plant, a block-making plant and a hardware store, with an operating profit of £11,000. The next year saw a loss of £16,000, due partly to breakdowns at the crusher, high fuel costs and rising interest charges. The delay in introducing the planned car-ferry also held back much of the economic development the islanders had anticipated. It is too early to assess the long-term viability of the co-op, but it seems to be under-capitalised and may well need to be subsidised for several years. Private industry is heavily subsidised in these areas, so it is not inconsistent to subsidise co-operatives.

The West Donegal team also sponsored a fishermen's and a knitters' co-operative. The fishermen's co-operative had a difficult first year but returned a profit in 1979. The project team's main anxiety was that the co-op depended over-much on its salaried manager and few members took an active interest in the management. The knitters' co-operative, composed of women producing high quality heavy woollen garments in their own homes, succeeded in raising the income of its members and increasing production, but by the end of 1979 it had run into severe marketing difficulties, with a decline in the American tourist trade and a national postal strike. Attempts at diversification were unsuccessful. The co-op did, however, win a grant from one of the state development authorities in 1980.

The North Leitrim project sponsored a small vegetable growers' co-operative, which provided an ancillary income for about a dozen households. The Connemara team subsidised an existing fishermen's co-operative, and work was done on fish farming at Connemara, Erris and Beara. A contract for a fish farming officer in Erris was signed in 1980 and the first rafts for cultivating shell-fish were put in position. The idea is to run the fish farms on a co-operative basis.

A tiny but interesting co-operative venture took place at the tip of the Mullett peninsula in Erris, where a dozen women of all ages met weekly to stitch quilts. Starting with no capital and most of them with no experience of the craft, they had by 1980 acquired a quilting frame and two sewing machines and were selling quilts to a department store in Galway.

Alongside these successes were a few failures, such as an unsuccessful island co-operative supported by the Connemara team.

(6.2.2) Other Economic Activities

The Beara team was unsuccessful in acquiring land for its intended model farm. Instead it helped a variety of small agricultural ventures including a lamb fattening co-operative. In Erris a start was made on a land drainage scheme, while North Leitrim ran a small holiday cottage scheme, using renovated abandoned dwellings. One of Beara's main ventures was a credit union, which was a source of cheap credit for about 150 families. With a capital of only £7,000 it could not be a source of development capital. Advice and support was also given to a multitude of other economic ventures in the six areas.

(6.2.3.) Non-Economic Activities

These formed a minor part of the projects' activities. Erris produced a local calendar and promoted an archaeological survey. West Donegal and North Leitrim organised local festivals and Beara raised a ladies' football team. Several community newspapers circulated at different times.

(6.2.4) Assessment

At a local level several hundred households have benefited directly from the producers' and users' groups set up by the projects, while many others benefited through the encouragement and advice given to existing groups. Hopefully this is only a beginning. The fish farms, for instance, were only just being established in 1980. These groups also give local people a chance to control indigenous economic growth, rather than leaving the localities' resources to be exploited entirely by outside developers.

At a national level the work with fishermen's co-operatives led to the revitalisation of NSIFA, for which Combat Poverty provided a salaried organiser. This was primarily a pressure group to influence government policy on fishing. In the wake of NSIFA the Beara team encouraged two small national organisations to combine to represent the interests of small farmers. The National Agricultural Institute was also given a grant from Combat Poverty to make a study of member participation in the rural producers' co-operatives.

The work of all the projects has shown up weaknesses in the system of development grants for western Ireland and underlined the need for extensive preparatory work in local communities before they are in a position to submit project applications.

Finally at European level the projects have illustrated some undesirable aspects of Community agricultural and fishing policies. Much of their experience is also relevant to Social and Regional Fund activities and we hope that it has been noted.

(6.3)   URBAN PROJECTS

This section covers six projects in urban locations, which like the rural projects already described each covered a broad range of local activities. They were, however, a far more diverse set than their rural counterparts. Three of the projects were in the Dublin area, one in the northern suburbs and two in the city centre. The others were at Cork and Waterford on the south coast and in the small inland town of Kilkenny. The South Centre Area Resource Project (SCARP) in Dublin and the Cork and Waterford projects were directly run by teams appointed by Combat Poverty. They were originally envisaged as a co-ordinated welfare rights project but this idea quickly faded and the teams were in general left free to develop whatever activities they found feasible and congenial. All three tended towards a community action model, seeing themselves to a greater or lesser extent as partisans of victimised groups. The Cork team was the most militant. The North Centre City Community Action Project (NCCCAP), based on the north Dublin dockland, also developed a tradition of militancy. This was one of Combat Poverty's earliest contracted-out projects, managed by a committee of local residents, priests and social service professionals. Combat Poverty's involvement with Bally-fermot Community Association in north Dublin was brief (June 1977 to June 1978) and limited to providing the salaries of a community worker and a welfare rights worker. The Kilkenny project was contracted out to the local social services council and was principally an exercise in intensive casework with a small number of families in a particular council estate. It was inspired by a visit by a group of Aide à Toute Détresse workers from the Continent.

(6.3.1.)   Conflict and Pluralist Strategies

The emergence of different strategies in the rural and urban projects occurred largely through force of circumstance rather than from any conscious policy of the national committee or the central staff. The field worker were also for the most part too young and inexperienced to have many preconceived ideas on strategy. Whereas in the rural areas the project teams gravitated to a community development approach ('all poor areas have the resources within them which can be developed to overcome poverty'[3]) the urban teams tended to identify themselves with disadvantaged groups struggling to win resources from an outside power structure. In some cases this was a campaign of bargaining and alliance building while in others there was a tendency to reject alliances and pose direct confrontations. Not that any team justified confrontation for its own sake, but they sometimes felt it was unavoidable.

As we have said, the NCCCAP and Cork projects were the most conflict prone. NCCCAP saw the only instance of civil disobedience we know of in the European Programme, when several members of the management committee blocked the traffic during the rush hour in protest against the city council's development plan for their area. One member suffered a few days in prison for refusing to be 'bound-over' to keep the peace, which attracted further protests.

The protest group also secured an hour and a half debate with the council officers on national television and the committee chairman later contested and won a seat on the city council.

The Cork project was likewise soon involved in a major dispute, this time between a local parents' group it had sponsored and the education and church authorities, about the type of primary schooling on their housing estate. No compromise was achieved in regard to their demands for co-education and in 1980 the parents were preparing to launch a court action against the Minister of Education.

The SCARP and Waterford teams avoided open conflict, preferring to help local groups bargain for resources. SCARP was closely associated with a well established council tenants' organisation, for which it provided many services. The Waterford team succeeded in opening a dialogue with almost every group in the city – employers, trade unions, central and local government, the church and voluntary groups – and developed an expertise in co-ordinating pressure group campaigns. It was a good example of pluralist community action.

The Kilkenny project was divided between intensive casework with a small number of families with difficulties and a general promotion of community life on the council estate where the team lived and worked. Its main achievements were in the casework area, where the team felt that the approach of living among those they served helped to establish closer and more trusting relationships.

(6.3.2.) Campaign Activities

NCCCAP not only protested against the city's development plan, but prepared and presented a counter plan. It was a partial success, forcing two revisions of the city plan which allowed rather more housing to be retained in the locality. Cork's 'education action group', although ultimately unsuccessful in securing co-educational primary schools in its area, did succeed in convincing the authorities that they had underestimated the number of school places that were needed.

The Waterford team organised several seminars involving a range of local groups, out of which arose a campaign for an arts centre and the appointment of a youth officer. In late 1979 it became involved in housing issues, setting up a flat-dwellers' association to press for an enlarged council building programme.

The Kilkenny team was at an early stage involved in forming a tenants' association to demand open fireplaces in the estate's houses. The association secured its fireplaces and lapsed into inactivity, preferring not to concern itself with the problems of the minority of poor families among its members.

SCARP was involved n a great deal of day-to-day work helping council tenants to get repairs. It also prepared a redevelopment plan for the area and held an exhibition to promote the rehabilitation of older houses.

(6.3.3) Welfare Rights

Although the three directly run projects began in theory as a single welfare rights project, progress in this field was at first very hesitant. The Waterford team brought together a claimants' group which soon metamorphosed into a co-op shop, trading in secondhand children's clothes. Only later did the team become indirectly involved in welfare rights by providing office space for a legal aid centre and through the flat-dwellers' association's housing 'clinic'.

The Cork team distrusted welfare rights, seeing it as a means of oiling the wheels of an inequitable system, but experience with a local industrial dispute prompted it to produce a 'Know Your Rights' booklet. In time it came to operate an active 'Area Education Rights Centre', combining casework and classes on welfare issues.

SCARP was the only project to employ a legal adviser. It operated an advice bureau in the main street, partly as a means of introducing itself to the residents. It also ran welfare rights educational activities, but the attempt to form a claimants' group was unsuccessful. NCCCAP and the Kilkenny team also gave individual welfare advice.

The hesitation in venturing into welfare rights arose in part from a lack of specialist knowledge among the project workers and a doubt whether it was an appropriate activity for community workers. Experience led not only to an acceptance of welfare rights but also, at least in Cork and South Dublin, to the acquisition of a significant expertise.

(6.3.4)   Youth Work and Training

This was another field where workers' attitudes shifted. The NCCCAP and Cork teams were both at first wary of becoming social control agents, keeping young people off the streets. Both eventually ran successful pre-vocational training courses, funded by the government industrial training service. NCCCAP's most successful course combined photography and basic literacy for a group of nine teenagers, samples of whose work were later published.[4] The Cork team ran a wide ranging sixteen-week 'School to Work' course with fourteen teenagers.

The Waterford team was instrumental in reviving the local youth service and greatly increasing the city's grant for youth activities. SCARP was involved in youth work with the tenants' organisation.

(6.3.5)   Cultural Activities

This was a particular forte of the Waterford group which ran two arts festivals and campaigned for an arts centre.

(6.3.6)   Playgroups

The more militant projects distrusted playgroups. NCCCAP included them in its submission to Combat Poverty, but later decided they were not relevant to the needs of working-class mothers. The Waterford team on the other hand was very proud of its playgroup, which won a prize in a national competition. The Kilkenny team's community work centred around the local playgroup, which it persuaded to appoint a local mother as salaried play-leader. It also encouraged some of the poorer families on the estate to join the group, but on the whole the group was not interested in their special difficulties.

(6.3.7)   Economic Activities

In contrast to the rural projects there were few urban activities of a directly economic nature. The co-op shop in Waterford had a very small turnover. The pre-vocational training schemes helped a few teenagers into skilled jobs, although the teams justified their work as much in terms of enlarging social awareness as in increasing employability. All the teams ran employment surveys to bring their areas' economic problems to public attention.

(6.3.8)   Resource Centres

The so-called Welfare Rights Scheme was later renamed the Urban Resource Scheme, and although the directly run projects never operated as an integrated scheme they all eventually ran resource centres, at first to serve their immediate localities and later to cover wider areas. By 1980 all the urban projects except Ballyfermot, which had dropped out of the programme, were giving out 'seed money' to local groups, helping them apply for grants, organising training courses, providing office services and putting them in touch with specialist advice. At the same time the teams became less involved in starting up new groups, although the availability of support services itself encouraged new groups to form. At the end of the programme the projects proposed to carry on as resource centres.

(6.3.9)   Assessment

There was very little direct economic impact from the work of the urban projects. This was not the route they chose to take, although self-help and co-operative ventures are possible in an urban setting as the Craigmillar project in Scotland demonstrates. The main objective in Ireland was to modify the relationship between the people and the administrations which controlled so much of their lives.

Many families may have benefited from the welfare rights advice given by the projects, although they were not the only agency in this field.[5] Some council tenants had their dwellings repaired more promptly through the teams' intervention. The Dublin city council was taught a lesson in consultation, and allowed 250 more houses to be built in NCCCAP's area. The Knocknaheeny estate in Cork secured more school places and precipitated a national test case on parents' rights.

All these were minor gains. No concessions were won on major issues and the community structures set up by the project teams were often still very fragile in 1980. At the same time various administrations have found themselves faced with a more demanding clientèle, which should discourage their more autocratic tendencies.

Some of these issues, notably the education dispute, have reached national level. If the government wished it could use these pressures to justify further measures of social reform. This may not have been alien to the Coalition Government's thinking in 1973, but with a different government in a different economic setting this seems unlikely.

At the European level the urban projects complement the work of the British ARCs in demonstrating the resource centre approach. Some of the project activities, especially in pre-vocational training, are relevant to the Social Fund, and indeed some are now supported on Social Fund money.

(6.4)   SPECIAL GROUPS AND SPECIAL ISSUES

This section covers the eleven remaining projects in the Irish National Programme. Two were minor involvements with organisations which were given office space in the Dublin HQ. The others included two directly run research projects and seven contracted-out arrangements, all concerned with special issues or special groups.

(6.4.1)   Social Welfare Allowances

This was to have been a major element in the Irish Programme, but in the event it was a minor component. It was envisaged as a descriptive evaluation of the government's new Social Welfare Allowances Scheme, due to come into force in 1976. In the event implementation was delayed until 1977, so that the Combat Poverty research team spent 1976 surveying the last 2,000 recipients of the Home Assistance scheme, which the new scheme was to replace. This was a residuary means-tested scheme for the extreme poor who had no other means-tested or insurance benefits for which they could qualify. The team also interviewed the senior officials responsible for the old and the new systems.

A seminar with the officials was held in 1979. Apart from this there has been no follow-up and the report has still (May 1981) not been published. Its general conclusions are that the problems of the old scheme persist in the new scheme – clients are unaware of their rights, benefits are too low, senior officials have too much discretion and too little guidance and the training system is inadequate.

(6.4.2) Social Service Councils

These are local bodies co-ordinating the work of non-government social welfare agencies. Several members of the Combat Poverty committee had links with these councils, and wished to survey their effectiveness. Accordingly a national survey of SSCs was carried out with a more detailed study in Co. Clare. The work progressed very slowly, due to staffing problems, and the two internal reports were not completed until 1979 and 1980. Neither has been published. The general conclusions are that SSCs are effective in co-ordinating services, identifying beneficiaries and spreading information. On the other hand they had contributed little to developing new services or discussing social issues, and they were not equipped to deal with income maintenance or housing problems.

(6.4.3) Old and Alone

The Irish Programme's third main survey was contracted out to the Society of St Vincent de Paul and focused on the housing conditions and social contacts of old people living alone, both in the Republic and Northern Ireland. The results were published in October 1980.[6] Over half the sample of 1,500 people was found to lack a hot-water supply and a bath or shower, and 10 per cent had no electricity. Only a small minority had telephones or any means of calling for help in an emergency.

The Society intends the results to be discussed by its local branches, which it is hoped will develop appropriate responses.

(6.4.4) Travellers

Combat Poverty's very first project was a contracted-out venture with Travellers Rehabilitation Industrial Aid (TRIAL), which ran a training centre for young people from 'Traveller' families at Ennis, Co. Clare. Shortly afterwards a 'one-off' grant was made to a similar centre, the Fairgreen Centre, for Traveller girls in Galway. The Travellers are Ireland's equivalent of Gypsies. There are estimated to be about 13,500 in the Republic, about 90 per cent of whom Combat Poverty reckoned to be illiterate.

Combat Poverty's financial aid enabled TRIAL to renovate its centre and extend it to include a girls' section, carpentry and metal-work shops and a literacy area. In 1978 a researcher was commissioned to carry out a participant observation study of the centre, and she submitted a detailed report to Combat Poverty.[7] The report, still unpublished, is a useful contribution to the literature on pre-vocational training for young people from cultural minorities.

The two centres are now supported by the national vocational training agency. Combat Poverty, while happy that their future had been secured, was anxious lest the tradition of Traveller participation in running the centres might be lost.

(6.4.5)   Battered Women

Irish Women's Aid provides 'refuges' for victims of family violence, a service pioneered in Britain in the 1960s. The organisation currently operates two refuges and a night shelter. In April 1977 Combat Poverty provided two workers for the Dublin refuge, which in that year handled over 200 families. One worker was to develop self-help activities and liaison with other organisations while the second was to stimulate research.

The two workers had a difficult relationship with the volunteers who ran the refuge and only partly succeeded in carrying out their tasks. The self-help objective was dropped, partly because of lack of space to organise activities. The liaison work was more fruitful; a government grant was obtained and a closer working relationship was developed with the city housing department. No attempt was made to link up with other women's organisations; Irish Women's Aid did not consider itself a feminist group.

The voluntary workers were not enthusiastic to carry out research. Two small surveys were, however, completed and prepared for publi-cation.[8] The researcher insisted that family violence was not related to social class, but her statistics show that use of the refuge clearly was. Most of the residents' husbands were unemployed and living on wel-fare payments. The wives usually attributed their husbands' violence to drunkenness. In 1976 the Republic had introduced 'barring orders' to protect battered wives, but the Combat Poverty researcher reported that none of the residents of the refuge had found these effective.

(6.4.6) Legal Aid

In 1980 no system of legal aid in civil cases existed in the Republic. Fortunately a number of barristers, solicitors and law students were prepared to give their services free, which they did through Free Legal Aid Centres Ltd (FLAC). This had twelve advice centres in Dublin. Its main objective was not so much to give direct service as to pioneer a public system of legal aid and advice.

During 1977–9 Combat Poverty grant-aided FLAC to employ a community law officer at its Coolock centre. This was intended as a prototype community law centre, run by a local management committee. The law officer was appointed to reinforce the welfare rights side of the centre's work. He seems to have been extremely active, giving individual advice, running courses, forming groups, conducting research and agitating for legislative reforms. By 1980 the government had put forward proposals for a legal aid service in civil cases, although FLAC found them inadequate in several respects.

(6.4.7) Housing Advice

For two years Combat Poverty grant-aided Threshold Ltd, a recently formed voluntary housing advice service. The service was very active, handling over 3,000 enquiries, but its organisers refused to be drawn into pressure group activities or forming client groups. Prior to the Combat Poverty grant it had, however, completed a critical analysis of rent control, which was included in the Combat Poverty report.

(6.4.8) Youth at Athlone

Combat Poverty was involved twice with the Community Services Council at Athlone, a small town in central Ireland. In 1976 it provided £10,000 to help build a youth centre and in 1980 it helped establish a swap-shop and an information centre for young people.

(6.4.9) Disabled and Homeless

Two outside organisations, the Disabled People's Action Group (DPAG) and Hope (an organisation helping homeless children) were given office space in Combat Poverty's Dublin HQ.

(6.4.10) Assessment

Neither of the two nationwide studies run by Combat Poverty has been published, so there has been no public reaction. The Old and Alone Study has been published and may prompt positive action from the Society of St Vincent de Paul.

The roll-call of agencies aided financially by Combat Poverty is indicative of its changing function. It too was becoming a resource centre, less often starting up projects of its own and more often helping other agencies, of every conceivable type. Most of them were single issue or special group projects, very different from the multi-activity local projects favoured in the early stages.

This may have been the most effective way for Combat Poverty to use its money, but it constituted a major change of direction undertaken without consultation with Brussels. Since the European Programme itself had little overall structure, the increasing fragmentation of the Irish Programme did it little harm. If, however, the Community should ever attempt a more coherent programme it would need to keep its national components operating within narrower limits. It was also very difficult for the European Commission to track which bodies in Ireland were the ultimate recipients of its money and what they used it on, for the contracted-out projects themselves often subsidised other projects. Moreover, the final recipients were often unaware of the European provenance of their aid ('Old and Alone' makes no acknowledgement of EEC support), so it bought no goodwill for Europe. In the Irish Programme there was a clear conflict between flexibility and accountability.

(6.5) CONCLUSION

In 1974 Combat Poverty declared its aim to be the reduction of inequalities in Irish society through practical interventions in deprived areas, increased public awareness, and contributions to the development of effective long-term policies.

There is a long list of practical interventions to the programme's credit and some of the structures it helped to establish, for instance some of the co-ops and training courses, will doubtless survive. This is less certain of the resource centres, although at least one is struggling on. Several outside organisations were helped through critical stages or enabled to expand with Combat Poverty's aid. Although the committee was disbanded in December 1980, it has left its mark.

On publicity and the development of long-term policy the achievement is less certain. Combat Poverty claimed to be responsible for almost all the publicity about poverty in the Republic in the last five years, but in general the programme was cautious about publicity, fearing it as a two-edged sword. Major policy issues have been raised, on agriculture, fishing, education, welfare law, housing and so on, but as yet it is difficult to identify changes that have flowed from this. We can only concur with the slogan on the cover of the Cork project's prospectus, 'All the flowers of Tomorrow are the seeds of Today'.

(6.6) POSTSCRIPT 1982

In December 1980 the Combat Poverty national committee was disbanded. The then Minister for Health and Social Welfare undertook to continue some aspects of the committee's work through a reconstituted National Social Service Board, but this was ignored when the new Board was set up in June 1981. In the same month, however, the general election returned the Fine Gael-Labour Coalition to power with the promise that 'the structure of the Combat Poverty organisation will be re-established with local involvement and the development of constructive community action against poverty'. The chairwoman of the old committee has been appointed to head the new organisation and legislation is expected in the spring of 1982 to give it powers to go back into business.

Notes

[1] Written by Edward James.

[2] United Nations, *Social Progress through Community Development*, New York, 1955.

[3] Quoted from the project manager for several of the rural projects, at a press conference in Dublin in 1980.

[4] *Inner Word*, published by NCCCAP and written by the nine trainees, 1980.

[5] A small network of Community Information Centres (CICs) was set up at about the same time that the Irish Programme was launched.

6 B. Power, *Old and Alone in Ireland*, Society of St Vincent de Paul, Dublin, 1980.

7 Ms Sinéad Ní Shuinear, *The Centre as a Nucleus for Traveller Development*, Irish National Committee for Pilot Schemes to Combat Poverty (unpublished).

8 According to Combat Poverty's research officer they were prepared for publication in the *Irish Journal of Sociology*, but the author was unable to trace them.

7
Italy[1]

(7.1) PADUA: THE REORGANISATION OF SOCIAL AND MEDICAL SERVICES

The Padua project, the largest in the European Programme, is an attempt to restructure the entire social and medical services of a town with a population of approximately 250,000.

(7.1.1) The Environment

Padua is a relatively prosperous town situated in the Veneto region of North-West Italy. The population has risen steadily over the last five years, mainly as a result of immigration from the rural hinterland. This has led to an imbalance in the average age of the population. Recent statistics show that 28.3 per cent of the citizens of Padua are under the age of nineteen and 16.4 per cent of the population is over sixty, 65 per cent of the latter group being female. Padua, being the seat of one of the oldest and most renowned universities in Europe, has a student population of about 60,000.

Padua is an important commercial and manufacturing centre with the result that it appears to be suffering less from the current economic recession than other towns in Italy.

Although the citizens of Padua seem to be quite well-off, there are roughly 4–6,000 people in the city whose sole source of income is social assistance. There are 3–5,000 handicapped persons not including the elderly handicapped.[2]

(7.1.2) The Project

The project had its origins ten years ago at a time where there was acute national and local concern over the adequacy of social and medical services. In 1972, following a survey of the population of Padua,[3] it was concluded that to remedy the ills of the city a new radical view of social welfare was required to replace the existing fragmented system which consisted of a plethora of unco-ordinated benefits and services. From this sprang the idea of a Unita Locale, a

Local Unit, which would provide integrated social and medical services on a local basis.

In June 1972 the first local unit was set up; four more were established the following Spring. The project became part of the European Programme at the instigation of the AAAII (Ammistratazione per la Attivita Assistenziali Italiana e Internazionale) a government-sponsored body which had, during the 1960s, advocated the local development of social services through the creation of Local Units.

Four main principles govern the project: *unification* of medical and social services; *prevention* of ill-health and poverty by means of the early diagnosis of social and health problems; *decentralisation* of services; *universality*, that is the provision of services to all citizens on a non-categorical basis. Initially the Commune decided not to provide services to specific groups of people identified as being in need in order to avoid their stigmatisation. However, when the project had been in operation for a number of years it became evident that certain social groups living in conditions of special hardship needed specific services over and above those available to the general population. These were, in particular, the handicapped and the elderly who were living alone. The project decided to set up special services to combat social isolation among these groups. These specialist services directed at certain clearly defined target groups were not felt to be a negation of the project's 'all for all' policy, but rather specific examples of such policy. The specialist services are available freely to all the citizens of Padua who are in need of them. There is no limit on the right to services based on geographic location, income level or any of the other criteria frequently used to confine the provision of welfare services to a limited number of recipients.

(7.1.3) The Local Units

There are ten local units in Padua each with a catchment area from 12,500 to 50,000 inhabitants. Each local unit provides a variety of social and medical services, the strongest emphasis being given to preventative socio-medical care for young children. In each unit there is a basic team consisting of two paediatricians, two health visitors, a social worker and two educational psychologists. For every three basic teams there is a specialist team comprising a neuropsychiatrist, a psychologist and, in the case of one team, a physiotherapist. The specialist team, in theory, deals with cases referred to it by the basic team although there is an increasing number of self-referrals. The four specialist teams are based in four local units but circulate among the others. There is also a speech therapy clinic. Preventative medical care is provided by the teams for children from birth until school-going age; thereafter it is normally provided through the medium of the schools.

The composition of the basic teams reflects the project's emphasis on inter-disciplinary co-operation. The educationalists and social workers work closely with the schools and the families of the children as well as co-ordinating the work of the basic teams with the other services provided by the unit.

The non-medical services provided by the local units include an information service whose task is to give advice to clients on welfare rights; a family aid service which provides domestic help to families with short-term problems (e.g. when a mother is ill or hospitalised) and on a more long-term basis to the elderly and the handicapped thus preventing, in many cases, their institutionalisation. The anagraphic service in each unit registers births, deaths, marriages and all other information on citizens required to be recorded under Italian law.

As mentioned above, special services are provided for those with particular needs: children from low-income families, the elderly, young offenders and the handicapped.

(7.1.4) Research and Evaluation

Prior to the setting up of the project little detailed information existed about the population. One of the main tasks of the project is the conduct of a survey of the population. A social register, designed to give a detailed and accurate profile of the entire city, is currently being compiled. It is hoped that this register will make easier the task of assessing the needs of the population and facilitate the effective provision of services.

(7.1.5) Conclusion

The Padua project undoubtedly satisfied the criteria set out in the Council Decision setting up the European Programme. It is innovatory in that it provides integrated social and medical services on a non-categorical basis to all citizens. These services are provided locally thus making them more accessible to the client population and enabling needs to be gauged more accurately than is usually the case with a more centralised system.

The level of *participation* in the running of the local units by the clients is virtually nil but there is a high level of client participation in the case of the specialist services. We can conclude from this that in the case of activities which citizens can organise themselves and where there is no call for professional expertise there is extensive client participation. Conversely, where professional skills are required there is hardly any participation on the part of clients who see themselves as passive recipients of services.

As to *transferability*, the project has attracted great interest both in Italy and in other countries. It has been visited by many of the other projects in the European Programme, all of which saw in it a solution to many of the problems of effective service delivery prevailing in their own Member States.

By all appearances the project has succeeded in replacing an out-dated fragmentary system of social and medical care with a new integrated system of services designed to meet the real needs of the people.

Lack of data makes it impossible to make a quantitative assessment of the effect of the project on the lives of the people of Padua. Many aspects of this project could theoretically be evaluated quantitatively in a scientific manner but the information necessary to carry out this type of analysis is not available. In spite of this, it can be concluded that the project must of necessity have improved the quality of life of the citizens of Padua. Services are more readily available to all and a high degree of socio-medical care exists for children. This project is exciting; it has many lessons for all of us regardless of where we live.

(7.2)   GIUGLIANO[4]

(7.2.1)   The Environment

Giugliano is situated north of Naples in the province of Campania, the poorest region in the Mezzogiorno. The area is one of impover-ishment, degradation and under-employment. The infant mortality rate is high, 23.3 births per 1,000. Unemployment is consistently high and 10 per cent of the population over six years of age is illiterate.

(7.2.2)   **The Project**

Giugliano was one of the second wave of projects to join the European Programme in 1977/8. Nevertheless, its origins can be traced back to 1974 when a group of doctors and para-medical personnel set up a Centre for Health and Social Services designed to provide polyvalent services, that is integrated social and medical services to the residents of Giugliano. Such services are directed towards: (1) children, young people, women and the elderly; (2) low-income families; (3) those who are in need of health, educational or social services. The responsibility for the project lies with the Director of the Centre, Dr Luciano Carrino. Project work is co-ordinated by a central team comprising a psychologist, a social worker, a secretary and two assistants. The project has rented premises in East and West Giugliano in addition to the Centre.

(7.2.3)   **Achievements**

With respect to the overall aim of the project, social centres have been created and sizeable numbers of persons from the target population have been involved in activities. The women and children have obtained an increased use of public transport facilities through negotiations with the local administration, as well as an increase in the number of children registered for summer holiday activities. Citizens' groups have succeeded in getting some rather nasty rubbish heaps removed.

Many reports have been made by the project team about their work. The project director has published a book, *Critical Medicine in Italy*, which expounds the intellectual basis of the project. Press conferences have been held, radio broadcasts made and staff have lectured about the project in Italy and in other countries. Many visitors from European countries have visited the project. Thus the project has shared its information, knowledge and progress locally as well as internationally. It has made an impact in the development of a regional health centre in Campania. Dr Carrino and his team have assisted in drafting regional legislation and in the development of a document expressing the need for polyvalent centres throughout Italy.

The concept of critical medicine based on effective participation of the recipients of welfare services is novel and may be particularly useful in poor economic areas such as the Mezzogiorno. It appears to depend on co-operation from local and regional administrators and union representatives; and on an adequate level of participation on the part of the clients.

(7.2.4.) Conclusion

This project has demonstrated that the quality of life, even in an economically poor community, can be increased by education about basic health, medical and social services and about ways in which to organise collectively and express needs. It has also helped prove that social and health services can be integrated and that multiple-service centres can be effective in dealing with problems occurring in the daily lives of those living under conditions of poverty.

Finally, the Giugliano project has demonstrated the relationship between effective practice and research. The staff's practice is based on data gathered in the process of doing their work, distinctly emphasising the importance of methodology in carrying out work with the poor.

Notes

[1] Written by Philippa Watson.

[2] Little data exists on these matters. All figures are approximate.

[3] Carried out by the Veneto Regional Centre for Research in Training in Social Welfare. The results are summarised in *Nuove Esperienze di Politica Sociale* published in Rome in 1975.

[4] This section draws heavily upon an evaluation made by Professor Tony Tripodi, who was engaged as an ESPOIR consultant during his sabbatical period at the University of Kent in the academic year 1979–80.

8
The United Kingdom[1]

(8.1) INTRODUCTION

(8.1.1) The Context

In 1972, when the Paris Summit committed the European Community to a new concern with social goals, the United Kingdom had still not formally become a Member State. The Poverty Programme has therefore broadly coincided with the first years of Britain's membership: years in which the relationship between Britain and her new partners has remained contentious in public debate.

Socially, politically and economically, moreover, the second half of the 1970s was a period of domestic turbulence. On the economic front, zero growth came to be the most optimistic goal for which policy-makers could aim, absolute decline the growing fear. Unemployment rose steadily and, apparently, ever more swiftly; inflation oscillated between about 8 per cent and 25 per cent. On the political front, the Labour government of 1974–9 attempted to forge a new 'social contract' between organised labour and government, intended to promote industrial peace and hence economic success within a framework of planned income redistribution; in the event, however, trade union discontent brought the experiment to an end and paved the way for a diametrically opposed approach to Britain's industrial and social problems by the new Conservative government. As Britain entered the 1980s, therefore, it was the bracing disciplines of the market and the dismantling of the apparatus of state planning that were being held out as the instruments of economic recovery.

(8.1.2) Poverty in the United Kingdom: the Research and Policy Agenda

The United Kingdom has a strong and long-standing tradition of social research into poverty. This has, nevertheless, a variety of different elements which combine and recombine in a changing kaleidoscope of research perspectives. To disentangle these contributing elements is inevitably difficult and, in a discussion as brief as this, crudely over-simplifying. Nevertheless, it may be useful to highlight three mutually interacting traditions and emphases.

First, there is a tradition of social arithmetic: the enumeration of families, households or individuals who fall below a particular 'poverty line' which is most conveniently defined in money terms. This is the tradition whose main representatives are Charles Booth's survey of London's poor in the 1880s, Rowntree's surveys in York in three successive periods in the years 1899–1950 and Townsend's studies of Britain in the 1960s and 1970s. The main focus is upon enumerating and categorising those who fall below whatever poverty line has been chosen; the main policy implications which are derived concern the levels of financial benefits which should be provided by the state through its system of social security. From this, various further questions are then commonly investigated: for example, the inferences that may be drawn as to the social and economic factors which precipitate individual poverty, or, at a very different level, the factors which deter individuals from making full use of the benefits already provided by the social security ystem.

Secondly, there is a long-standing tradition of concern with the family and with patterns of child rearing. Particularly during the later part of the nineteenth century, the eugenics movement was closely associated with this concern over the capacity of lower-class parents to raise children capable of making an effective contribution to the nation's economic and, indeed, its military strength.[2] Such fears were reformulated in the early 1970s by the then Secretary of State for Health and Social Security, Sir Keith Joseph, in a research programme he launched on the 'cycle of transmitted deprivation' which supposedly condemned the children of poorer families to a lifetime of poverty. More generally, however, this tradition of concern with the family has addressed itself to the capacity of the nuclear family, in a rapidly changing urban-industrial society in which traditional networks of social support have been disrupted, to provide children with the domestic support and the competences they need to survive and succeed in a society based on individual achievement.[3]

Thirdly, there is a long-standing tradition of self-help and mutual aid hailing, for example, from the Methodist chapels of the eighteenth century and the early trade unions of the nineteenth century. Here the main focus is upon the disruption of community networks which results from urban and industrial change; the counter-measures which this tradition highlights centre in political education and community self-help in order that occupational and/or urban communities particularly exposed to the costs of social change may better be able to cope with and challenge these changes. The main focus of research is upon the wider processes of change which may threaten such communities; the main focus of policy recommendations is upon providing resources to facilitate self-help and a creative community response to these changes. In the 1960s and early 1970s, the programme of Community Development Projects (CDPs) launched by the Home Office gave renewed expression to these perspectives. At the level of action, these projects proved a seminal influence in promoting new forms of community development throughout the United Kingdom, bringing together trade union groups with the residents of deprived areas; at the level of research one of the main results was to emphasise the impact of the rise and decline of industries on patterns of deprivation in the local communities immediately dependent upon them.

Each of these traditions of research and experimentation has had its counterpart in developments at the level of global social policies. The United Kingdom is distinguished from its neighbours by the major role which social assistance (Supplementary Benefits) plays in income maintenance, as well as the extent of critical research on poverty that this has helped to provoke.[4] For example, in recognition of the plight of the elderly poor, revealed in part by social researchers in the 1960s, there were various efforts at pensions reform; these culminated in the Labour government's plan of 1975, incorporating 'dynamisation' of benefits, on the Continental model.[5] At the same time, however, political pressures for restrictions upon public expenditure, coupled with a growing challenge to the discretion exercised by social assistance officials, led to a variety of reviews of the Supplementary Benefits system itself.

Particularly in the later part of the decade, both major political parties gave increasing emphasis in their policy statements to support of the family. A new system of child benefits was introduced in the middle of the decade, partly in recognition of the plight of many one-parent families.

Finally, throughout the 1970s, the Home Office in particular held to its interest in the support of community development approaches to combating deprivation, not least through its Voluntary Services Unit established early in the decade.

(8.1.3)   The British Projects in the European Programme

It would, of course, be misleading to suggest that the British projects were selected for the European Programme in terms of their systematic representativeness of this agenda of research and policy debate. Nevertheless, it would equally be misleading to disregard the fact that the British projects between them have spanned the principal axes of this debate. The welfare rights projects in Wolverhampton and Belfast have addressed themselves to the low levels of take-up of cash benefits by those living below the 'official' poverty line which is defined by the social assistance system. The Family Day Centres have attempted to develop new forms of support to one-parent families and other households whose livelihood and well-being are continually threatened by the lack of wider kinship networks. The Area Resource Centres and the two Edinburgh projects (Social and Community Development Project and the Craigmillar Festival Society) have built upon the traditions and models of community development established by the CDPs and other innovators in the 1960s and early 1970s.

(8.2)   NEW MAPS OF MISERY: THE NORTHERN IRELAND PROJECTS[6]

(8.2.1)   Introduction

Northern Ireland is the poorest part of the United Kingdom, and the province hardest hit by the current recession. The two short projects which featured in the European Programme of pilot schemes vividly portray, in their different ways, the human misery which this entails.

The two projects can best be viewed as two phases of a continuing project which embraced many other activities. Like most good social planning exercises it began with a survey, the Areas of Special Social Need (ASSN) survey. This was the first project supported by the European Community. The survey's sponsors, the Northern Ireland Department (the government department with overall responsibility for the province), then convened a committee of all the agencies which the survey results indicated as relevant to the problems they outlined. This Belfast Areas of Need (BAN) committee succeeded in mobilising a large amount of public money for projects in the special need areas, including a further project in the European Programme, the Belfast

Welfare Rights Project. This was focused on the low take-up of means-tested income maintenance benefits in certain districts.

The entire set of projects took place in greater Belfast, the urban area in which almost a third of the province's population lives.

(8.2.2) The Areas of Special Social Need Survey

The work had been commissioned before the European Programme was launched. It followed from a series of similar surveys on the mainland of Britain sparked off by the launching of the Urban Programme in 1968 and the policy of positive discrimination in favour of poor districts. In a broader sense it was part of a tradition dating back to the Booth and Rowntree surveys a century ago, mapping out the distribution of poverty in urban areas.

The bulk of the survey was a paper exercise, plotting data from the last census (1971) and operational data from the social services on to city maps. A doorstep survey of two areas was carried out to check the validity of the data and to invite opinions on several issues. The three stated objectives of the project were to use small area indicators to describe the concentrations of poverty in Belfast; to examine the statutory services and their effectiveness in combating social need; and to see if the methodology could be applied to the rest of the province. The ulterior motive was to stimulate action to alleviate poverty in districts where the research team knew full well that it existed in dramatic concentrations.

The survey used thirty-nine indicators of social need and calculated a separate rate for each 200 metres square of the urban area. Eighteen electoral wards were identified as 'high need' areas. Four need syndromes were observed. The first linked unemployment, low incomes, overcrowding and large families; the second linked old housing, low incomes, private renting, a high proportion of elderly people and a high proportion of children in care; the third linked mental handicap and educational subnormality; and the fourth, various other aspects of educational disadvantage. The first syndrome was considered the most important and was concentrated on the Catholic areas of both the inner city and the outlying council estates. The second syndrome affected both Catholic and Protestant areas of the inner city. The third and fourth syndromes were less concentrated and less important statistically. Roughly equal proportions of Protestants and Catholics lived in high-need areas, although Catholics more often suffered multiple deprivation, having larger families and higher levels of unemployment. In each of the two areas chosen for doorstep interviews, the Catholic Falls Road, and the Protestant Shankhill, 90 per cent of the population suffered some aspect of social need.

The spatial distribution of the public services designed to combat poverty was found to be inversely related to social need. No comparable concentrations of poverty were found in the follow-up survey in the rest of the province.

The survey was completed in 1976 and the results were published by HM Stationery Office the following year.[7]

(8.2.3)   Belfast Welfare Rights

The ASSN survey was a success in that it served as the basis for bringing together a number of agencies which made a reality of positive discrimination in public spending. Although some of the spending plans have since been postponed, a Belfast Co-ordinating Committee is still in existence whose BAN working group continues the work of the first BAN planning team.[8]

One of the findings of the survey was that there was a very low level of take-up of means tested cash benefits in certain poor districts. The second project supported by the European Community was an experiment designed to compare different methods of raising the level of take-up. The original intention was to survey the take-up rate of seventeen benefits in four areas (one inner city Protestant, one inner city Catholic, one outer area Protestant and one outer area Catholic) and then to attempt three different methods to raise the take-up rate. For various reasons the experiment did not work out quite as planned. This was, however, the only project in the European Programme to have a clear-cut experimental design.

The project was led by a university researcher and was based on local teams recruited in each area, which each set up and staffed an information bureau. It was eventually decided to run all three methods to increase take-up (door-to-door canvassing, leaflets and information bureaux) simultaneously in all four areas, relying on record keeping to distinguish the effectiveness of each method.

The preliminary survey of 1,100 households in 1979 collected a great deal of information not only about take-up rates but about housing, employment and incomes, which corroborated in vivid detail the findings of the ASSN survey. Taking into account the retired, single-parent families and the unemployed, only a minority of heads of household in the four areas were in employment. Nearly two-thirds of the population was below the projects' austere poverty line. 'In large parts of Belfast poverty is a mass rather than a minority condition' (*Poverty*, April 1980).

The survey report made special mention of the province's draconian policy on recovering debts, which has since been relaxed in response to this and similar protests.

Take-up of different means-tested benefits varied from 92 per cent to 33 per cent. It was considered that many applicants were deterred by out-of-date folk-knowledge of benefit criteria and fear of being rejected as undeserving claimants. On techniques to improve take-up, the researchers concluded, on the basis of 4,000 queries and several hundred successful claims, that leaflets were ineffective and the best results could be obtained from information bureaux publicised by door-to-door canvassing. This differs from findings in mainland Britain, which are mainly based on experience in areas of much less marked concentrations of poverty.

Although designed as a social planning exercise focused on a tightly defined problem, the Belfast Welfare Rights project was in some ways a community development venture in disguise. The local workers in the information bureaux were anxious to help 'their' people in whatever way they could (there were perhaps as many queries on housing as cash benefits) and much community work went unrecorded in the survey report. The project leader herself won a test case on sex discrimination arising from an incident in the course of the survey.

The findings have been published by the Child Poverty Action Group.[9]

(8.2.4) **Assessment**

The linked series of projects has been very successful in documenting poverty in Belfast, influencing the pattern of public spending, and exploring the particular problem of take-up of cash benefits. It has been in many respects a model social planning exercise. Hundreds of Belfast residents are undoubtedly better off as a result of its work. Unfortunately the projects have had to work in a climate of worsening economic depression and continuing political violence, both of which have struck hardest in the special need areas. The BAN projects have included a number of employment initiatives, but the problem they face is massive.

> It is easy to demonstrate statistically that the basis of much social need is the serious lack of employment, which if it were remedied would remove many other aspects of need.
>
> (ASSN report to the Commission, 1977)

(8.3)   THE WOLVERHAMPTON PROJECT

(National Association of Citizens Advice Bureaux Tribunal Representation Unit)

(8.3.1)   Aims

The overriding objective of the project is to make social welfare benefits more accessible to claimants by improving the quality of welfare rights advice and the provision, through the medium of the Citizens Advice Bureaux (Cabx), of representation before social welfare tribunals. To achieve this the project operates as a support unit, organising training for volunteers from ten Cabx in the West Midlands and providing a back-up service.

More specifically, the *primary goals* of the project are: (i) to equip generalist workers within the bureaux with the skills necessary to identify benefit problems; (ii) to equip those same workers with the ability to inform, advise and effectively intervene on behalf of their clients to maximise their income as far as possible; (iii) to enable all bureaux to have the capacity to represent appellants before social welfare tribunals; (iv) to encourage poor people with social security problems to use the services of the Cabx. The *secondary goals* of the project are (i) to aid other agencies and groups to develop welfare rights activities and to become aware of Cabx services; (ii) to aid the development of welfare rights services within the Cabx in regions which do not have ready access to similar support units; (iii) to establish welfare rights as an important element in Cabx development.

(8.3.2)   Organisation, Structure and Activities

The project team is small, having on average five members. An advisory group helps and advises on the running of the project and in planning and executing action and research programmes.

The project offers two types of training: in-bureaux training designed to teach workers about the social welfare system and so improve the quality of advice given to clients, and specialist training for those who are interested in tribunal representation. In-bureaux training, as its name suggests, consists of talks given by the project team to groups of volunteers in the bureaux. Specialist training is by means of residential courses on advocacy skills, coupled with mock tribunal hearings using video tape. The project offers a back-up service which ranges from advice over the telephone to bureaux workers on specific cases to joint interviews with the claimant and sometimes to joint representation.

From the outset the project has aimed at expanding its work both locally and nationally. Project staff have given a massive number of training courses up and down the country and have actively participated in the national debate on the provision of adequate representation at social welfare tribunals.

(8.3.3) Conclusions

Although it is difficult to measure accurately improvements in the quality of advice and representation offered as a result of the project's work, it is clear from discussions with the project team that bureaux volunteers show an acute awareness of the importance of welfare rights advice and considerable ability in providing it, a state of affairs which certainly did not exist before the project was set up.

The results of the project's work have been felt not only in the West Midlands but in many other areas of England and Wales. Although it is impossible at this stage to assess the full impact of the project, suffice it to say that it has stimulated a national awareness of the importance of integrated welfare rights services, that is the unified treatment of welfare rights problems from pre-claim advice to representation on appeal, and it has made moves to ensure the provision of such services in the West Midlands. All this is no mean achievement for what began as a small specialised project.

(8.4) THE FAMILY DAY CENTRES[10]

The Family Day Centres (FDCs) component of the European Programme comprised seven distinctive projects with the common objective of experimenting with new forms of non-residential care to help families in need. After the first year of the programme, the Institute of Community Studies was appointed to act as co-ordinator and overall assessor of the FDC projects.

Six of the projects were based in London, the seventh in Liverpool. Thus they were situated in areas which had long been particularly vulnerable to social and economic disruption, and where networks of community support and mutual aid had been weakened. In these areas, the more vulnerable members of society had been most badly affected. The FDCs provided a particular service (such as the care of children during the day) and provided a focus for community interest and a framework for rebuilding networks of mutual aid and support.

(8.4.1)   Aide à Toute Détresse (ATD)

ATD London is a member of an international federation which operates in many different locations and which ran several other projects in the European Programme. ATD's activities are concerned with promoting social awareness of what they term the 'Fourth World', that is, the 'bottom' 2 per cent of society which forms a sub-proletariat which is excluded from the normal social, political and economic systems, and to combat this exclusion by helping such families to develop the means to represent their interests collectively.

The sub-proletariat with which ATD worked in London came to the attention of the movement first when they were referred by housing authorities in South London to the ATD residential centre in Surrey, which provided short-term accommodation for disadvantaged families. Several of these families expressed an interest in maintaining contact with ATD after leaving the centre, and they formed the nucleus of the FDC project.

ATD's strategy for publicising the plight of the Fourth World was to provide a forum for regular meetings and discussion between representatives of the Fourth World and members of the mainstream society. These meetings were supplemented by home visits, telephone calls and letters to Fourth World families and a newsletter was launched giving information about 'Fourth World Evenings', written by the families themselves. ATD project workers also helped individuals compile their autobiographies, to be used to make the rest of society aware of the conditions in which the 'poorest of the poor' live. In addition, Fourth World families participated in rallies, meetings and conferences with their counterparts in other countries.

(8.4.2)   Camden Drop-In

The Drop-In Centre was based in one of twenty-three Family Service Units (FSUs) which had been operating in the UK since 1948. FSU families were referred by social services departments for help in dealing with their multiple problems. The Centre employed trained social workers to work intensively with a small proportion of the total number of FSU families in an informal setting, providing a warm and welcoming environment where people could discuss their problems openly and honestly with each other and with the project staff, could learn how their behaviour affected others and could, if they wished, try to develop new social (and domestic) skills. In the long term, the project workers aimed to help families become more confident of their skills and their role in the community, to promote mutual aid between members, and to help users develop social relationships outside the Centre.

Apart from traditional social work techniques, project staff also used video equipment and role playing which gave users the opportunity to see their social behaviour from an outsider's viewpoint and to 'learn' appropriate social behaviour for dealing with individuals and institutions. The Centre also had an active social side, with users organising communal outings and activities. The project staff kept individual diaries giving 'profiles' of the Centre users to which the latter could add their own comments and versions of events. Many of the Centre users seemed to benefit considerably from intensive social work in an informal setting and local social services department were very impressed.

(8.4.3)   Croydon Gingerbread

Gingerbread is a national self-help/mutual aid organisation whose members are lone parents. It aims to provide inexpensive social activities for single parents and their children; to provide practical help and advice; and to draw public attention to the economic and social needs of lone-parent families. Single-parent families are particularly vulnerable to economic hardship since adequate child care facilities are prohibitively expensive or simply not available. Gingerbread is particularly concerned with the safety of children who are left alone after school and during school holidays, who are at risk of road accidents and accidents in the home. The Croydon project provided a much-needed service for looking after the school-age children of single parents during these periods.

Project staff collected children from schools in the area and took them to their base, a large and comfortable Victorian house, where they looked after them until their parents could collect them after work. In school holidays this was extended to full day care. The project was obliged to limit places to children in the five to eleven age range since care of pre-school children is strictly controlled by local authority regulations and children over eleven are considered to be slightly less at risk. Even in this age range, the demand for places was overwhelming. Ideally, if resources permitted, the Gingerbread organisation would like to extend the service to include all children of lone parents. This would seem to be an invaluable service to provide to all children, regardless of their parents' marital state.

(8.4.4)   Defoe Day Care Centre

The Defoe project is a community nursery situated in the grounds of a college in Hackney, an inner London borough with many of the problems of deprived inner-city areas, and showing very high indices of poverty.

The project's main aim was to provide good quality care for pre-school children for the whole working day, thus enabling parents to work or to retrain or complete their education so as to improve their position in the labour market. It offered day care to six babies and to about twenty other children under five. As in the Croydon Gingerbread project, demand for places far exceeded supply and so places were allocated on the basis of greatest need, together with consideration of a balanced sex/race composition of the group. The baby places were allocated to young mothers who had become pregnant and left school before the end of their secondary education. They were able to attend courses in the college and visit their babies in the nearby nursery frequently. The other places were allocated to toddlers whose parents were in particular need: i.e. single parents, families on very low income, people in poor housing, parents with poor health.

The nursery combined good quality child care with education which educationalists and child care specialists who had contact with the nursery rated very highly. The project was slightly less successful in its attempt to provide a focus for community activity; the main obstacle to success was that the nursery was 'invisible', being tucked away in the college grounds.

(8.4.5) LVSC Family Groups

The London Voluntary Service Council (LVSC) is a co-ordinating body for a variety of voluntary and charity organisations which has a history of involvement in family group work dating back to 1948. LVSC supported about thirty family groups in the Greater London area, eight of which were funded by the European Programme.

Family (or neighbourhood) groups were aimed to attract people from the community who were so lacking in self-confidence that they were unable to sustain normal outlets for social expression and personal contact with others. Family groups comprised about ten to fifteen members, including a group leader, a playleader and (usually) an assistant playleader, who were paid a wage based on recognised salary scales.

First the group personnel were recruited from the local population and trained by the project staff in LVSC to establish and maintain their own family groups in the community. Then family groups were established in two contrasting London boroughs. The group leaders arranged their own accommodation (usually in community centres or church halls) and recruited their own group members. The groups usually met for about two hours, once a week. Group members had the chance to share their skills with others and discuss topics of common interest while the playleader and her assistant looked after the children. Many people who were socially isolated, lacking self-confidence and self-esteem, clearly benefited from the family-like hospitable atmosphere of the family groups, and in many cases friendships and support networks flourished. Their success was largely due to the considerable personal qualities of the group leaders and the fact that they belonged to the same community as their group members.

(8.4.6) The Downtown Family Centre

The parent body of this project was Cambridge House, a charitable institution concerned with furthering the 'new careerist' philosophy; that is, that helpers should be recruited from the target groups themselves and be paid on recognised salary scales (in common with the LVSC approach).

Downtown is an area in the inner London borough of Southwark at the heart of London's dockland, known locally as the 'island' because it is effectively cut off from the rest of London. The Surrey Docks, which isolated Downtown from the rest of London but at the same time provided its community with work, have become derelict. The disappearance of virtually the only source of work produced a drift in population unknown to the community for many generations, producing an irreversible disruption of the extensive kinship networks which were once prevalent. The Downtown population is traditionally hostile to outsiders so the 'new careerist' approach was particularly appropriate here.

Local people were involved from the beginning. Although the local tenants' association was initially hostile to the scheme, it soon came to support it fully. At first the project was aimed at all young families in the neighbourhood, but later the centre was reserved for the use of children under three and their parents. Older children were excluded since there were excellent nursery school facilities on the 'island' which would be threatened with closure if they were not fully exploited. The centre successfully attracted a very high proportion of their target group: mothers of very young children who tended to be socially isolated. The centre was open for several hours every weekday and the centre users organised social and handicraft activities. In addition, a literacy group helped a small number of people considerably. As in the case of the other FDC projects, of very great importance were the support networks which developed among users.

(8.4.7) The Newby Street Clubhouse, Liverpool

The parent organisation of this project was the Liverpool Personal Service Society (LPSS), a long-established voluntary social work agency with a large family casework component. LPSS activities were supported by a local housing association, Merseyside Improved Houses (MIH), which provided suitable premises at the outset of the project.

Newby Street is in the Kirkdale district of Liverpool. In 1976 it was the only remaining street, surrounded by wasteground, in a very depressed area due for redevelopment by Liverpool Corporation. Community recreational facilities for adults and children in the area were virtually negligible. Moreover, the indices of poverty were particularly high. The presence of such large numbers of particularly vulnerable people was partly explained by MIH's policy of providing accommodation in that area to people in particular need.

The project was small-scale, even by FDC standards, employing only one full-time leader and a part-time assistant for most of the duration of the programme. It was a centre where anyone could drop in and stay to chat, take part in discussions or more structured activities. It was particularly successful as a step-off point for further community action by local residents and for providing a focus for mutual aid and support.

It was generally very favourably received by local agencies in the area. LPSS was certainly convinced of the usefulness of this particular approach for helping people with problems and it went on to establish a similar clubhouse for recent psychiatric patients.

(8.5) THE AREA RESOURCE CENTRES[11]

(8.5.1) Introduction

As seen in the opening section of this chapter, there is a long-standing tradition in Britain of community self-help and community development as a strategy for combating poverty. During the 1970s, central government expressed its interest in part through the establishment of the Voluntary Services Unit within the Home Office; in the voluntary sector, the Gulbenkian Foundation was a leading innovator.[12] Both played an important part in sponsoring the three area resource centres which were included in the European Programme, although the centres are indebted to – and have contributed to – a much wider stream of innovation in this field. The Community Work Service (CWS) of the London Voluntary Service Council (LVSC) is located in central London and serves the whole city. The South Wales Anti-Poverty Action Committee (SWAPAC) has been based in Merthyr Tydfill, between the mining valleys of the South Wales coalfield and rural mid-Wales. The Govan Area Resource Centre (GARC) is based in Govan, a small shipbuilding area of central Glasgow. They have collaborated in a programme of joint monitoring and evaluation, sponsored by the European Commission and the Gulbenkian Foundation.

The areas in which the three centres have been working are in many ways very different: in population, in geographical area covered, in their patterns of industrial development and in their traditions of local organisation and community self-help. Shipbuilding transformed the inner-city community of Govan into an industrial centre by the end of the nineteenth century, its expanding labour force (drawn from the Highlands and Ireland) accommodated in over-crowded tenements. South Wales was transformed over a similar period by the coal and steel industries and has similarly gone into decline during the twentieth century. London's economic base is more varied: but this very complexity tends to mask the disadvan-tages and deprivations suffered by substantial minorities within the population. The city's manufacturing industry is in decline; and in coming years the introduction of microprocessors threatens office work, another major source of employment. Finally, there are varia-tions in the community networks of the three areas: in South Wales, for example, many of the community self-help groups and organisa-tions which once existed have crumbled in the face of depopulation; in London there is a much richer range of local community groups, but the size, heterogeneity and administrative complexity of the city tend to isolate them from each other.

(8.5.2)   Resources for Communities

In a complex and rapidly changing urban-industrial society, the processes whereby life chances are distributed are increasingly obs-cure, especially to more disadvantaged members of society. The disadvantaged lack the networks of information, expertise and mutual support necessary in order to articulate their interests and to press for alternative social arrangements; and these disadvantaged communities are often characterised by traditionalism, parochialism and deference towards established authorities.

All three projects have therefore set out to provide the resources whereby these communities can learn to participate actively in chang-ing their social environment, rather than fatalistically adjusting to changes imposed upon them. Each resource centre has sought to establish a 'communications system' among the community groups in its area, enabling them to speak more effectively to each other and to policy-makers whose decisions affect local patterns of deprivation and their relief. The threefold aim has been: (i) to illuminate, demystify and give early warning of the wider processes of socio-economic change which impinge upon these communities; (ii) to explore, demonstrate and publicise the alternative social arrangements which can be successfully pioneered by local self-help groups, thereby stimulating innovation by other community groups; (iii) to provide local self-help community groups and, more especially, federations of such groups with (a) the information, resources and expertise they need to negotiate their way in a bureaucratised world, and (b) the political knowledge and skills to articulate the interests of the disadvantaged within the political arena. The resource centres are, in short, concerned with the *power* inequalities within our society and the way these shape regional, employment and social policies in the interests of more advantaged groups.

The Govan project has used seminars, courses, a community newspaper, libraries and occasional publications to monitor, explain and publicise the effects of impending changes in government policy, particularly in the fields of housing and employment. Community responses have then been fed back to government. The resource centre has also encouraged and supported a variety of new community ventures capable of challenging disadvantage and of promoting debate and the learning of new skills: particularly in the field of employment, where various producer co-operatives have been attempted under very difficult conditions. Thirdly, the Govan centre has provided a wide range of services to local community groups which are seeking, directly or indirectly, to combat the deprivation of the area: secretarial equipment, feasibility studies for employment initiatives, training in administrative skills, etc. [13]

Based as it is within the London Voluntary Service Council (LVSC), the London Community Work Service has inherited a wide network of links to professional community workers and local community groups throughout the capital. It has built upon these in order to carve out a distinctive role for itself as a *regional* resource centre. First, it provides a city-wide communication and 'early warning' system. Through its newsletter and conferences it monitors and publicises developments in social and economic policies which affect disadvantaged groups and communities in London; and it allows a wide variety of groups to use these mailings to publicise their responses to those developments. During 1980, for example, CWS monitored and publicised government proposals for changes in its Urban Aid programme and plans for major changes in the administration of London's council housing. Secondly, CWS co-ordinates and services the federations of community groups and the campaigns which often develop around metropolitan issues such as cuts in health services and school closures. Thirdly, where these federations and campaigns endure, and are in evident need for a continuing specialist support service, CWS has sought to create such a specialist agency, e.g. to help local communities scrutinise development proposals which affect them. However, as the funds available for voluntary activities have become scarce, it has become increasingly difficult to hive off such specialist services in this way.

The South Wales project (SWAPAC) has made several important changes of emphasis in the course of its work. First of all, it initially devoted a lot of energy to support particular local initiatives, especially in the fields of employment, housing, and social and legal services: as concrete measures to combat deprivation, as models of new forms of mutual aid and as the building blocks of regional federations similar to those which CWS has built. After the early years, however, this direct sponsorship of local initiative was reduced: in part because many became self-sustaining and could be built into regional federations, and in part because the rising levels of unemployment encouraged the project to work increasingly with the trade unions on measures of job protection across the region as a whole. Secondly, the project has increasingly emphasised the importance of political education in the development of self-help community groups, if they are not merely to administer their own poverty. This involved not only the creation of links between community groups and organised labour but also less obvious fields of political education, such as self-help groups of the elderly. Third, instead of feeding the views of community groups merely to policy-makers, the project has increasingly sought to influence a wider range of interest groups and public opinion: in regard, for example, to the exclusion of South Wales, the 'valley city', from government funds which are restricted to inner city areas of deprivation.

(8.5.3)   Conclusion

The resource centres demonstrate how disadvantaged communities can be enabled to participate in the formulation and implementation of policy. Such participation does not, however, involve a harmonious partnership between voluntary efforts and statutory resources; rather, as often as not, the new skills and opportunities which the resource centres provide, lead these disadvantaged groups to express their grievances and hostility towards the policy-makers upon whom their lives have so long been dependent.

(8.6) SOCIAL AND COMMUNITY DEVELOPMENT PROGRAMME, EDINBURGH[14]

Like the area resource centres, both of the Edinburgh projects in the European Programme have been concerned with local areas of multiple deprivation. The Social and Community Development Programme (SCDP) was established jointly by the city and regional government. It aimed to tackle four areas[15] of multiple deprivation in the city, by means of a twofold strategy: greater co-ordination of the various instruments of government, and simultaneously, activation of the energies of the communities concerned.

In the early years the emphasis was upon promoting networks of community groups in the four areas; and more specifically, upon assisting them in articulating their views of the local authority policies which affect them. However, the project's location within the local authority raised high expectations in the four areas concerned, and prompted these communities to voice their resentment over their long-standing neglect by local government. The credibility of the project with the community groups in the four areas was therefore always fragile. Secondly, SCDP has striven to forge a more integrated approach to deprivation by different local authority departments. At least initially, there was no systematic procedure for debating the balance which should be struck between programmes oriented towards particular areas (bringing together the variety of local authority services) and, on the other hand, service-oriented programmes (which husband and develop scarce professional expertise). In consequence, the committees and departments administering these service-oriented programmes have been reluctant to commit themselves to the area-oriented policies advocated by SCDP. In 1979, the city government withdrew its collaboration in the project; the regional authority, however, strengthened its commitment to urban regeneration and to SCDP as an instrument of policy co-ordination.[16] Latterly, therefore, the project has been centrally concerned with managing the 'creative tension' between area-based and service-based policies within the regional authority. Thirdly, SCDP has increasingly aimed to build links between local communities and outside sources of funds – including Urban Aid, the Manpower Services Commission and others.

Like the area resource centres, therefore, the SCDP emphasises that disadvantaged communities lack the information and resources to influence the formulation and implementation of social policies. The area resource centres build a communication system principally by promoting 'horizontal' networks of community groups. SCDP, in contrast, has emphasised the 'vertical' dimension of such a communication system, negotiating and interpreting between local government and outside funding bodies on the one hand, and community groups on the other. This is possible because of its location inside local government (which incidentally distinguishes it from most other projects in the European Programme). It should be added, however, that although the project prefers to present its activity as the provision of a neutral communication system, it is perceived by local authority departments and by the community groups in the areas concerned, more as a political negotiator and 'broker', wielding a significant amount of political influence. Moreover, the system of direct consultation which the project promotes between local people and officials by-passes the traditional system of representative democracy through elected councillors, even though the project, as part of local government, is itself formally responsible to those elected councillors. In pioneering these new channels of communication, therefore, the project, if only by implication, raises more fundamental questions about consultation, participation and representation in the government of a bureaucratised society.

(8.7)   THE CRAIGMILLAR FESTIVAL SOCIETY[17]

Craigmillar is an area of 25,000 population on the outskirts of Edinburgh, consisting largely of families rehoused from the inner city. It ranks as the most deprived area within the Lothian region: in terms of high unemployment, poor housing and social amenities, and rates of delinquency.[18] Craigmillar is stigmatised as one of the 'black spots' of Edinburgh; the local authority has tended to dump its 'problem' families there, and over the decades the residents have become frustrated, resentful and resigned to their fate.

In the early 1960s, however, a handful of residents launched an annual Arts Festival which, unlike the Edinburgh International Festival, would be accessible to the people of the Craigmillar estate and would indeed be a direct expression of their local traditions and creativity. However, those involved soon moved from the arts to a wider programme of 'cultural action' in Craigmillar: attempting to mobilise local resources of leadership, enterprise and particular skills in a collective and creative response to the major problems afflicting the area. By the early 1970s the Festival Society had widened its range of activities to virtually all areas of the community's life: housing, employment, welfare rights, transport, and services to the elderly and handicapped; and it had begun to promote a sustained analysis of the wider social, political and economic processes impinging upon Craigmillar from outside, in order to be able to modify the governmental policies upon which the estate is dependent. The Festival Society had begun an exercise in retrieval: the retrieval of self-governing and creative community networks which are not dependent upon capricious decisions taken by power centres outside the community.

During the period of the European Programme the Festival Society has been developing 'a comprehensive plan for action' by drawing together the people of Craigmillar and representatives of local government, and by piloting innovatory schemes for combating particular aspects of the estate's deprivation. It has won funds from a variety of external agents, both statutory and charitable, as well as from the European Commission. The wide-ranging programme of planning and innovation remains centred, however, in the Arts Programme with which the Festival Society began its work.

Nevertheless, the various forces which combined in the past to make the estate an area of multiple deprivation have continued and in some cases grown more severe. Unemployment has worsened here, as it has elsewhere; public and social services have been cut; there has been a resurgence of vandalism and delinquency. Secondly, although co-operation between the Festival Society and statutory welfare agencies has often been mutually fruitful, there have also been tensions and 'demarcation disputes'. The wide range of activities in which the Society is now engaged and the power and patronage which it therefore wields have also led it to be criticised by other community groups, both inside and outside Craigmillar, as well as by elements of local government.

The Craigmillar Festival Society demonstrates, nevertheless, that within any disadvantaged community there may exist a variety of latent skills which can be mobilised into action. It also demonstrates, however, the extended period of time which is necessary in order to cultivate these skills; and its work over two decades contrasts with the shorter-term funding which policy-makers conventionally provide for 'pilot' anti-poverty projects.

Notes

[1] Sections (8.1) and (8.5) to (8.7) have been written by Graham Room; Section (8.2) by Edward James; Section (8.3) by Philippa Watson; Section (8.4) by Jane Dennett.

[2] See, for example, B. Semmel, *Imperialism and Social Reform*, Allen and Unwin, 1960.

[3] See, for example, the literature produced by the Study Commission on the Family.

[4] See R. Lawson, *Social Assistance in the Member States of the European Community* (Report prepared for the European Commission), 1979, esp. paras. 1.4, 2.5–2.6, 2.22.

[5] Cf. T. Wilson (ed.), *Pensions, Inflation and Growth*, Heinemann, 1974.

[6] Edward James acknowledges the assistance with earlier drafts given by the two project leaders.

[7] *Belfast: Areas of Special Social Need, Report by Project Team, 1976*, HMSO Belfast, 1977.

[8] See Annexe 1 to Chapter 24, Volume III of *Europe Against Poverty*, ESPOIR report to the Commission for the European Communities, 1980, contributed by the Northern Ireland Central Economic Service.

[9] Evason, E. *Ends that Won't Meet, a Study of Poverty in Belfast*, Poverty Research Series 8, Child Poverty Action Group, June 1980.

[10] Jane Dennett wishes to thank the projects' staff for their assistance with an earlier draft of this section, as well as Phyllis Willmott and Susan Mayne at the Institute of Community Studies.

[11] Graham Room acknowledges the help given not only by the staff of the three resource centres, but also by Ray Lees and Marjorie Mayo at the Polytechnic of Central London, who have acted as research staff to the joint monitoring exercise held under the auspices of the Gulbenkian Foundation. Their final report to the European Commission provides a detailed analysis of the area resource centres: see *Resourcing Communities* (1980), obtainable from the authors at Polytechnic of Central London, 76–78 Mortimer Street, London W1.

[12] See, for example, the Gulbenkian-sponsored report which proposed such resource centres, *Current Issues in Community Work*, 1973.

[13] It has also, however, stimulated conflict among these groups and questions have been raised about the continuing viability of the centre in its

present form: see F. J. C. Amos, *A Review of Govan Area Resource Centre*, January 1980.

[14] Graham Room is grateful to Dorothy Dalton and other members of the SCDP team for their assistance with earlier drafts of this section. He has also had access to a valuable external evaluation report commissioned by SCDP in 1978: see F. J. C. Amos, *Appraisal Report*.

[15] Georgie-Dalry, Leith, Pilton and Wester Hailes.

[16] The project was able simultaneously to move into a fifth area, one of rural depopulation and 'deindustrialisation' in the west of the region, rather than remaining concentrated in Edinburgh.

[17] Graham Room is grateful to Helen Crummy and Steve Burgess of the Craigmillar Festival Society for their assistance in the preparation of this section.

[18] *Multiple Deprivation: Report of a Working Party*, Lothian Regional Council, January 1976.

9
The Cross-National Studies[1]

(9.1) INTRODUCTION

The Council Decision of 1975 provided for studies to be launched which would 'improve understanding of the nature, causes, scope and mechanics of poverty in the Community' (Article 1). In principle at least, these have all been cross-national studies.

During the first phase of the European Programme, two cross-national studies were undertaken:

> Institut Français d'Opinion Publique (IFOP, Paris), *The Perception of Poverty in Europe*, 1977.
> P. Willmott (Institute of Community Studies, London), *Poverty and Social Policy*, 1977.

In the second phase of the programme, several further studies were carried out:

> B. Van Praag (Leyden University, Holland), *Research Project on the Size, Aspects and Causes of Poverty in the European Community.*
> P. Willmott, *Unemployment and Anti-Poverty Policies.*
> G. Schaber (Institut Pédagogique, Luxembourg), *Persistent Poverty. Poverty in Nomad Populations* − studies by Etudes Tsiganes (Paris) and the Centre pour l'Analyse du Changement Social, Louvain, Belgium.[2]

Two of the cross-national studies − those by IFOP and Van Praag − investigated the subjective perceptions of poverty held by members of the population at large in the different Member States of the Community. Three more of the studies − those by Willmott and that by Schaber − aimed to investigate the objective patterns of deprivation among poor households and to assess the effectiveness of alternative patterns of social provision. Finally, two of the studies were concerned with the poverty of nomad populations.

These are academic studies which can be judged by conventional academic standards; at the same time, however, they must be judged as 'pilot' studies within the European Programme. This chapter attempts to raise some general questions about each study, to draw some broad comparisons and to suggest some general conclusions for future cross-national research. More specifically, in section (9.2) each of these studies is considered in terms of:

   (i)   the intellectual and social context of the questions to which it is addressed;

  (ii)   the methods it employs and the difficulties encountered;

 (iii)   its significance as a *pilot* study within the European Programme:

      (a)   in contributing to an understanding of the dynamics of poverty within the European Community;

      (b)   in developing new methods and raising new questions for future European studies in this field;

      (c)   in producing 'concrete information' of relevance to policy-makers at national and European levels. (Cf. Council Decision, Article 1).

Certain difficulties should however be noted in making this assessment. First, when the ESPOIR evaluation began, two of these cross-national studies were already complete but the rest would not produce their final reports until November 1980. At least in regard to the second phase of studies, therefore, this evaluation must be regarded as highly provisional. Only when the researchers have been able to present their final reports for discussion by European policy-makers and the academic research community will it be possible properly to judge the contributions they have made. Secondly, the studies are very diverse in their assumptions, the questions they pose, their research methodologies, etc. so that any detailed comparison is neither easy nor, probably, very worthwhile. Finally, *cross-national* research poses problems and demands methods which are still relatively under-developed; the studies in the present programme, although in general they have tackled these problems bravely, have been limited in what they could achieve within the period available to them.[3]

(9.2) THE INDIVIDUAL STUDIES

(9.2.1) IFOP, the Perception of Poverty in Europe (1977)[4]

(i) *Introduction: the study and its questions*
This study focuses upon the perceptions of poverty held by the

populations of the different Member States and the social values which these perceptions express.

Since 1973 the European Commission has conducted regular 'Eurobarometer' surveys of public opinion using market research agencies in the different Member States. In 1976 a series of questions was added in order to investigate (a) respondents' perceptions of their incomes in relation to those of other people and in relation to their own requirements; (b) their general degree of satisfaction with their conditions of life; (c) their awareness of the existence of poverty and their 'images' of the poor. The co-ordination of the survey and the analysis of the data were carried out by IFOP (Institut Français d'Opinion Publique), the French agency involved in the Euro-barometer.

The data collected were used (a) to distinguish different types of attitude towards the poor and (b) to suggest the wider social values embraced by those holding these different attitudes. From these conclusions, recommendations were derived for a programme of public information and education, aimed at transforming attitudes and mo-bilising popular support for more effective policies to combat poverty.

It is now widely accepted by policy-makers and social researchers that poverty must be defined in *relative* terms, that is, in relation to the standards of living prevailing in the society and at the time concerned.[5] This in turn 'directs our attention to the values and perceptions (held by members) of the wider society and away from an exclusive concern with the poor themselves',[6] for at least two reasons: (a) because it directs attention to the ways of life and patterns of expenditure and consumption which are prescribed by the society at large as 'normal' for its members; (b) because these wider values and perceptions will affect the political support available for policies to combat poverty. The inclusion in the Poverty Programme of research into these normative life styles and social perceptions is therefore to be applauded.

(ii)   *The methods*

As already noted, the method used to collect data was a set of questions appended to the regular Eurobarometer survey. It was probably unavoidable, therefore, that a highly structured form of questionnaire should be used, with only a very limited number of possible answers being offered to respondents. This hardly suffices, however, to explore the qualitative variations in people's subjective perceptions and it gives them little opportunity to provide the researcher with their own categories and images of the world. Nor, of course, can such a questionnaire properly investigate the strength or fragility of the attitudes and attributions which people hold; still less can it analyse the social milieux in which these diverse attitudes to, and images of, the poor are generated and maintained, threatened and transformed.

(iii) *The results*

(a) *The dynamics of poverty in the European Community*   The IFOP study maps out the awareness of poverty and attitudes towards the poor across different social groups. It uses the data collected to construct attitude clusters among different groups of the population. These categories or groups are then labelled as 'cynics', 'militants for justice', etc., their proportions varying between countries.

Attitudes are found to be specially harsh in the British Isles. In all countries it seems to be those least vulnerable to poverty themselves – the educated and those with higher incomes – who are least harsh. Among these, the report singles out a minority of 'militants for justice' – perhaps 10 per cent of the population, on average – who are sufficiently concerned to commit themselves actively to measures aimed at changing wider attitudes and policies.

Nevertheless, any study – including those under consideration here – can be guilty of invalid inference from the data collected, or it may insufficiently recognise how the methods used constrain and shape the findings that emerge. Thus, for example, as Golding has argued, the IFOP study largely fails to recognise that the sorts of psychological factor found to be important in 'explaining' perceptions of poverty are in fact 'rooted in the prior construction of the research'. The differences found between different countries may not in fact reflect different patterns of attitudinal predispositions, but point rather to 'different structural and political systems and . . . the different dominant cultures'.[7]

(b) *New questions and new methods*   One of the aims of a research study, especially a *pilot* study, should be to advance and even transform the research agenda, opening up new questions for further enquiry and generating new hypotheses. It is, however, the gaps and omissions in the IFOP study that highlight the questions to which future research should address itself, rather than any positive contribution which this study makes.

What, for example, are the social mechanisms which determine the visibility of the poor and the perceptions and attitudes towards the poor held by members of the wider society? What are the social factors determining the moral credibility of the poor? Why in recent years have there been significant and relatively rapid shifts in public attitudes towards the poor? These are questions upon which *cross-national* study can throw valuable light – not in terms of supposed differences in 'national character' and attitudes, but rather in terms of social, cultural and economic processes.

(c) *Policy implications* What 'concrete information' of policy relevance does the IFOP study provide and what new strategies for combating poverty does it suggest? The report seems to centre its recommendations on a programme of public information and education, aimed at the population at large, in order to sensitise them to the poverty in their midst. Again, however, as Golding has argued, 'values, attitudes and opinions are rarely reducible to individual traits, and seldom changeable by information campaigns alone'. Such campaigns would themselves be moulded and distorted by 'just those processes and mechanisms which create the unsympathetic and censorious attitudes to poverty under attack'[8] – as Golding's own research elsewhere demonstrates.[9] Again, therefore, policy-relevant research on perceptions and values would need to attend to specific instruments of policy rather than to public attitudes and awareness seen *in vacuo* as timeless personality predispositions.

In short, therefore, the report rightly emphasises the constraints which public attitudes place upon policy-makers; what it neglects are the ways those attitudes are affected by *existing* policies and can perhaps be shaped by new policy initiatives and reforms as much as – or more than – by information campaigns. Willmott's study of *Unemployment and Anti-Poverty Policies*, to be discussed below, suggests certain useful lines of enquiry here: for example, it contrasts the different patterns of stigmatisation of the poor (and of the means-tested benefits on which the poor often depend) in countries with different combinations of social insurance, social assistance and other methods of income support.

(iv) *Conclusions*

The IFOP was widely reported in the European press. Indeed, of all the projects and studies included in the programme, this is probably the one which has so far had most public recognition. It may well have contributed to highlighting poverty as an issue of European debate. It is not difficult to criticise the methods used and the quality of the data collected by opinion poll agencies. Nevertheless, as Golding concludes, the 'aims of the study are vitally important (and) . . . deserve an extended response in investigating more closely the complex relationships between culture, economic change and social policy'.[10]

(9.2.2)   The Van Praag Study (1980)[11]

(i)   *Introduction: the study, its questions and its concepts*
Like the IFOP study before it, the van Praag study focuses upon the subjective perception of poverty. Also like its predecessor, it investigates these perceptions by means of opinion surveys carried out by established polling or market research agencies. These are the only two studies within the present programme to have covered all the Member States of the Community, excepting only Luxembourg.

The Council Decision of 1975 directs attention in its definition of poverty to the 'minumum acceptable way of life' in the different Member States. It is upon this that van Praag focuses his attention, recognising, however, that 'acceptability' is a subjective concept and may, therefore, differ among different groups of the population. It is upon the adequacy of each individual's own resources and standard of living, as he himself perceives it, that van Praag concentrates. (This contrasts somewhat with the IFOP study, which focuses upon the perception of the poor held by different categories of the wider population.) Van Praag then derives from the responses obtained across the society as a whole a national poverty line which expresses the *vox populi*. He thereby addresses himself to a range of issues which overlap with the concerns of the IFOP study: for example, the minimum way of life prescribed by society as a whole for its members and the implications for policy-makers of these different perceptions.

Van Praag first takes empirical data on individuals' subjective assessments of different levels of income and provides a theoretical interpretation of these in terms of levels of individual welfare. Secondly, he seeks empirical data on the incomes which individuals reckon they will need to 'make ends meet' and provides an interpretation of these in terms of subjective poverty lines. Finally, given both sets of data, his theoretical framework can then explore the relationships between levels of individual welfare and the subjective poverty lines which individuals hold. Each of these analyses is further refined by using more detailed data on the respondents concerned: their family size, their region of residence, etc. (Van Praag also builds upon these basic results in a variety of other ways: for example to calculate the 'poverty gap' in different countries and to estimate national distributions of income.)

The IFOP study approaches the collection and interpretation of its data within a broadly socio-psychological paradigm or framework. Van Praag, in contrast, proceeds within a theoretical and methodological framework rooted in econometrics and welfare economics. This theoretical framework is daunting in its degree of elaboration; but it also has certain limitations.

First, this study tends (like the IFOP study) to treat individuals' perceptions as *given*; it thereby diverts attention away from the dynamic social processes which continually shape and transform individuals' aspirations and perceptions. Secondly, the national poverty line is interpreted by van Praag as expressing the *vox populi*, a broad social consensus.[12] However, consensus in regard to the requirements the respondents themselves need may not, of course, be identical with the consensus over what others — and, in particular, the poor — need. Furthermore, in societies where sharply conflicting social and political values are being paraded in competition with each other, it can be misleading to assume that van Praag's national poverty line expresses some sort of 'consensus', rather than merely a statistical average. Thirdly, the elaborate examination of the relationship between individuals' welfare and their subjective poverty lines seems either to be a mere semantic exploration of the meanings which individuals give to various questions regarding their subjective well-being or, alternatively, to risk confusing scientific and technical findings with political judgements on the welfare of different social groups.

Like the other cross-national researchers, van Praag is writing for the academic research community as well as for European policy-makers. The theoretical issues which his work raises will continue to generate debate within the academic community. What is, however, probably of more interest to the policy-making community are the concrete results which van Praag produces or which, given more time, could be generated by the extensive data base which he has accumulated. Before considering these results, however, it will first be necessary to consider the methods of data collection and analysis which he employs.

(ii) *The methods*

Like the IFOP study, van Praag has used a network of market research/opinion polling agencies to gather his data. Within a period of only eighteen months, around 24,000 respondents have been questioned and the data analysed. The data collected mainly concern (a) respondents' subjective assessments of income and of 'making ends meet'; (b) respondents' income, demographic, occupational and other characteristics. Several important questions of method arise.

1. The definition of *income* is fundamental to this study, as it is to several of the others. It figures in the subjective perceptions which respondents are asked to register; it also figures as one of the objective characteristics of the respondents which van Praag uses in order to explain differences in their perceptions. Among researchers on poverty, there have been long-standing and by now highly-refined debates on the variety of definitions and conceptualisations which may be used. Van Praag, however, confines himself to only limited questions about income and leaves this defined only loosely. It is of course true that in such questionnaires, only a limited number of income questions could be posed; this may excuse, but it can hardly compensate for the problem.

2. The data collected about respondents' demographic, occupational and other characteristics are equally fundamental to the investigation. In part, they stand proxy for the various and complex factors which determine respondents' ways of life – the expectations they have as to an acceptable standard of living and the resources which this standard demands. It would, however, be unreasonable to expect this particular cross-national study to produce detailed findings about these concrete processes, especially given the limited time and resources available. Van Praag must, rather, be judged by his success in generating plausible hypotheses as to how these different ways of life concretely affect the levels of income and other resources which people subjectively reckon to be necessary.

3. Like the IFOP study, van Praag can be criticised for offering only a limited number of possible answers to respondents – a limitation particularly serious for exploration of cross-national variations in people's perceptions of ways of life. To a considerable extent, the use of polling agencies for gathering the data may have made this unavoidable for both studies; nevertheless, it places severe limitations on the validity of the data collected. Postal questionnaires (except in Italy and Ireland where personal interviews were undertaken) can

hardly have avoided reinforcing these problems.[13] It is questionable, therefore, whether the quality and validity of the empirical data on subjective perceptions are such as to warrant applying to it the elaborate theoretical apparatus which van Praag has developed – even assuming the usefulness of the latter when applied to higher quality data.

(iii) *The results*
It is important that even the critic who has major reservations about van Praag's theoretical framework should not overlook the potential usefulness of the data which are being collected. Equally, however, it is important that those readers of the van Praag reports who are impressed, daunted or even intimidated by this theoretical super-structure should not flinch from judging the research in part by the concrete results which it has produced.

Van Praag offers findings relating to (i) differentiated family poverty lines; (ii) cross-national comparisons of poverty ratios (the proportion of the population in poverty) and poverty gaps (the aggregate income deficiency of those in poverty); (iii) the individual characteristics most likely to be associated with poverty; and (iv) some preliminary assessment of the impact of income maintenance policies on poverty. O'Higgins summarises some of these results: 'High (subjective) poverty levels appear to be explained by low national incomes (Ireland, Italy, UK), more unequal incomes (France) or relatively high expectations (Denmark)'.[14] Nevertheless, quite apart from the problems of method discussed earlier, it is the interpretation of these results that remains problematic, particularly their implications for policy.

The policy implications of the work are at best tenuous and ill-defined. It is, first of all, not altogether clear what policy implications van Praag would himself wish to advance. Would he argue, for example, that if the national poverty lines revealed by his study are wildly out of line with income support scales for the poor (e.g. social assistance benefits) then policy-makers are being overly paternalistic in imposing their views of appropriate relativities and risk undermining their own political legitimacy? What inferences, if any, would van Praag draw from his results in regard to people's willingness to pay for income support policies?

Secondly, it is doubtful whether the data and results he has produced suffice to generate *any* clear policy implications. For example, individual perceptions are treated by van Praag as though they were independent of, and prior to, the policy-making process. However, in order to draw policy implications it is first necessary to know more about how the subjective perceptions of poverty which have been investigated are themselves affected by current policies: e.g. prevailing social assistance scales in different countries. In a reworking of van Praag's interim results, O'Higgins maps out some of the possible effects of current policies on subjective perceptions and warns of the consequential difficulties in deriving clear policy implications. Moreover, as O'Higgins argues, 'the (potential) value of (van Praag's) subjective assessments of poverty . . . lies less in the possibility of thereby defining a (new sort of) poverty line as in investigating the extent to which public policies may generate extra resistance' to anti-poverty measures: issues which are left largely uninvestigated.[15]

(9.2.3)   Willmott: Poverty and Social Policy (1977)[16]

(i)   *Introduction: the study and its questions*
This study was carried out by Professor Willmott at the Institute of Community Studies and two institutes with which he had previously collaborated, INFAS in Bonn and CREDOC in Paris.
    It was deliberately and self-consciously a *pilot* study in wanting (a) to test out methods of research that could subsequently be used in nationwide sample surveys and (b) to demonstrate how such surveys could contribute to the comparative analysis of how social policies actually operate and hence to more effective efforts to combat poverty. It did not, therefore, address itself to specific policy questions on the extent and dynamics of poverty; however, it intended of course that the comparative survey would throw interesting light on the operation of different policies and would suggest what sorts of policy question might most suitably be tackled by these methods.

(ii)   *The methods*
In each of the three countries concerned, a sample survey was undertaken in a rural and an urban area. Three main problems of definition and method were tackled: (a) the definition of poverty; (b) the inclusion of sufficient numbers of the poor within a general sample of the population; and (c) the development of questionnaires suitable for cross-national research. The researchers discuss the various possible

solutions to these problems and justify the ones they have themselves chosen. Here comments are limited to the first and second.

(a) *The definition of poverty* Willmott addresses five basic questions to be answered in defining an income 'poverty line': (i) the level of income signifying poverty; (ii) the unit of analysis — family or household; (iii) the inclusion or otherwise of housing costs; (iv) the allowance to be made for dependent members of the family or household; (v) the value of national versus international poverty lines. In regard to the first of these questions, for example, Willmott proposes that in future national sample surveys a line placed at two-thirds of the net median income might be most appropriate; in the present study, however, he chooses to focus on the bottom 20 per cent in each country, in order to compare the social composition of the poor in the three countries and hence to suggest the relative effectiveness for different groups of different policy 'mixes'. Willmott also attends to other aspects of poverty — housing, health, etc; and he explores the patterns of social isolation and non-participation associated with poverty of resources (emphasising, for example, the particular isolation of the poor in Germany). Nevertheless, it might have been possible to exploit the survey data still more, to explore how far alternative definitions of poverty lead to different conclusions regarding patterns of poverty in the three countries concerned.

(b) *Representation of the poor* One of the principal innovations which the study aimed to pioneer was a technique for ensuring that within a general sample of the population sufficient numbers of the poor were included. This would then permit larger-scale nationwide sample surveys in a programme of further research. Willmott's method was to over-sample in poor areas (as indicated by census and other official data). Only in Germany, however, was this method as successful as had been hoped; in Britain it may well be that, because the data used to select areas for over-sampling were somewhat out of date, changes in population composition had subsequently occurred. Willmott argues that the reasons for this incomplete success have been identified and that the wider application of the method would therefore be justified. However, it is not a method that he developed further in his subsequent study of unemployment and poverty.

(iii)   *The results*
Among the principal findings which Willmott produces, he points to the relative success of French social policies in supporting families at

risk of poverty, of the Germans in supporting the elderly (especially through 'dynamised' pensions) and of Britain in preventing extreme poverty, using a system which emphasises flat-rate benefits. Willmott also emphasises that the British housing and health systems appear to reach the poor more effectively than do their counterparts in France and Germany. Finally, however, he points out that in all three countries, the poor lack the information they need to make full use of these services.

Nevertheless, there are of course some difficulties in interpreting Willmott's findings. For example, as Lawson has observed, those groups whose representation among the poorest 20 per cent of the population is higher in one country than elsewhere, may nevertheless be treated better relative to the non-poor of their own country, than their counterparts elsewhere. Moreover, the analysis of social policy in the three countries could have been much more detailed and rigorous, rather than dealing in very general terms such as 'universalism and selectivity'; and Willmott's presentation of information about national policies could have been complemented by study of the practical operation of local services. As will be seen, however, this is a gap which Willmott in his subsequent study of unemployment and poverty seeks to avoid.

(9.2.4)   Willmott: Unemployment and Anti-Poverty Policies (1980)[17]

(i)   *Introduction: the study and its questions*
Like its predecessor, this study by Willmott has involved collaboration among the Institute of Community Studies, CREDOC and INFAS, with ICS acting as general co-ordinator. The study focuses upon poverty among the unemployed in Britain, France and Germany. It is concerned principally but by no means exclusively with *income* poverty. It aims to suggest how social policies might be made more effective in preventing and combating such poverty.

Within most of the countries of the European Community, there are regions of long-term unemployment. Only in the last few years, however, with the deepening recession, have unemployment and the poverty it produces become a prime concern of policy-makers and the public at large. Moreover, as Willmott observes, continuing technological change is likely to keep unemployment high on the political agenda, at least over the next few decades, and to heighten the relevance and value of studies such as this. Willmott justifies cross-national studies of unemployment and poverty in terms of the social policy lessons which countries facing these common problems may learn from each other. More particularly, countries with little history of industrial unemployment may well find that their social policies are ill-equipped to cope with such problems and the social consequences of long-term unemployment.

As Trinder has pointed out, relatively few comparative studies of unemployment have previously been undertaken: Willmott's is a pioneering work. Trinder anticipates, moreover, 'an explosion of research into the unemployed in the 1980s and 1990s'. He concludes: 'It would be a great pity if the national efforts of individual countries were not matched by a similar growth of EEC initiatives. Partly it would be an opportunity missed because there is no easier time to incorporate the cross-national needs into the work of individual governments than when they are expanding their own efforts in that area'.[18] Nevertheless, Trinder also suggests that there are key questions in this emerging policy debate to which Willmott's cross-national study has inadequately addressed itself. For example, in Britain at least, policies for assisting the unemployed are constrained by public fears over the supposed work disincentives of such assistance, even in a time of few job opportunities. Cross-national comparisons on the treatment of the long-term unemployed might have questioned how well founded are these fears.

(ii)   *The methods*
The study concentrates upon selected areas of Bristol, Reims and Saarbrücken. These three cities were carefully chosen, on the basis of census and other data, so that (a) they would broadly resemble each other, (b) they would not be atypical of their respective countries and (c) they would reveal recently rising unemployment to levels higher than average. The last of these conditions means that it is only during the current recession that substantial numbers of families have been plunged into poverty as a result of rising unemployment. These areas can, therefore, reveal particularly clearly the social consequences of such rapid change and the inadequacies in existing social provisions. The methods of investigation have been threefold.
1. A questionnaire survey has been undertaken among the populations of the three selected areas. A general survey was chosen (a) in order to include not only the unemployed themselves, but also the

'disguised' unemployed and the under-employment of workers on short-time, married women without hope of employment, etc.; and (b) in order to compare the poverty of the unemployed with (i) that of other groups in the target areas and (ii) the general standards of living there. In addition, more intensive and structured interviews have been carried out.

Such an approach can provide illuminating comparisons of individuals' different unemployment biographies. Nevertheless, there is little systematic investigation of the position of the unemployed within the labour markets of the three areas. Moreover, if Willmott is indeed interested in the generally depressing effect which rising unemployment has on the prosperity of such areas, it would have been valuable also to have area studies of the local economies, for example, rather than relying on a method of sample surveys which is most suited to identifying poor individuals submerged within a population of general affluence. Nevertheless, within the constraints of time and resources available, this could perhaps hardly have been undertaken in addition to the general sample surveys.

2. Interviews have been conducted with a variety of local agencies which deal with the unemployed − including, most obviously, employment exchanges and social security officials. The aim has been to explore the local operation and effectiveness of these agencies, rather than relying upon official descriptions of their intended effects or on details of national legislation.

One of the principal goals of the whole study, indeed, is to assess the relative effectiveness of different social policies in alleviating and preventing poverty among the unemployed. In spite of this, the research into the local operation of social policy agencies has been largely confined to these interviews; considerable freedom appears to have been given to the different teams as to the agencies selected; and it is by no means clear that the issues posed in these interviews were tightly related to those which the pilot questionnaire among the area populations had revealed as significant. In consequence, the study exhibits rather less coherence and consistency than might have been hoped. Nevertheless, this very wide combination of sources of data can at least provide valuable illustrations of the relative effectiveness of different policies.

3. The researchers have collected background information about the three geographical areas and about the wider social policy frameworks within which local services are provided. It remains to be seen how far

Willmott, in the published version of his study, will be able to present the conclusions of his local enquiries within this broader context of information about national policies, drawing upon previous research materials and official documentation.

(iii)   *The results*

(a) *Poverty and unemployment in the European Community* By focusing upon a general sample of the population, Willmott generates findings which may be compared with those of his previous study. They are broadly consistent: for example, in regard to the protection of the elderly in Germany, and the prevention of *extreme* poverty in Britain — defining poverty, of course, in terms relative to the income levels of the areas concerned. Willmott generates a wide range of new questions for more detailed and intensive studies: for example, in respect of youth unemployment, early retirement policies, and employment-related welfare benefits. Nevertheless, as in his previous study, these findings and suggestions for further research tend to emerge somewhat haphazardly from the comparison of data from the three sample surveys, rather than in response to specific questions which the study was intended to address.

(b) *Policy implications* Similarly, Trinder comments that 'it was not clear what policy issues the study intended to examine specifically'. For example, 'the survey seems to collect much more data on the job placement side of the Government's role in unemployment, than on the income support role'. Trinder emphasises the need for further and more systematic monitoring and comparing of how these various policies operate, especially bearing in mind that 'even with unchanged policies, the effect of increasing levels of unemployment may well affect (the way) the services (are in practice) provided'.[19]

Nevertheless, Willmott does point to a variety of policy suggestions on unemployment and poverty, albeit somewhat less systematic than might have been hoped. He points to the apparent accessibility of the British social assistance system and its lower degree of stigmatisation, enabling it to provide more adequate protection against extreme poverty. Secondly, he points to the greater and more flexible opportunities for early retirement in France and Germany and the lesser need for the early retired to depend upon social assistance. In all three areas, however, existing social provisions fail to prevent large numbers of the unemployed falling into poverty; only the more privileged at work are likely to enjoy extra earnings-related protection. Finally, in regard to re-employment, he finds Germany offers more vigorous job placement schemes and youth training programmes, promoting thereby a more flexible and active manpower policy. Again, however, Willmott advances these as tentative conclusions meriting more intensive and systematic investigation.

(9.2.5) Schaber, Persistent Poverty (1980)[20]

(i) Introduction: the study and its questions

The persistence of poverty in our advanced Western societies is, of course, a presupposition of launching a poverty programme. What Schaber and his team set out to investigate is the extent to which particular households may persist in poverty, both intra- and inter-generationally. More specifically, these researchers are, as Münster-mann has summarised, centrally interested in 'the transmission of poverty over time primarily by factors fostered in the socialisation process and sufficiently independent from social change to use traits of the parental family of origin as predictors of present poverty'.[21] This investigation has been carried out in the 'Greater Luxembourg' region – that is, Luxembourg itself and the adjacent regions of Germany, the Netherlands, Belgium and France. It therefore offers an opportunity to compare the significance of persistent poverty in seven different regions, enjoying a common social, cultural and industrial history but contrasting in their political systems, languages and institutions.

The research has been carried out by six regional teams (each based on a research or educational institute), co-ordinated by a central team in Luxembourg itself. This central team includes members of the field teams on a rotating basis.

(ii) The methods

The investigation proceeded through three main phases. In Phase (A), the researchers built up a list of their target population, namely, those families with children born in 1970. At Phase (B), they took a sample of 1,400 families from the base population (200 in each of the seven regions) and studied the incidence among them of various forms of deprivation. This allowed the researchers to produce indices or indicators for easily recognising which families in the original population are at high risk of poverty. One consequence of the choice of base population, however, is that the parents are now mostly aged 30–50, at the peak of their occupational and earnings careers; those parents in the regions concerned who are now at highest risk will tend not to be included.

Finally, in Phase (C), these indicators are used to retrieve from the base population (listed in Phase (A)), extra families at high risk of poverty. This new sample, containing disproportionate numbers of those at high risk, are then subjected to more intensive interviews in order to reveal the extent and dynamics of persistent poverty and the use which the respondents make of different social, educational and income maintenance provisions. In addition, this final phase involves drawing upon comparative information on the operation of social policies and services in the different regions, in order to explore the implications of the research findings for policy.

(iii)   *The results*

(a)   *The dynamics of poverty in the European Community*   The research of Phase (B) indicates that two groups of families are at high risk of being in multiple deprivation. The first are single-parent families; but there is little evidence that significant numbers of the parents were themselves from broken or incomplete homes. Rather, the social, economic and political factors which tended to generate single-parent families a generation ago — including the impact of war — are very different from those of significance today. The rates and incidence of single-parent families a generation from now will, similarly, depend less upon the socialisation patterns within today's one-parent homes, than on wider changes in marriage and career patterns, etc.; and these, in turn, will be moulded by a much wider range of social policies than those concerned specifically with the poor.

The second group at high risk of being in multiple deprivation are immigrant families. Nevertheless, the parents themselves are in general better off financially and in terms of amenities than they were in their regions of origin. They may lack skills; what they do not lack is personal initiative and determination.[22] Consequently, whether or not their existence in their new milieu is secure depends principally upon the civil, political and social rights granted them by the host society. As for their children, their persistence in poverty within the host society is likely in general to depend not so much upon the socialisation process they have enjoyed as upon the opportunities extended to them for education, job training, etc. The extent to which these opportunities will indeed be available is more a matter of policy decision than scientific forecasting.

In short, then, as Münstermann summarises, 'the main result of the study . . . is that there is *no* stationary segment or stratum in society, in which the same correlates of poverty prevail now as a generation ago and in which a given set of behaviour patterns, attitudes and values are passed from parents to children that keep them from moving up'.[23]

(b) *New methods and new questions* The Schaber research points (if only by implication) to a range of major new questions – new, that is, by comparison with the original interest in the transmission of poverty through the socialisation process within the family. First, it focuses attention upon structural changes in and between societies which determine what types of individual and family are thrust into poverty. Secondly, it invites more concentrated attention on intra-generational persistent poverty and the patterns of upward and downward mobility between states of poverty and non-poverty. This, in turn, suggests the value of a follow-up longitudinal study over a period of several years.

(c) *Policy implications* Schaber appears to have carried out little empirical research into the operation of the local services upon which these families are dependent, including, for example, the perceptions and behaviour of officials, teachers, etc. A *fortiori* no comparative investigation of these local processes has been undertaken, even though the five-nation study surely invited such comparison.

Nevertheless, the directions of new research opened up by the Luxembourg study emphasise the importance of such policy-oriented studies: in regard, for example, to (a) educational and employment opportunities for second-generation immigrants at a time of rising unemployment and (b) the wide range of policies having long-term effects on rates and patterns of family break-up.

(iv) *Conclusions*
The supposed transmission of deprivation primarily through socialisation processes within the family has also been the subject of a major recent government-sponsored research programme in the United Kingdom. What the British studies and the Schaber research both reveal, however, is the tenuous evidence for such a diagnosis of persistent poverty.[24] This is not an insignificant or unimportant result – whether anticipated or otherwise by the researchers themselves – at a time when public opinion and political decision-makers seem unlikely to be especially ready to recognise the wider social, economic and other policies upon which the persistence of poverty is more fundamentally dependent.

(9.2.6) Poverty in Nomad Populations[25]

(i) *Introduction*

The European Community expresses the aspiration to closer economic, social and political co-operation, harmonisation and even integration among the peoples of the different Member States. However, at the fringes of the economies of most of the Member States, socially and culturally separate and only recently politically articulate, stand various nomad populations of travellers, Gypsies, tinkers and others, moving around the edges of the dominant host societies. It is upon the poverty that some at least of these people suffer, that various studies in the later years of the Poverty Programme have focused. In France, Etudes Tsiganes have sponsored research in Toulouse, Strasbourg and Paris; while the Centre pour l'Analyse du Changement Social at the University of Louvain has engaged in a three-nation study covering Holland, Germany and Belgium.

(ii) *Research on Gypsies: principles and problems*

Gypsies have always been dependent on continuous economic relations with the wider society, rather than being self-sufficient. In the industrial economies of western Europe, they have long performed jobs avoided by members of the dominant population. Increasing urbanisation of this population and of economic activity has drawn the Gypsies also into the urban environment, but there is no reason to suppose they cannot find new economic roles.

However, increasing political control on the unconventional use of urban land – in this case, by non-sedentary populations – has made their nomadic way of life, their cultural integrity, their kinship networks and their opportunities for establishing an economic niche for themselves, increasingly fragile and vulnerable. The social legislation of an increasingly interventionist state and official enforcement of the formal obligations of citizenship (for example, the obligations of parents to send their children to school) have further eroded Gypsies' traditional way of life. The result is to expose them to multiple impoverishment.

As Okely has emphasised, therefore, the current Gypsy 'problem' – including the poverty which many may now suffer – is centred less in economic than in political developments and in the mutually antagonistic stereotypes and perceptions that they have fostered between Gypsies and non-Gypsies. As a concomitant to such political developments, it has become increasingly common for formal political 'representatives' of Gypsies to be consulted by policy-makers of the dominant society, but their representative status and views are questionable.

These, Okely argues, are some of the issues of policy-relevant research to which current studies should be addressed. She also, however, points out some of the principles and problems of method which research into Gypsy and nomad populations should confront. The Gypsies' own perception of their situation may differ radically from that held by non-Gypsies or 'Gorgios' – but to an extent and in ways which the latter rarely appreciate, because 'evasion and secrecy' are the Gypsy's means of self-protection. The evidence gained through intensive and long-term interaction and acquaintance with even very small 'samples' of Gypsies can therefore be more reliable than that acquired from more ambitious mass surveys of a conventional type. Any study which ignores these considerations will be methodologically inadequate and it will tend to give a misleading account of Gypsies' needs, priorities and actions, as also of current changes in the relationship between Gypsies and the wider society.

Finally, therefore, Okely reminds us that policies affect the interests of different groups differentially: 'Policy questions . . . are not value-free, nor politically neutral'.[26] Where the interests of Gypsies and non-Gypsies collide or conflict, the policy recommendations which researchers advance should make clear the implications for these various interests. Okely calls for policy-relevant research which can demonstrate how far the interests of Gypsies and of different groups in the wider society can be reconciled, retaining for the Gypsy a range of choice in regard to his way of life and his relations with the dominant society.

(iii)   *The studies*

(a) *The Toulouse research project*   Initially, the Toulouse team concentrated on collecting considerable quantitative information about Gypsies' living conditions, using, for example, conventional sociological questionnaires. Increasingly, however, they shifted to qualitative methods of participant observation. This has drawn upon the long experience which the field workers have of local Gypsy communities and the relations of trust and confidence they have built up.

The researchers demonstrate that Gypsies are well able to find economic opportunities in advanced economies. In the Toulouse area, however, Gypsies are becoming increasingly immobilised on over-crowded sites, as a result of pressures from the dominant society. The researchers map out these pressures and the consequent disruption and impoverishment of the Gypsies' way of life: not least, of their networks of mutual aid, social control and informal welfare provision.

Okely applauds the methods which have been used and the accurate picture it has provided of Gypsies' current circumstances. In particular, she emphasises that the evidence 'is neither filtered nor possibly mistranslated through the formalised techniques of "objective" researchers lacking firsthand observation of Gypsies.'[27]

(b) *The Strasbourg research*   The Strasbourg researchers have been involved in two principal projects. First, over a period of many years, they have built up a computerised documentation centre as a base for research and, simultaneously, as a resource available to individuals and groups working with Gypsy communities. Secondly, they have engaged in action-research into the patterns of intervention by Gorgio (non-Gypsy) officials and voluntary welfare organisations into the life of Gypsy communities, especially the most impoverished. This research reveals the priorities and concerns of the Gorgios and the responses they perceive the Gypsies as making. The research team, although not themselves specialists on Gypsy and nomad studies, have drawn in local voluntary organisations, as well as the documentation centre, as resources in the research.

The Strasbourg team appears not to have confronted and sur-mounted fully the practical problems of discovering the Gypsies' own responses to these interventions; the definition and analysis of the interventions therefore reflect the bias and role of the Gorgio intruders. Nevertheless, Okely welcomes the information which the research is likely to produce on the 'images' and perceptions which the Gorgio intruders hold of Gypsies.

(c) *The Paris research*   The third of the Etudes Tsiganes studies included in the European Programme focuses upon the perceptions which Gypsies and non-Gypsies hold of each other, using both quantitative and qualitative techniques. The researchers have attempted to develop explanations of variations in the perceptions and stereotypes which the non-Gypsies hold, for example as between rural and urban populations. They also explore the increasing external controls upon Gypsies, the consequent destruction of traditional kinship networks and the metamorphosis of the Gypsy into a welfare recipient dependent upon the wider society's formal system of social support.

Okely applauds the clarity of the research, noting that its efficient conduct has been possible because of the researchers' long experience of Gypsy studies. The researchers have made an important contribution to our knowledge about the views of officials, policy-makers and the wider public, in particular. They have also been sensitive to the methodological problems of approaching Gypsies which were discussed above.

(d) *University of Louvain*   This research study began only in October 1979 and it therefore had only thirteen months to complete its work. The team has focused upon the problems experienced by nomads in Belgium, Holland and Germany and the policy interventions undertaken by the official authorities. Okely welcomes some of the work undertaken by the Louvain team, particularly in 'drawing attention to the major mistakes and injustices in public policy towards the Gypsies'.[28]

Nevertheless, she stresses the inadequacies in the methods employed to investigate Gypsies' own wishes, needs and activities and questions whether reliable findings are likely to result. She emphasises again that it takes an extended period to build up relationships of trust and mutual confidence with Gypsy communities and consultations with their formal 'representatives' can be no substitute. She concludes that it was unrealistic for the Louvain researchers, who apparently had little previous experience of research in this field, to carry out a study in a period of only thirteen months; in such a short period, only specialist researchers with long-term knowledge and well established contacts with Gypsy communities could have met the Commission's expectations.

(iv) *Conclusion*

As Okely emphasises, poverty among nomadic populations should remain an important item on the research agenda of the European Community. She highlights the recommendation by Etudes Tsiganes that 'legislation within the European Community should be harmonised, especially in order to resolve certain contradictions when the Gypsies cross frontiers'. If Gypsies' needs are not recognised, their 'cultural, political and economic impoverishment will accelerate'.[29]

(9.3)   GENERAL CONCLUSIONS

Cross-national research poses formidable theoretical and practical problems. The researchers must define questions of common interest; they must surmount barriers of language and intellectual tradition; they must cope with logistical and communications problems which, if only because of geographical distance, can be considerable; they must balance uniformity and coherence in the overall enterprise against flexibility and sensitivity to local circumstances within the different countries being studied. It follows that researchers must not be too ambitious in the goals they set themselves; equally, policy-makers who fund such research must not be too demanding in their expectations.

(9.3.1)   The Questions

The studies under consideration vary greatly in the questions they pose and in their conceptualisations of poverty. This reflects in part much wider theoretical debates and disagreements on the definition and conceptualisation of poverty and deprivation.[30] So too, it may partly reflect the different research and policy agendas in the different Member States of the European Community, as well, of course, as the distinctive intellectual positions from which the different research teams hail.[31] Nevertheless, this diversity may also reflect a somewhat *laissez-faire* attitude on the part of the programme's sponsors.

How far are the questions to which these studies address themselves those which are highlighted by the current agenda of policy and research? Their policy relevance has been touched upon within the preceding sections of this chapter. It must, however, be added that many of these studies make little effort to justify their concerns in terms of the wider debates within the research communities of which they are members; and little attempt to relate their findings to those emerging from elsewhere in those communities. It may, of course, be that since their reports were prepared primarily for the Commission, the researchers did not feel bound to present and justify their work in terms relevant to their peers. Nevertheless, it would be unfortunate if cross-national studies sponsored by the European Commission failed to serve as bridges among the wider research communities in the different Member States.

(9.3.2) Methods

The obvious first source of material in any scientific enquiry is the existing corpus of relevant research material and documentation. In the social policy field, both academic and official documentation abounds. Trinder's comments upon Willmott's study of *Unemployment and Poverty* have a more general applicability. He lists a considerable number of secondary sources upon which such a study might, at least in part, have drawn and upon which, indeed, some previous attempts at cross-national comparison have been content to base themselves. Much of this existing data may, of course, lack comparability cross-nationally, as well as being less up-to-date than the fruits of fresh empirical enquiry – a deficiency particularly serious if, for example, one is studying unemployment at a time of deepening recession. Nevertheless, as Trinder concludes, Willmott's sample surveys (and, it may be added, the surveys carried out by various of the other research teams in the present programme) 'cannot be fully exploited in a vacuum'.[32]

The other methods used in these studies are multiple: the analysis of existing literature and documentation, sample surveys, opinion polls, participant observation and evaluation of the effectiveness of local services. To some extent, the researchers have chosen particular methods in the light of their questions and their previous experience; equally, however, the methods available have been constrained by the peculiar problems of any cross-national study.

It is probably not insignificant, therefore, that the studies which have used a broad range of research methods have been those which have been most concentrated in their geographical extent or have even, indeed, not been cross-national at all. The studies by Etudes Tsiganes are an obvious case in point. At the opposite extreme, the IFOP and van Praag studies are far more ambitious in the number of countries covered; and while it is easy to pick holes in the quality of the data collected, it is difficult to see what alternative methods could have been employed, within the time and resources available.

(9.3.3) The Fruits of the Research

One of the results of a research study – and especially of pilot studies – should be to advance and transform the research agenda, opening up new questions for further enquiry and generating novel hypotheses. It will be evident from this chapter that while some of the studies have made positive contributions in this respect, it is the gaps and omissions within some of the others that highlight the questions inviting further research.

So too, few of the studies have successfully generated clear implications for policy, whether at national or European levels. This is in part because of the difficulties of combining, especially on a cross-national basis, empirical investigation of the poor themselves with study of the practical operation of local services and policies. This problem has been particularly marked and obvious in the case of the Gypsy studies, where investigation of the perceptions held not only by actual policy-makers but also by the Gypsies themselves is especially demanding; but, albeit for varied reasons, several of the other studies have found it similarly over-demanding to cope with policy analysis as well as the dynamics of poverty.

Nevertheless, this chapter has highlighted some of the new issues for policy-relevant research. What they have in common is a more strongly sociological approach. Again, however, no attempt will be made here to summarise or bring together what has already been said in earlier sections.

(9.3.4) A Role for the European Commission

The studies in the present European Programme establish a clear case for cross-national research in this field: first, in order to help national governments to learn from the social policies developed elsewhere and secondly, in order to illuminate common problems in the Community of interest to the Community institutions.

The conceptual and methodological problems of such research are considerable. In addition, however, there are major institutional barriers, including a lack of sponsors. Most obviously, national governments and funding agencies commonly give a relatively low priority to such comparative research. The European Commission is in a unique position to promote cross-national research studies which (a) have a clear policy relevance for co-ordinated action by the Member States and (b) are integrated into a coherent programme of action and research.[33]

Nevertheless, cross-national research sponsored by the European Commission should not be carried out in isolation from the wider research communities of the various Member States. First, it is important that the fruits of this research should be published and disseminated across the Community as a whole. Secondly, some of the research efforts supported by the Commission could profitably be concerned with existing research material and official documentation in the different Member States, rather than engaging in new empirical study.

Notes

[1] Written by Graham Room.

[2] One of the cross-national studies was stillborn. During the first phase of the programme, Hywel Griffiths at the New University of Ulster carried out a study of voluntary organisations in Northern Ireland and their role in combating poverty, entitled *Yesterday's Heritage or Tomorrow's Resource?* (1977). A cross-national extension of this study was planned but various accidents prevented its execution. However, studies of the role of voluntary organisations were subsequently included in the national reports on poverty which the Commission sponsored in 1979–80.

[3] The materials upon which this chapter has drawn are threefold: first, the reports and materials provided by the research teams themselves (although there has not been time to take full account of the draft reports produced in September 1980 and the final reports); secondly, consultants' reports which were commissioned on each study; finally, the proceedings of a colloquium which we organised for three of the second phase of studies in July 1980. We are extremely grateful to the research teams for their collaboration in the evaluation exercise in spite of their heavy workloads.

[4] This discussion draws heavily upon a consultancy report prepared by Peter Golding, Research Associate at the Centre for Mass Communication Research, University of Leicester. The study itself is available from: DGV, Commission of the European Communities, 200 rue de la Loi, 1049 Brussels.

[5] See also Chapters 10 and 11 below.

[6] Golding, *op. cit.*, p. 1.

[7] *Ibid.*, pp. 15, 6.

[8] *Ibid.*, pp. 21, 18.

[9] See, for example, P. Golding and S. Middleton, *Images of Welfare*, Martin Robertson, 1982.

[10] *Op. cit.*, pp. 20–21.

[11] Information regarding this study can be obtained from Professor van Praag at the Economic Institute of Leiden University, Hugo de Groot-straat 32, 2311 XK Leiden, Holland. A published version of the final report is likely to be forthcoming during 1981–82.

This discussion draws heavily upon a consultancy report prepared by Michael O'Higgins, Lecturer in Social Policy at the University of Bath.

[12] As O'Higgins points out, it is also said to distinguish between those whose income is or is not subjectively sufficient to make ends meet; O'Higgins demonstrates the tension between these two interpretations, not least in regard to van Praag's calculation of the poverty ratio.

[13] O'Higgins, moreover, expresses his worries about the response rates achieved.

[14] O'Higgins, *op. cit.*, Part 2, p. 14.

[15] *Ibid.*, Part 1, p. 4.

[16] It is unlikely that this report will be published in its entirety; copies may, however, be obtained from the European Commission (see note 4 above).

This discussion draws heavily upon a consultancy report prepared by Roger Lawson, Senior Lecturer in the Department of Sociology and Social Administration, University of Southampton.

[17] Willmott is preparing a revised version of the final report for publication in 1981/2.

This discussion draws heavily upon a consultancy report prepared by Christopher Trinder, research fellow at the National Institute for Economic and Social Research.

[18] Trinder, *op. cit.*, p. 22.

[19] *Ibid.*, pp. 12–13.

[20] This discussion draws heavily upon a consultancy report prepared by Jörg Münstermann, an associate of the Forschungsgruppe Arbeit und Gesundheit (FAG), Rosental 25, 4600 Dortmund 1, Germany. Information regarding this study can be obtained from Professor Schaber at the Institut Pédagogique, Walferdange, Luxembourg.

[21] *Op. cit.*, p. 3.

[22] They are, in general, the cream of their society of origin. Cf. S. Castles and G. Kosack, *Immigrant Workers and Class Structure in Western Europe*, Oxford University Press, 1973.

[23] *Op. cit.*, p. 8, emphasis added.

[24] See, for example, some of the interim reports emanating from this

programme of DHSS/SSRC sponsored research: e.g. R. Silburn, 'A Report Summarising and Comparing the Sub-Contracts of the "Socio-Economic" Group' (mimeo), August 1978.

25 In contrast to the studies discussed so far, this section relies entirely upon an evaluation report produced by our consultant, Judith Okely, Lecturer in Social Anthropology at the University of Durham.

26 *Op. cit.*, p.7/7.

27 *Ibid.*, p.7/28.

28 *Ibid.*, p.7/84.

29 *Ibid.*, p.7/95.

30 These concepts can, indeed, be said to be *essentially* contested, in the sense that competing theoretical frameworks express more fundamental differences in philosophical assumptions which cannot be resolved by appeal to empirical evidence. See, for example, G. Hawthorn and H. Carter, *The Concept of Deprivation* (Report prepared for the DHSS/SSRC Working Party on Transmitted Deprivation, January 1977).

31 This raises the question as to whether cross-national research is inherently 'asymmetrical', in addressing itself primarily to questions arising within *one* nation's research and policy agenda; or whether cross-national research can be 'symmetrical', in the sense of addressing itself to truly *common* problems.

32 *Op. cit.*, p.7.

33 Within the United Kingdom, the SSRC held a series of workshops during 1979 to consider the value of intra-UK comparative social policy research, focusing upon the different regions and nations within the UK. One of the main issues discussed was the institutional barriers to such research, including the lack of sponsors and the lack of contacts among experienced researchers working on similar problems in different regions. It followed that a more adequate communications network among researchers was required in order to promote information exchange and cross-regional comparative studies. (See G. J. Room, *Report on the SSRC/DHSS Workshop on the Comparative Study of the Social Services in the United Kingdom*, 20–22 September 1979).

PART III

The Programme as a Whole

10
The Definition and Measurement of Poverty[1]

(10.1) INTRODUCTION: THE COUNCIL DEFINITION

The Council Decision of July 1975 provides a definition of poverty:

> For the purposes of this Decision, the following definitions shall apply:
> — persons beset by poverty: individuals or families whose resources are so small as to exclude them from the minimum acceptable way of life of the Member State in which they live;
> — resources: goods, cash income, plus services from public and private sources.
>
> (Article 1, para. 2)

The definition of poverty — and hence also its measurement — is far from straightforward. The difficulties are in part technical; more fundamentally, however, the use of a definition involves choosing among the various theoretical assumptions about the causes of poverty which underlie competing definitions. Indeed, the definition, the measurement and the explanation of poverty are closely interdependent, as also are the policy implications which the social investigator may draw. This chapter therefore complements — and at points anticipates — the discussion of explanations of poverty to be presented in Chapter 11.

The Council definition was not formulated *ex nihilo*. In order to appreciate the assumptions which lie behind it, section (10.2) will briefly survey the pre-history of competing definitions. Within the Poverty Programme, the participating projects and studies have employed definitions of poverty and of their target populations which to varying extents elaborate upon, diverge from or contest the Council definition. These various definitions will be the subject of section (10.3). Finally, in the light of the research and action carried out within the present programme, it will be possible in section (10.4) critically to reconsider the Council definition, as a pre-condition for developing a revised definition to be used in future programmes.

(10.2)   A HISTORY OF DEFINITIONS[2]

In the different Member States of the European Community, social research and political debate on poverty have taken different forms over recent decades, as also have the definitions of poverty which have been used. It is most obviously to the Anglo-Saxon debate that the Council definition is heir.

More specifically, in the United Kingdom there is a longstanding tradition of social enquiry into poverty which has focused upon enumeration of the numbers of the population falling below some 'poverty line' defined in money terms. Charles Booth in the 1880s and Seebohm Rowntree were the pioneers of this tradition; its most recent exponent is Peter Townsend, with his study of *Poverty in the United Kingdom* (1979). Rowntree and Booth attempted to compute the physical necessities of life required for subsistence and thence to derive the minimum income which an individual, a family or a household would require: Rowntree's successive surveys over half a century revealed a declining proportion of the population of York living in such 'absolute' poverty. During the post-war period, Townsend has been one of the principal researchers concerned to promote a *relative* definition of poverty, which will recognise that the 'needs' which an individual or family must satisfy in order to live as a member of his society are *socially* rather than physically determined. These researchers have been a continuing critical influence upon the evolution of the 'official' poverty line — that is, the level of income guaranteed by the state through its social assistance system.

This has, to repeat, been one of the dominant traditions of social enquiry into poverty in the United Kingdom and, indeed, the Anglo-Saxon world at large. Townsend's definition of poverty is similar to that adopted by the Council of Ministers, although there are also significant differences: 'that section of the population whose resources are so depressed from the mean as to be deprived of enjoying the benefits and participating in the activities customary in that society can be said to be in poverty'.[3] This definition, like that employed by the Council, focuses upon the various resources which an individual needs to have at his disposal in order to meet certain needs

– whether these are defined in physically absolute or in socially relative terms.[4] However, the Townsend definition also concerns itself with the patterns of social participation and intercourse in which people may be involved and which, indeed, they may consider as great a priority for their energies as securing the means of physical existence: a priority which the Council (although recognising in its requirements that the pilot projects should include the 'participation' of the poor) does not explicitly include in its definition of poverty as such.

The definition of poverty in terms of the patterns of social intercourse in which people are able to participate is still more central to other traditions of enquiry and debate. For example, American writers in the tradition of Oscar Lewis not only explain but also define poverty in terms of the sub-culture in which its members are involved.[5] As we shall see, however, these definitions do not exhaust those which have been used by the studies and projects within the programme, the diversity of which points to a more profound and richer definition which might be used in future.

(10.3)   THE DEFINITIONS USED IN THE PROGRAMME

It is some of the cross-national studies that most obviously take the Council definition as their point of departure. As seen in the previous chapter, Willmott's approach is particularly close. Schaber develops indicators of multiple deprivation which reveal to what extent different aspects of disadvantage cluster together for particular categories of families. Both of these research teams develop objective definitions of poverty, in the sense of identifying patterns of objective disadvantage.

As Willmott's careful discussions demonstrate, however, even the definition and measurement of *income* poverty are far from straightforward.[6] Golding is highly critical of the IFOP study's carelessness in this regard;[7] van Praag seems similarly to have overlooked the complexities involved.[8] Indeed, Willmott himself is criticised by both Lawson and Trinder for not testing more carefully the stability of his results, i.e. how much they would be affected by adopting somewhat different definitions of income.[9] It remains to be seen how Schaber's indicators of multiple deprivation will stand up to similarly critical scrutiny.[10]

Both the Willmott and Schaber research teams recognise, of course, the social context in which such disadvantages arise and the need for their definition to be made relative to the societies concerned. Willmott is studying three societies with significantly different levels of prosperity; in both studies he avoids employing any cross-national line and instead accepts the Council's implicit invitation to consider the poor of different Member States in relation to their own societies. In Schaber's case, a more homogeneous region is under consideration and the findings can therefore be pooled, ignoring national boundaries.[11] However, Schaber's concern with the persistence of poverty *inter-generationally* confronts him with major long-term changes in the 'minimum acceptable way of life'; while the high numbers of immigrant families located by his indicators highlight the problem of what relative deprivation standards to use when looking at migration between societies with very diverse levels of prosperity.[12]

These definitions of (relative) poverty involve judgements by social researchers as to the resources necessary for participating as a member of a particular society – albeit judgements based upon careful empirical study of the ways of life of different sections of the population. Van Praag, however, offers an alternative: a national poverty line based upon the subjective perceptions held by citizens themselves, which supposedly avoids relying on judgements by experts (or indeed by politicians). The value of such an approach was examined in Chapter 9 and will not be re-examined here. Its theoretical interpretation and significance for policy remain at best unclear.[13]

Finally, the Gypsy studies highlight still further the complexities of using a socially relative definition of poverty. The Gypsies' way of life differs significantly from that of the dominant society; the resources, both material and non-material, necessary for sustaining it are likewise distinctive. As Okely argues, therefore, 'problems of poverty and deprivation should be considered in the context of the group's own defined priorities'.[14]

The action projects offer a variety of conceptualisations and definitions of poverty – implicit, if not always explicit – which reflect the diverse goals of their work and which complement their diverse attempts to *explain* poverty (which will be considered in Chapter 11). First, many of the projects echo Townsend's concern with the patterns of social consumption and participation which society enjoins upon its members. The poor are those who are excluded from such social intercourse: the isolated, the invisible, the hidden and the overlooked; their attempts to obey these social injunctions tend also, however, to leave them with inadequate resources even for physical subsistence. [15] Secondly, many projects use a definition of poverty which focuses upon the citizen as *par excellence* a participant in political processes of decision-making. Sudden job redundancy, low wages and arbitrary allocation to sub-standard housing are outward and visible signs of the lack of effective participation which particular groups of the population enjoy in the formal and informal decision-making processes of industry, government, trade unions, and even the social welfare agencies which are intended to relieve their poverty. Thirdly, various projects articulate a definition of poverty in terms of the legal and social *rights* which the poor are denied – in terms, that is, of *social injustice*. [16] Finally, various projects conceptualise poverty straight-forwardly in terms of a lack of opportunity and choice. [17] (This is a definition which may likewise be the one most suited to the poverty revealed by the Gypsy studies. [18]) In short, therefore, the projects (and studies) in the present programme, taken together, point towards a new definition of poverty which recognises the economic, social and political inequalities of a stratified society. [19] They point also towards an explanation or understanding of poverty as the outcome of the irresponsible exercise of overly concentrated social, economic and political power.

(10.4)   THE COUNCIL DEFINITION RECONSIDERED

The Council definition focuses upon (i) 'individuals and families'; (ii) 'the minumum acceptable way of life of the Member State in which they live'; (iii) the resources of 'goods, cash income, plus services' without which a person is excluded from society. The diversity of definitions which have in fact been employed by the projects and studies in the present programme – and the insights which these alternative definitions have provided – point to various inadequacies in this Council definition of 1975.

(i) 'Individuals and families'
The focus upon individuals and families may hold the danger that poverty is assumed to be (a) the fate of merely a residual minority; and (b) largely the result of mischance in the biographies of individuals, rather than the manifestation of wider societal processes. As seen in

the previous section, the action projects in particular use (or search for) definitions which can take account of these wider structural factors – factors which, as will be seen in the next chapter, are central to their explanations of poverty in the European Community.

(ii) *'The minimum acceptable way of life'*
The work of the studies and projects points to inadequacies in this aspect of the Council definition. First, as the van Praag study for example reveals, what is seen as the 'acceptable minimum' may vary greatly between different social strata of the population (as also may people's awareness of poverty in their society); there is a hierarchy of life-styles within our West European societies and the 'acceptable minimum' is variously defined by members of these different strata.[20] Moreover, what people see as the minimum acceptable for themselves may differ from the minimum they are prepared to guarantee their less fortunate fellows.

Secondly, the poor themselves may have very limited aspirations and may tend to restrict the range of goods and opportunities of which they feel a need: the standard of life which they take as a legitimate aspiration is deflated by their longstanding experience of want. Their sense of subjective deprivation relative to other members of the society is often surprisingly restricted. To be poor is, after all, to have little option over whether or not the 'way of life' which is available is 'acceptable' or not.

(iii) *'Resources'*
The Council definition implies that poverty consists primarily in a lack of resources, including goods, cash and services. It focuses attention upon the way in which these resources are distributed in society. To this extent it contrasts with the Townsend definition, failing to focus upon the social participation from which the poor are excluded; and it contrasts with various of the projects discussed in the previous section which define the poor primarily by their lack of opportunities for participating in the decisions which affect them or, alternatively, by the violation of their legal and social rights.

The Council definition also tends to imply that simply providing more resources to the poor will be a sufficient anti-poverty policy, without any structural changes being necessary in the larger society. The programme, however, points to the wider mechanisms of inequality at the heart of our societies which must be transformed if poverty is to be eliminated.

Notes

[1] Written by Graham Room.

[2] This section is brief in the extreme. For more thorough and extensive discussion, see P. Townsend, *Poverty in the United Kingdom*, Allen Lane, 1979, especially Chapters 1, 5–7, 11.

[3] P. Townsend (ed.), *The Concept of Poverty*, Heinemann, 1970, p. 19.

[4] Both definitions thereby reflect the English tradition of liberal political economy: see G. Room, *The Sociology of Welfare*, Martin Robertson, 1979, pp. 29–30.

[5] See e.g. D. Moynihan (ed.), *On Understanding Poverty*, New York, Basic Books, 1968.

[6] Willmott, *Poverty and Social Policy*, Chapter 3; *Unemployment and Anti-poverty Policies*, Chapters 3 and 5.

[7] See above, Section (9.2.1).

[8] See above, Section (9.2.2), esp. sub-section (ii).

[9] See above, Sections (9.2.3) and (9.2.4).

[10] See above, Section (9.2.5).

[11] It remains a pity however that no comparative empirical study of the operation of local services in these different countries has been undertaken.

[12] See above, Section (9.2.5).

[13] See above, Section (9.2.2).

[14] Consultancy report on Gypsy studies (see above, Section 9.2.6), p. 7/11.

[15] See, for example, the UK Family Day Centres and the Cologne project's work with the elderly: see Sections (8.4) and (5.2) above.

[16] The German projects, dealing particularly with *Randgruppen* or marginal groups of the population (paupers who traditionally suffered diminished civil, social and political rights), have been especially inclined to this definition of poverty. They have used the new citizenship rights defined by the BSHG (Federal Social Assistance Law) as a critical benchmark by which to evaluate existing social provisions and injustices.

[17] For example, SCDP in Edinburgh – see above, Section (8.6).

[18] See above, Section (9.2.6).

[19] Cf. Max Weber's essay, 'Class, Status and Party' in *Essays from Max Weber* (edited by H. H. Gerth and C. W. Mills).

[20] See above, Section (9.2.2.).

11
Understanding
Poverty [1]

(11.1) POVERTY IN THE EUROPEAN COMMUNITY

The post-war decades have been a period of unprecedented economic growth and affluence in the Member States of the European Community, contrasting with the austerities of the 1930s and 1940s. Particularly in the 1950s and 1960s, this prosperity promised rising living standards which would be available to all, not least to those previously vulnerable to poverty. During the same period, there has been a dramatic expansion in the social services provided through statutory agencies and/or independent welfare organisations, accompanied by a general growth in governmental expenditure. As George and Lawson therefore conclude, 'there was abundant national wealth and government activity to deal with problems of excessive income inequalities and poverty'[2].

It was in this context of growth, prosperity and optimism that the European Community was established and developed over its first decade and a half. Partly out of confidence that economic growth would automatically guarantee attainment of *social* goals, partly out of national governments' unwillingness to surrender their powers in the social field, it was only in regard to agriculture and transport that precise social objectives were included in the Treaty of Rome.[3] Such social measures as were included tended, moreover, to focus upon the worker and his working environment and to be defined principally as an adjunct or lubricant to the creation of a common market.

In the Anglo-Saxon world at least, the 1960s saw a 'rediscovery' of poverty. Economic growth and the expansion of the public sector might have reduced the numbers of people in *absolute* poverty; as seen in the previous chapter, however, it was increasingly in terms of *relative* deprivation that social policies were coming to be evaluated and found wanting. In the United States, the 'War on Poverty' was the most obvious expression of this new awareness; later in the decade, similar experimental programmes were launched in Britain alongside a burgeoning corpus of academic research.[4] On the Continent also, increasing attempts were being made by movements such as ATD Fourth World to sensitise public opinion to the persistence of poverty in Western Europe.

During the early 1970s, this diminished confidence in the social beneficence of post-war economic expansion entered the political agenda of the European Community also. As seen in Chapter 1, the 1974 Social Action Programme, including the Poverty Programme, was intended to put a 'human face' on the Community. In the event, however, the period of the Poverty Programme has been one of arrested economic growth and restrictions on the growth of public expenditure: a challenge to the basic assumptions on which the Community had been built. There has been rising unemployment and in several countries — notably Germany — this would have been still higher had not restrictions been tightened on the entry and residence permits of immigrant workers (*Gastarbeiter*).[5]

These developments have exposed major gaps in the social insurance schemes which in most of the Member States were designed to support income during short-term dislocations, but which, it is now evident, are much less adequate to cope with long-term unemployment, for example, and tend to neglect women, the young and the unskilled in particular.[6] It is hardly surprising, therefore, that during the 1970s, and especially during the period of the programme, there have been significant changes in the numbers and categories of the population dependent on social assistance — and hence living at or below the 'official' poverty line. In general, the number of elderly people on social assistance appears to be falling, at least in *relative* terms, partly because of more adequate pensions provision; but young people, the unemployed and single parents have increased as a proportion of recipients. There is clear evidence that many of those formally eligible for such benefits do not claim them, either because of ignorance or out of fear of stigmatisation. Moreover, as Lawson has noted, 'there is evidence in some countries, most notably the UK, that the growing numbers of unemployed receiving benefits is leading to pressures for more stringent policies and controls in this field'.[7]

The action-research projects and the cross-national studies in the present programme shed light on many of these developments. Albeit incompletely and unsystematically, they reveal the changing patterns and dynamics of poverty in our rapidly changing societies and the changing social relationships between the poor and the more advantaged. In this chapter, three broad questions will be considered by means of which their findings can be brought to bear on the current agenda of political and academic debate:

(i)   Why is there poverty in an affluent society? In what ways has the current recession accentuated the extent and changed the patterns of poverty in the European Community?

(ii) Why is it that existing social policy measures, particularly those specifically designed to combat poverty, are not more effective? Why, instead, do they tend to reinforce the long-term dependence of the poor or, alternatively, to deter the poor from making use of them?

(iii) In what senses — and for whom — is the persistence of poverty a *problem*?

It is these questions which provide the principal focus for the three main sections of this chapter. Nevertheless, this attempt to bring together the findings of the projects and studies can be only schematic and tentative; and it provides only the outline of common trends and processes in the Community, rather than detailed comparisons between the member states. It should therefore be regarded as an agenda for more systematic future comparative research and action-research, based upon the disparate and fragmented results yielded by the present programme.

(11.2) THE GENERATION AND PERSISTENCE OF POVERTY

In the 1950s and 1960s, the expanding consumer societies of Western Europe held out new aspirations towards material advancement and self-development for the individual citizen. Policy-makers, social researchers and the wider public embraced two confident assumptions.

1. It was assumed that economic prosperity and the expansion of the social services would ensure that all citizens, at least in some measure, would be able to partake of these new opportunities. One of the results would be that poverty would be progressively eliminated.

It has, however, become increasingly evident that in order to appropriate these new opportunities, individual citizens need a variety of new skills, credentials, information and other resources which are themselves unevenly distributed. For example, although there has been considerable expansion of educational opportunities, this has tended to raise the level of credentials which an individual requires in order to secure access to more desirable occupations and work milieux.[8] The extent and quality of individual citizens' participation in the production and consumption milieux of our societies therefore remains highly competitive and unequal, despite the apparent expansion of individual opportunities.

Recognition of this demands as its corollary that poverty be understood in terms of *relative* deprivation. The poor are those who lack the new skills, credentials and other resources which are required in order to gain access to the more desirable — or at least tolerable — segments of society's production and consumption milieux. Indeed, such relative deprivation may involve increasing rates of *absolute* deprivation, at least among particular sub-groups of the poor: first, for example, because irregular employment, low income and physically deleterious working conditions continue to endanger health; secondly, because the cultural imperative to participate in society's expanding range of consumer activities may lead the poor to reduce their expenditure on the physical essentials of life.

2. It was equally assumed that the costs of social and economic change, which were in any case limited, would be remedied by the new infrastructure of the welfare state. For example, the social insurance systems which were established following the war provided a system of income maintenance designed to protect its members against the vicissitudes of a rapidly changing market society — at least in regard to employment income — or, alternatively, to compensate them for the losses they incurred through no fault of their own.

Nevertheless, it has become increasingly apparent that the role which these welfare state provisions have been able to play has been limited by the wider political, economic and social contexts in which they have operated. For example, those in more insecure employment are often inadequately protected by such a social insurance system. More generally, a variety of other costs of social and economic change tend to lie where they fall, with no compensation for those who bear them. Indeed, it is those individuals, communities and regions least benefited by the expanding range of opportunities of the post-war period which tend also to suffer disproportionately the social costs and social insecurities which our rapidly changing societies tend perennially to produce. Virtuous and vicious circles of cumulative advantage and disadvantage have tended therefore to develop, with only those groups and communities who are already relatively advantaged having the power to escape bearing the costs of change.

The various projects and studies within the European Programme provide a prism through which it is possible to view the combined impact of these new opportunities and aspirations on the one hand and the social costs of change on the other upon patterns of disadvantage and deprivation.

(11.2.1) The Benefits and Costs of Economic Change

Many of the projects and studies within the European Programme reveal *the impact of economic change* upon patterns of deprivation.

(i) Some of the projects are located within neighbourhoods or regions whose economic and industrial history has produced distinctive and striking patterns of deprivation and poverty. The projects point to the ways in which the creation of wealth in one region can promote the creation of poverty in others, thereby shaping the context for the projects' work.

The Mezzogiorno, north-east Bavaria, Brittany, South Wales, Scotland, Northern Ireland and the west of Ireland are all regions peripheral to the Member States of which they form a part and, furthermore, to the European Community as a whole. The inhabitants of these areas have long suffered relatively high rates of unemployment and under-employment; wages are low and so too are levels of investment in industry and in social infrastructure. Emigration of those of working age to the economically more prosperous regions of the Community is longstanding. Some of this migration is to the industrial heartland of the Community and involves the crossing of national frontiers; some is to the more prosperous regions of the countries concerned, such as Dublin and north Italy; some is merely to local growth points, such as Naples and Cork.[9] All of these flows involve an export of human capital for which the regions concerned receive no direct compensation;[10] and all undermine the networks of mutual aid and informal social support in these regions. In other respects, of course, the similarities among these regions are only limited. The peripheral character of southern Italy is that of an under-developed and pre-industrial economy as, in some measure, is that of Brittany and the west of Ireland;[11] in contrast, the economic weakness of north-east Bavaria has been strongly reinforced by the post-war political divisions of Europe;[12] again in contrast, the South

Wales region, Scotland and Northern Ireland are areas which have long been based upon a few traditional heavy industries whose decline has accelerated over recent decades.[13]

Other projects are working in inner-city areas and many point to the impact of changes in the local economy upon patterns of inner-city deprivation. Some are areas of industrial decline: for example, the Govan area of Glasgow was traditionally based on the ship-building industry and is now, like inner-city Dublin, suffering the impact of 'de-industrialisation'.[14] Some other city areas, although not suffering such longstanding decline, have been hit especially badly by the recession of the 1970s: for example, Duisburg in the heart of the Ruhr, which is heavily dependent on the coal and steel industries.[15] In such areas it is not merely the unemployed who suffer the social costs of economic change and recession: others within the population are made to work short-time, skills are under-utilised and there is a general deflation of purchasing power and prosperity.[16]

In other cities, however, general economic prosperity has been no less able to generate deprivation. This is particularly obvious among migrants from the peripheral regions of the European Community, the Mediterranean and (in the case of Britain) from the Caribbean and the Indian sub-continent, who have been recruited to low-paid and unskilled jobs. For example, the ATD projects in France work with formerly landless migrants jettisoned from the rural economy and forced to seek unattractive jobs on the fringe of the urban economy.[17] These migrants tend to be concentrated and segregated either in the inner cities (most obviously in the case of Britain) or in housing estates on city outskirts (most obviously the *cités de promotion* of France, the successors to the *bidonvilles*). They are in general badly organised and especially vulnerable to redundancy in times of recession; the ethnic minorities among them commonly suffer further discrimination.

As already hinted, however, urban growth and urban deprivation are not peculiar to the industrialised regions of the Community. For example, Naples is an area of rapid urban growth within an under-developed region; and Giugliano is one of its rapidly expanding satellite towns, absorbing its population overspill as well as migrants from the hinterland. The population is heavily weighted towards the younger age-groups and public services are under strain in coping with rising demands for housing, etc.[18]

This brief discussion touches on only a few of the interactions between, on the one hand, the varied economic and industrial histories of different regions and, on the other hand, the different administrative regimes for providing services, housing, etc. — and their combined effect upon patterns of poverty and deprivation. It remains an obvious area for further cross-national comparison.

(ii) Many projects monitor the impact of economic prosperity, change and decline upon particular occupational groups and demographic categories. They point to the persistence of low pay, despite post-war economic growth, among the unskilled sector of the labour force, which includes disproportionate numbers of immigrant workers, the handicapped, women and the educationally unqualified. These tend also to be those with the least satisfactory employment-related welfare benefits (including, for example, pensions) and job security.[19] They form a 'reservoir' of unskilled labour within a stratified labour market; they keep only a tenuous hold upon their niche at the edge of the economic system; in consequence, they have been particularly vulnerable to the rising unemployment of the 1970s and are disproportionately represented among the increasing numbers of people dependent upon social assistance benefits,

These are then the people least able to cope with rising rents and fuel bills: they are those with the least financial reserves to insulate themselves against such threats and the least political resources to combat the policies responsible. Debts and rent arrears are common, especially among families with children: this is highlighted, for example, by the Belfast Welfare Rights project and the Duisburg and Craigmillar projects.[20] Schaber's research in 'Greater Luxembourg' indicates that among families, it is immigrants and one-parent households who are most vulnerable to these related forms of deprivation; the 'map of misery' may differ in its detail in other Member States and regions, but its overall outline seems broadly uniform.

(11.2.2) The Benefits and Costs of the Welfare State

The expansion of the post-war welfare states has had obvious costs in terms of public taxation and government expenditure. The projects and studies within the European Programme, however, point to certain less obvious costs of this expansion.

(i) *The governmental role in economic change*
To an increasing extent, Western governments have become actively

and directly involved in monitoring and steering the processes of economic change discussed above, albeit with economic more than social goals in mind: for example, through their macro-economic management of the economy, their regional aids to industry and their role as substantial direct employers. Some of this intervention is, moreover, carried out in partnership with the European Commission.

A few of the projects – for example, the British Area Resource Centres[21] – have monitored the effects of this government intervention on the way in which the social costs of economic change are distributed. It is clear that some of the basic heavy industries, such as steel, coal and ship-building, for which governments have taken a particular responsibility in recent decades, are the industries where unemployment is mounting particularly fast during the current recession. In addition, employment in social and public services run by governments has been restrained or even reduced in some Member States during recent years, again adding to the pool of unemployed.

(ii) *Gaps in the welfare state*

The expansion of public and social services during the post-war period has by no means benefited different sections of the population equally. National studies (including the National Reports on Poverty conducted as a separate part of the European Programme[22]) reveal that, despite the vast increase in provision, relative inequalities among different social classes persist: for example, in respect of educational opportunities and health care.[23]

What the projects in the European Programme do is highlight those groups and communities within the population which have been particularly neglected in this expansion of social provision. They point, for example, to (a) the educational neglect of lower working-class children (Duisburg, ATD); (b) neglect of the housing needs of immigrants and ethnic minorities (Amberg, Belfast Welfare Rights project, Roubaix); and (c) inadequate pensions for women and those with an interrupted record of social insurance contributions (Cologne). The studies by Willmott compare the patterns of neglect associated with different patterns of social provision in the different Member States.[24] Many of the projects also point out how more advantaged groups of the population have been able to manipulate and benefit from these expanded services, especially because the bureaucratisation of these services has tended to deter their use by less educated, knowledgeable and organised people. Finally, they monitor the impact upon these same groups of current reductions in levels of welfare provision.

It is, finally, by no means only the projects working *outside* the statutory agencies of the welfare state that point to these gaps. From inside local government, the Padua project centres its attention upon the inadequate co-ordination of health and social services. Likewise, the SCDP project in Edinburgh and the COPES project in Paris point not only to the malco-ordination of conventional local authority services but also to their inaccessibility to the disadvantaged.[25] What the evidence from the other projects suggests, however, is that this insensitivity and inaccessibility are not merely *technical* problems of communication etc., but are also symptoms of the success of more advantaged groups in manipulating these services.

(iii) *Victims of the welfare state*

Finally, in various ways this expansion of governmental social policies has tended unintentionally to create *new* forms of deprivation and disadvantage. Redevelopment policies in the inner city (for example, the Marolles area of Brussels) and the establishment of new housing estates containing migrants from less developed areas and/or the displaced population of the inner city (Chorweiler in Cologne, Craigmillar in Scotland and the *grands ensembles* in France) tend to disrupt or neglect informal community networks of social control and mutual aid.[26] The Giugliano project points to the socially incapacitating effects of many institutionalised forms of health care, which again disregard the informal caring networks within local communities.[27]

Finally, the social legislation of an increasingly interventionist state tends to be unintentionally intolerant of nomad populations. Economic changes have certainly challenged Gypsies and similar groups to seek out for themselves new occupational roles; but within the urban economy, it is the increasing *political* controls that constrain their traditional nomadic existence and now threaten them with impoverishment. The informal welfare systems of traditional Gypsy communities are disrupted and the individual Gypsy often becomes dependent upon the formal welfare system of the larger society.[28]

(11.2.3) The Social Consequences of Change

The individuals and communities who bear these costs of economic change and governmental intervention tend to remain or become socially isolated. They lack the income and other resources to participate in the social activities enjoined by a consumption-oriented society.[29] Women, the unqualified and the low paid tend not to be unionised and to be separate, therefore, from traditional forms of working-class organisation, mutual aid and solidarity.

Such networks of mutual aid as they have been involved in tend to suffer disruption. Peripheral regions which lose those of working age experience a concomitant decline in the strength and vitality of these networks: the South Wales project, for example, points to the decay of the traditional social fabric and of community groups in the valleys. A similar fate can afflict inner-city areas: some of the Family Day Centres in London, for example, work with isolated poor families where networks of informal community support have been disrupted by depopulation.[30] The Cologne project's inner-city work exposes the social isolation of the elderly poor; PACT points to their similar isolation in rural Brittany.[31] Reception areas of the inner city offer few opportunities for welcoming and integrating newcomers, especially ethnic minorities (see, for example, the Marolles area of Brussels); the populations of new housing estates are separate from established social networks in the host area and therefore become a ready focus for resentment and hostility.[32]

Their social isolation and the disruption of established networks of informal support increase the need of such groups and communities for social services; in general, however, they lack the political power to ensure that these services are provided. Moreover, without these extended networks of mutual support, the disadvantaged tend also to lack the information and informal expertise with which to understand and confront these various economic, political and social processes impinging upon them: they suffer an enforced parochialism.

(11.3) THE PERCEPTION AND TREATMENT OF POVERTY

(11.3.1) The Mystification of Poverty

Economic change and governmental intervention have their casualties and costs, but the processes whereby these are generated are not readily visible: (a) because of the complexity of our rapidly changing industrial-bureaucratic societies; (b) because the disadvantaged who bear these costs lack the resources and skills to monitor and publicise them, still less to organise and oppose them; (c) because those who generate such costs have every interest in concealing their responsibility; and (d) because the equal opportunities ostensibly offered by the educational system and the market place make inequalities of outcome appear to be the necessary result of individual talent and effort on the one hand, or of ineluctable economic forces on the other.

In consequence, these disadvantages are commonly perceived not as the precipitate or fruit of wider social processes, but rather as characteristics of the communities or individuals concerned. Moreover, the very similar social processes of precipitation to which they have fallen victim are left unnoticed and particular expressions of disadvantage are perceived as a variety of marginal categories and communities – the homeless, social assistance recipients, etc. Poverty appears and is treated as a fragmented and individual problem, even where whole communities suffer deprivation.

It is these processes of mystification which the German projects are particularly concerned to expose. Over the post-war period as a whole it is only the *Randgruppen* – i.e. marginal groups – who have been acknowledged by policy-makers in Germany as a social problem; poverty was long assumed by most commentators to have disappeared. Only in the 1970s has a new debate begun which, in some degree, recognises the persistence of poverty. As a contribution to this debate, the German projects set out to demystify the persistence of 'marginal groups' such as the *Obdachlosen* (people in emergency accommodation) and *Nichtsesshaften* (vagrants): they demonstrate how such people are recruited from the unemployed and homeless, channelled to assistance agencies which segregate them from the rest of the population and metamorphosed in public consciousness into a separate and distinct type of sub-human being.[33]

(11.3.2)   The Stigmatisation of Poverty

Separated from the society at large by these disadvantages, the poor then readily become stereotyped as morally and intellectually inferior. Especially where social links of mutual aid and support have been undermined or were never strong, sympathy towards the anonymous disadvantaged is very limited: for example, between established residents of metropolitan areas on the one hand and, on the other, ethnic minorities in the inner city and in their rural or under-developed areas of origin. The unemployed are stigmatised as 'workshy'; one-parent families, as the work of the British Family Day Centres reveals, are denigrated as feckless and irresponsible; the single homeless of Copenhagen and Stuttgart are metamorphosed into 'vagrants', the objects of public hostility and revulsion.

Once they have been designated incompetent and potentially disruptive, the disadvantaged are then perceived by society at large as requiring paternalistic supervision, in their own interests as much as in those of the society at large. Alternatively, such incompetence is often taken as justifying a policy of neglect and of limited commitment to the removal of disadvantage: especially where the threat of disruption is limited, for example from the population of poor regions peripheral to the mainstream of society.

(11.3.3) Official Treatment of Poverty

These popular attitudes towards poverty also underpin many of the social and public services ostensibly designed to combat deprivation. These services tend, therefore, to be oriented primarily towards the *symptoms* of disadvantage: emergency accommodation for the homeless, regional aid to attract industry to economically peripheral areas, short-term training opportunities for the unemployed. In consequence, they are at best ameliorative rather then preventive; and they tend still further to obscure public recognition of the processes which *generate* deprivation and disadvantage. They tend to segregate the poor from the rest of the population, to deny them any participation in the design and control of these services and to discourage the poor both from claiming their rights and from becoming independent again.

Many of these measures involve incentives and disciplines which tend to inhibit self-help on the part of the individuals and communities concerned. First, they tend to place upon the disadvantaged themselves the onus or responsibility of seeking out and proving a need for assistance: only in law, if at all, is assistance to overcome poverty a *right*. The effectiveness of these benefits therefore depends upon the information available to their intended beneficiaries: but both the Wolverhampton and Duisburg projects, for example, point to its paucity. The effectiveness of these benefits also depends upon the way in which officials exercise their discretionary powers: again, various projects point to the unfavourable stereotypes which many officials, like the wider public, hold of their clients.[34]

Secondly, social assistance, in particular, often creates a 'poverty trap' by denying or reducing benefits if the recipient secures an increased income from elsewhere. Other measures to assist the poor, such as the traditional German provisions to assist 'marginal groups' like the *Obdachlosen* and *Nichtsesshaften*, create a supervised long-term existence for the poor which disables them from re-integrating themselves into the wider society.[35] More generally, the 'helping professions' (including conventional social workers) tend often to disregard the latent skills among the poor themselves, which might be mobilised in new forms of creative mutual aid.[36]

One overall result then is that a high proportion of the poor feel too humiliated and stigmatised to seek out these forms of assistance; official measures designed ostensibly to relieve poverty remain only very incompletely effective. Nevertheless, some of them have a significant regulative role vis-à-vis the labour market: for their deterrent effect and the disciplines which they involve impel the poor to seek out low-paid casual and unskilled work.

(11.4)   THE CONSEQUENCES OF POVERTY

For whom, then, is poverty a 'problem' — and what precisely *is* the problem? For the poor themselves, the 'problem' is, first, the low and insecure income on which they have to survive, the poor housing and amenities they are able to enjoy and the lack of educational qualifications to which they seem inevitably condemned; secondly, it is their lack of opportunities to participate in the communal activities customary in the societies of which they are members, and hence their social isolation; thirdly, it is their almost complete lack of control over the wider economic, social and political decisions which impinge upon their lives and hence their perennial insecurity; fourthly, it is the humiliation of their continuing dependence on the charity of the wider society and, more particularly, upon the officials who administer relief; finally, it is the unlikelihood of any improvement in this situation, whether for themselves or their children.

Enjoying few of the opportunities held out by a wide range of social institutions as the normal aspirations of modern citizens, exposed to the perennial insecurities of a rapidly changing urban-industrial society, socially isolated and stigmatised by officialdom and the wider public, the poor are confirmed in their fatalism, mistrust and lack of self-esteem. They tend to lose the skills and know-how required to manipulate the agencies of the wider society, except, to some extent, those which deal directly and exclusively with the poor. (This is not to deny, however, that they may be very creative and skilful in manipulating the stereotyped images which the wider society thrusts upon them. The vagrants of Stuttgart, for example, 'sell' their poverty and degradation, exploiting bypassers' sense of guilt.[37]) They limit their horizons and expectations: partly out of ignorance of the opportunities available, partly out of realism; and they often give their children little encouragement and support to seek educational success. These consequences of poverty are then identified by members of the wider society as pathological defects which justify the continuing segregated treatment and supervision of the poor.

The children who grow up in such families may well be at risk of 'inheriting' the poverty of their parents. Nevertheless, both the studies and the action projects in the European Programme provide clear evidence against popular theories of 'transmitted deprivation' – the argument (as Münstermann summarises it in his report on the Schaber study) that 'there is . . . (a) stationary segment or stratum in society, in which the same correlates of poverty prevail now as a generation ago, and in which a given set of behaviour patterns, attitudes and values are passed from parents to children that keep them from moving up'.[38] Instead, the wider social, economic and political factors which thrust families into poverty have changed markedly over the last generation and may well do so over the next; whether or not the children of today's poor also grow up poor will depend principally not upon the socialisation patterns within these families, but rather upon policies regarding the broad pattern of social and economic opportunities which are made available to them. These implications of the Schaber research are consistent with what is revealed by the work on the UK Family Day Centres, for example, and various of the other projects working particularly with families.[39]

Whether or not poverty is recognised as a 'problem' by the wider society, is, however, more questionable, in view of the continuing low priority which poverty is given on the political agenda of most Member States. *Contra* the IFOP study's recommendations, merely to increase public awareness of poverty will hardly suffice to secure a widespread political commitment to its elimination.[40] Nevertheless, the findings of the present programme suggest that there are three main senses in which poverty is indeed a significant problem for the wider society, and one whose significance may well grow through the 1980s.

(11.4.1)   Poverty as a Public Burden

The 'poverty trap' or 'Armutskarussel', in which the poor often find themselves moving from one agency of segregated relief to another, tends to reinforce their long-term and expensive dependence upon public support. Furthermore, the agencies of official intervention commonly disregard the latent resources and skills among the disadvantaged communities and people concerned and the potential voluntary effort which might be mobilised. In contrast, the action projects in the present programme demonstrate the cost-effectiveness of self-help efforts, as compared with the conventional services of which the poor become the long-term dependents. It is true that the action projects in the present European Programme have typically mobilised highly skilled and highly motivated teams and have involved an intensive and expensive use of resources; nevertheless, there are grounds for believing that they are cost-effective and could be made the basis of wider-scale policy reforms which would reduce the public burden of maintaining the poor.[41]

(11.4.2)   Poverty as Social Injustice

Poverty and deprivation involve social injustice rather than individual irresponsibility and fecklessness. First, the economic and social costs of change are imposed disproportionately and without adequate compensation upon those groups and communities who have least resources and skills to bear them and the fabric of whose lives is put in jeopardy. Secondly, official agencies, ostensibly designed to provide compensation and to restore such individuals and communities to full participation in the wider society, in practice commonly operate to reinforce their exclusion and stigmatisation, subjecting them to paternalistic supervision. The promises of an affluent society are proved empty; the rights of full citizenship are rendered ineffective. A variety of political theorists have, in recent years, called attention to this gap between promise and performance in our western societies and the consequent corrosion of their moral and political legitimacy: the poverty exposed by the European Programme gives concrete expression to these theoretical debates.[42] The European Programme serves, however unsystematically and incompletely, to confront members of the wider society with an understanding of this unjustice and of the social, political and moral options among which they must now choose. It challenges the growing tendency among the more advantaged and policy-makers to regard poverty not so much as an evil to be remedied but as an economic necessity.

(11.4.3)   Poverty and Social Disorder

How the poor express their resentment and sense of deprivation depends very much on the local traditions of community action which they have inherited. The disorganised and isolated tend to withdraw into sullen apathy; amongst themselves they are often quarrelsome and disorderly. The negative images of poverty promulgated by opinion-leaders in the wider society often lead to mutual denigration and hostility among different groups of the poor: for example, the different ethnic groups on the Bergsteig estate, where the Amberg project team is working. Where community networks of social discipline are broken down, the young often turn to delinquency and vandalism.

However, where there are more organised community organisations and traditions of collective action, the resentment of the poor is likely to be expressed in more violent disorder directed against the wider society. The increasing numbers of able-bodied workers, whether employed or made redundant in the current recession, who are becoming dependent upon social assistance and who are newly vulnerable to social deprivation may here be of considerable significance for the future: both because of the suddenness with which such deprivation has been thrust upon them, after the rising expectations of the 1960s, and also because of their links with the trade unions and organised labour, who previously had been only peripherally concerned with the problem of poverty. Various of the projects warn of the possible social disorder which this new poverty may generate: for example, in areas of traditional working-class solidarity and militancy, such as South Wales, and in areas with high proportions of ethnic minorities suffering higher than average unemployment.

At the same time, however, the increasing proportion of the population dependent upon public relief may also invite increasing resentment from more advantaged sections of the community and increasing supervision and control of the ways in which these benefits are distributed. (Indeed, as the IFOP study reveals, this resentment may be greatest among the lower working class, i.e. those whose own independence is least secure.) In short, therefore, there are serious dangers of a spiralling polarisation of mutual suspicion and hostility between the 'new poor' and those sections of the population who have been relatively successful in insulating themselves against the insecurities and costs of the present austerity.

(11.5) CONCLUSIONS

(11.5.1) Poverty in the European Community

The findings of the action-research projects and cross-national studies strongly suggest that poverty and deprivation within the European Community

(a) are *European* problems, in the senses (i) that they take many similar forms in the different Member States and (ii) that they are associated with wider social, economic and political changes which transcend national boundaries and which include many of the traditional areas of activity of the European Commission;

(b) have worsened during the period of the programme, partly as a consequence of the deepening recession;

(c) arise and persist among certain communities and categories of the population not so much because of their inadequacies and incompetences, but rather because (i) they are especially vulnerable to the costs of social change, both in times of prosperity and, still more, in periods of austerity; (ii) they are commonly stigmatised or disregarded by the population at large and denied adequate or just compensation for bearing these costs; (iii) they are segregated by many conventional welfare services from the rest of the population, denied participation in the design and control of these services and discouraged from claiming their social rights;

(d) tend to alienate the disadvantaged from the principal social and political institutions of their societies, with consequent dangers to the effectiveness of those institutions and even to social and political order.

As noted earlier, the evidence of other recent studies is that the numbers of the population dependent upon social assistance — and hence living at the 'official' poverty line — has been increasing as employment opportunities have fallen. It is likely that unemployment will persist and even grow in importance as a social problem of the 1980s and 1990s, as a consequence of recurring energy crises and technological change, notably that resulting from the introduction of micro-processors. At the same time, the proportion of one-parent families may well continue to increase and this, together with an ageing population, will further add to the proportion of the population dependent upon the state rather than upon the labour market for their primary income. These developments challenge still further the basic assumptions upon which the social market economies of Western Europe and the Treaty of Rome were based.

How will this growing dependence on state benefits be perceived and defined, both by the state itself and by independent members of our societies? Will those dependent upon the state become a stratum of second-class citizens — stigmatised, supervised and resentful — or will new rights to share in society's prosperity, irrespective of employment status, be worked out? It is to these emerging political and moral questions of the 1980s and 1990s that the present European Programme points. Many of the innovations which have been developed at local level[43] and the wider policy implications which these suggest demonstrate the beginning of the quest for answers.[44] These innovations highlight the importance of public services which do not segregate the poor from the rest of the population, which facilitate participation by service users in the formulation and implementation of social policy measures and which do not attempt to tackle poverty independently of policies in the labour market, the housing market, etc.[45]

Nevertheless, it is impossible to be optimistic about these future developments. The poor lack any significant political power and influence and their advocates are heard only with impatience, especially at a time of austerity. Popular ideologies which identify the poor as 'scroungers' are as likely to wax as to wane. Whether or not poverty is recognised as the social problem it is, as seen in Section (11.4), is likely therefore to depend crucially upon the directions of political leadership exercised at national and European levels.

(11.5.2)   Understanding as Demystification

Those who attempt, in the words of the 1975 Council Decision, to promote an improved understanding of 'the nature, causes, scope and mechanics of poverty' address their findings to a public which is simultaneously embarrassed and concerned, ignorant and dismissive. In some Member States of the European Community, there is now a considerable body of research into poverty and it is no longer an inadequate understanding that is the principal barrier to effective counter-measures: instead, it is the political will that is lacking.[46] In other Member States, it is the lack of interest in poverty that is most striking and that highlights the lack of any voice which the poor enjoy in articulating their needs and grievances.

To publicise the extent and dynamics of poverty is inevitably, therefore, a political act: whether at the local level where most of the projects have been working, the national level with which the national reports are principally concerned or the European level at which the cross-national studies and, indeed, the ESPOIR report are pitched. Research into poverty is inevitably illuminating, prompting attention to the invisible, the forgotten, the overlooked; it is simultaneously research into the most surveyed, supervised and scrutinised segment of our population. Such research may furnish 'concrete information' for policy-makers, as demanded by the Council Decision of 1975; it is equally likely, however, to be ignored or distorted by those from whom it demands a response.[47] Those who research and disseminate are unavoidably involved in the continuing mystification and demystification of poverty, the continuing competition among the paradigms paraded by different societal interest groups.

Notes

[1] Written by Graham Room.

[2] V. George and R. Lawson (eds.), *Poverty and Inequality in Common Market Countries*, Routledge and Kegan Paul, 1980, pp. 234–5.

[3] D. Collins, *The European Communities: the Social Policy of the First Phase*, Volume 2, Martin Robertson, 1975, pp. 28–9.

[4] See, for example, R. Lees and G. Smith (eds.), *Action-Research in Community Development*, Routledge and Kegan Paul, 1975.

[5] George and Lawson, *op. cit.*, pp. 209–11.

[6] See, for example, Section (5.1) above on the situation in Germany, the home of the 'economic miracle'.

[7] R. Lawson, *Social Assistance in the Member States of the European Community* (Report prepared for the European Commission), 1979 para. 2.2.4.

[8] F. Hirsch, *Social Limits to Growth*, Routledge and Kegan Paul, 1977.

[9] See, for example, Sections (6.3) and (7.2) above.

[10] S. Castles and G. Kosack, *Immigrant Workers and Class Structure in Western Europe*, Oxford University Press, 1973.

[11] See Sections (4.4) and (6.2) above.

[12] See Section (5.5) above.

[13] See Sections (8.2), (8.5) − (8.7) above.

[14] See Sections (6.3) and (8.5) above.

[15] See Section (5.3) above.

[16] The second study by Willmott, *Unemployment and Anti-Poverty Policies*, looks at these more general aspects of deprivation suffered by areas newly afflicted by high rates of unemployment. See above, Section (9.2.4).

[17] See Section (4.3) above.

[18] See Section (7.2) above.

[19] The second Willmott study (see above, Section (9.2.4)) is looking in part at sickness- and handicap-related unemployment and poverty, as well as at the redundancy payments associated with unemployment. Willmott is also looking at the qualifications of those who have most recently become unemployed. Nevertheless, what would be valuable is a systematic cross-national study of the relationship between such employment-related welfare benefits and the incidence of poverty.

[20] See Sections (5.3), (8.2), (8.7) above.

[21] See Section (8.5) above.

[22] See Section (1.4) above.

[23] In the case of Britain see, for example, A. H. Halsey *et al.*, *Origins and Destinations*, Oxford University Press, 1980.

[24] See Sections (9.2.3) and (9.2.44) above.

[25] See Sections (4.2), (7.1), (8.6) above.

[26] See Sections (3.2), (4.5), (5.2), (8.7) above.

[27] See Section (7.2) above.

[28] See Section (9.2.6) above.

[29] See, for example, Willmott, *Unemployment and Poverty*, October 1980, Chapter 5, discussed in Section (9.2.4) above.

[30] See Section (8.4) above. See also Willmott, *Poverty and Social Policy*, p. 123, discussed in Section (9.2.3) above.

[31] See Sections (4.4) and (5.2) above.

[32] See, for example, the work of ATD in France (Section (4.3) above).

[33] See Sections (5.1), (5.3.2), (5.4.2), (5.6).

[34] See, for example, Sections (5.2.2) and (5.3.2).

[35] See, for example, the Stuttgart project's analysis of vagrancy. (Section (5.4.2) above).

[36] See, for example, the work of the UK Family Day Centres and the Craigmillar Festival Society (Sections (8.4) and (8.7) above).

[37] See Section (5.4) above.

[38] See Section (9.2.5) above.

[39] These findings run counter to what the ATD movement appears to believe: namely that the extreme poor share a common history and a collective identity inter-generationally: analogous, in some respects, to that of the Gypsies (see above, Section (9.2.6)), whose collective identity is also threatened by the dominant society.
It is disturbing to note Willmott's finding that existing income support policies in several of the major Member States are far from adequate in keeping larger families out of poverty, even where the head of the household is employed (Willmott, *Unemployment and Poverty*, October 1980, Chapter 6).

[40] See Section (9.2.1) above.

[41] Various projects have attempted to assess the cost-effectiveness of the innovations they have undertaken.

[42] Writing from within the liberal tradition, see C. B. Macpherson, *The Political Theory of Possessive Individualism*, Oxford University Press, 1962; and F. Hirsch, *op. cit.* From the neo-Marxist tradition see J. O'Connor, *The Fiscal Crisis of the State*, New York, St Martin's Press, 1973; and C. Offe, 'Structural Problems of the Capitalist State', in K. Beyme (ed.), *German Political Studies*, Volume I, pp. 31–57.

[43] See below, Chapter 12.

[44] See below, Chapter 14.

[45] See, for example, Section (5.6) above.

[46] Cf. J. Higgins, *The Poverty Business*, Martin Robertson, 1978.

[47] Compare the reception given to Townsend's study, *Poverty in the United Kingdom*, Allen Lane, 1979.

12
Combating Poverty[1]

(12.1) STRATEGIES FOR SOCIAL CHANGE

(12.1.1) Introduction

A wealthy society which combats poverty is struggling with itself, to counter its own practices which leave some of its citizens poor, unhealthy, ill-housed, ill-educated and unemployed. It is trying to achieve a redistribution of resources in favour of its weaker members and, more difficult, to secure that this redistribution is maintained, which must entail some redistribution of power as well as resources.

The European Programme of Pilot Schemes for the most part offers a set of community work strategies to achieve this goal. It can be argued that some of the very small projects were experiments in social casework or groupwork (e.g. the Camden Drop-In or the Copenhagen project), but few projects had more than an incidental concern with providing advice or therapy for individuals.

To say that they are mainly community work projects is not in itself very helpful, however, for we lack a universally agreed definition of community work.[2] We can say that community work concerns working with groups to achieve wider changes in society, but so does politics and religion. Rather than search for an overarching definition, it is more useful to say that there are several different strategies of intervention in society in favour of its weaker members which go under the name of community work, all of which are represented in the European Programme. In this chapter we try to identify these major strategies.

The purpose of the classification we have developed is not simply to divide up a long chapter, but to clarify some basic differences between projects, and to help explain their activities, assumptions and objectives. This is a classification of strategies rather than projects, for we recognise that strategies blend and change over time, and that different actors can operate different strategies in the same project. We hope that our classification will help understand these shifts and tensions.

(12.1.2)   Three Traditions of Social Work

Before America's War on Poverty there were two main traditions in community work. One derived from the Charity Organisation Society of mid-Victorian England and was greatly developed by the major voluntary bodies in North America, who became very sophisticated in organising joint fund-raising activities and operating integrated patterns of service delivery. The Social Service Councils which figure in the Irish Combat Poverty Programme are directly in this line of descent. With the growth of public social services, these skills in manipulating bureaucratic organisations became highly valued in the public sector. Thus in the European Programme we find COPES in Paris assisting in the co-ordination of six agencies providing child care services, while in Padua the *comune* is redeploying its health and welfare services in new geographical, administrative and professional patterns.

Meanwhile, a parallel tradition had emerged. This can be traced back to the Settlement movement in late nineteenth-century Britain and America, although its major development came in the context of Western aid to the developing countries after the Second World War. Schemes for economic and social development in these countries ran up against a cultural gap between local people and outside experts. On the one side was a population more motivated to protecting its traditional pattern of life than to economic change and suspicious of outsiders whose main concern in the past had been to collect rents, taxes or loot. On the other side, the scientific experts often had little understanding of the land tenure systems and kinship patterns which made nonsense of their attempted innovations. The answer seemed to lie in participatory arrangements, allowing local people to determine their own priorities and getting them to co-operate with each other in their achievement. Thanks in part to the work of Oscar Lewis,[3] who popularised the theory of a universal cultural gap between poor people and the rest of society, the technique was imported to America's cities for the War on Poverty.[4] The technique was already known in Europe, particularly through the work of the Dutch Ministry of Social Work.[5]

For many people, this second tradition became the only true form of community work, as evidenced by basic textbooks such as Murray G. Ross, *Community Organisation, Theory and Principles*.[6] The two traditions were sometimes differentiated as community organisation (the Social Service Council tradition) and community development (the UN tradition). [7] The United Nations provided its own definition of community development in 1955:

> Community Development can be tentatively defined as a process designed to create conditions of economic and social progress for the whole community, with its active participation and the fullest possible reliance on the community initiative. [8]

Several of the European Programme's projects conform closely to this model. The Irish rural projects, with their emphasis on economic structures, come closest to it, but it also fits urban projects in Edinburgh, London, Naples and elsewhere.

The Committee and staff of the Irish National Programme still seemed to see community work polarised between these two models in their internal disputes in the mid-1970s. A statement from the programme's second director to the management committee in 1976 vigorously asserts the primacy of the community development approach:

> It would be very easy . . . to put into effect a programme of service orientated projects which would simply have the effect of alleviating poverty, e.g. projects improving residential facilities for vagrants, meals on wheels, etc. . . . They would bring us no nearer to the eventual elimination of poverty . . . However, it does seem possible . . . to carry out projects which will, hopefully, bring us a little way towards a society where poverty will no longer exist. The projects can do this by beginning a process of social change.
> The greatest scope for bringing about desired social change is through the promotion of *participation* within the local projects. In this way poor people will understand their situation better, will be better able to articulate their needs and will be better equipped to press for the satisfaction of their needs. . . . Participation is not only a way towards achieving an end, but is an end in itself if one sees poverty as social exclusion.

However, when Jack Rothman came to elaborate his models of community organisation in 1968, [9] he identified three models. The first two were the traditions we have outlined above, which he christened 'social planning' and 'locality development'. The third, which he called 'social action', was born of the War on Poverty and its chief exponent was Saul Alinsky. [10] The UN style of community development had been aimed at securing collaboration between people and authority, smoothing out conflicts to make way for the march of progress. Alinsky and his confrères turned the concept of cultural difference on its head; cultural patterns of poor people were to them a response to the pressures of the larger society, and poor people could only behave differently and survive if they could break down the constraints imposed upon them by the wider social structure. His ideal of community work, put forward as early as 1946, is rather different to that of the UN:

> A people's organisation is a conflict group. This must be openly and fully recognised . . . A people's organisation is a banding together of a multitude of men and women to fight for those rights which ensure a decent way of life . . . A war is not an intellectual debate and in a war against social evils there are no rules of fair play.

These three models were postulated over ten years ago, and do not cover all the strategies used in the European Programme of the mid-1970s. However, it is useful to consider the salient features of Rothman's three models put forward at the height of America's War on Poverty and at the time when anti-poverty schemes were beginning to appear in Europe.

Social planning is defined as 'task oriented', that is, committed to achieving certain specific results. The process whereby these results are achieved is a subordinate consideration. Participation by the client group may be involved, if this is considered useful. Being 'task oriented', social planning projects are often happy to submit to 'scientific' evaluation.

The basic assumption of a social planning project is that there are a number of substantive problems to be solved. The basic strategy for change is to gather all the available facts on which to work out rational solutions. Its tactics are fact-finding and analysis. This may involve conflict with groups opposed to change or it may be achieved by consensus.

In such a setting the practitioner is a recognised expert, experienced in manipulating formal systems, particularly inter-organisational groups. Normally the sponsors of the project are part of the established 'power structure', whether they are public or semi-public bodies or major non-government organisations. It is a system of reform from above. The 'boundaries' of the project are in one sense geographical, but they are also usually categorical, in that the clients are people with particular problems. These problems are often associated with poverty, but the poor as such are seldom an operational category. There is no assumption that their needs are in conflict with the rest of society or vice versa, as in other types of project. Rothman describes this as an 'idealist' approach, believing that the common good arises from the expert's exercise of judgement and conscience. The clients are basically viewed as 'customers', active in consuming services rather than in determining them.

The *locality development* strategy is, by contrast, 'process oriented'. The process of building co-operative relationships and community structures takes precedence over whatever substantive reforms are made or services delivered. The goal is to increase what Murray Ross termed 'community capacity'. For this reason there is a tendency to distrust evaluation directed at assessing 'results'.

The basic assumption is of a local community overshadowed by the wider society. The basic strategy for change is to help the community express its felt needs. The basic tactic is discussion and communication, with a search for consensus. The practitioner of this strategy does not push his own technical expertise, he is an expert 'enabler' or 'encourager' operating mainly through small groups. He sees the whole community as his client, including the local power structure. His employer is usually an agency from outside the locality. The project 'boundaries' are geographical rather than categorical, although there may be a particular attention to certain categories, such as women (but never men), young people, farmers, and so on. The practitioner normally sees conflict as damaging, stressing the compatibility of different interests. His approach is 'rationalist', seeing the common good as arising from discussion and agreement, with a faith in broadly based representative institutions. The clients are seen as participants with the practitioner in a common endeavour. Clearly they suffer from some form of inadequacy or they could do without the practitioner, but despite all the culture of poverty theories, the strategy rests on a conception of the client population possessing certain strengths and energies which need to be focused and released. In his concern to address the whole community, the practitioner often rejects categorising the poor as a group or styling his activity an anti-poverty project.

The *social action* project may be task or process oriented. Its practitioners' view of society is of a hierarchy of privilege and power, in which certain groups or areas are deprived or ignored. The basic change strategy is to defeat the forces which oppress them; the tactic is organised conflict. The practitioner assumes an 'advocate' or 'activist' role, with recourse to mass organisation when necessary. Frequently sheer numbers are seen as the only resource of the oppressed. The power structure is the enemy. The project therefore needs an autonomous power base, ideally with the client group as the employer. The 'boundaries' of the project may be formally defined in geographical terms, but it is difficult to constrain it geographically for there will be a constant tendency to seek solidarity with fellow groups in other areas. There is usually no hesitation in categorising the poor or the working class (or the Fourth World) as a separate entity – the fear of stigma is replaced by a search for solidarity.

The assumption of inevitable conflict between interests leads to a 'realist' view in which there is no common good to be unveiled by the expert or arrived at by honest discussion between men of goodwill. Rather, public policy reflects the balance of power in society at a particular moment. The client population is seen as a victim of the system, and one school of social action workers places great emphasis on living among them and sharing their standard of living. Rothman identifies 'social reform' as a variant of social action, with the difference that the practitioners do not operate from within the victim population.

(12.1.3)   A Pattern of Projects

The Rothman analysis illuminates many aspects of the European Programme. For instance in Ireland we can see two social planning projects, the Social Welfare Allowances project and the Social Service Councils project. There are five rural projects which conform to the locality development model, and we can see at least two urban projects which adhere to the social action model. But the Irish National Committee at one time or another supported twenty-six projects, so where do the others fit in?

Rothman himself admits that projects may blend strategies. He could also add that the dominant strategy may change over time, and that different practitioners, sponsors and clients with a project may promote different strategies. Indeed this is the source of a constant state of tension in many projects. Furthermore projects may choose to present themselves to the world in different guises. The most notable example of this is that social action projects frequently do not have an autonomous power base, and are faced with seeking support, financial or other, from elements of the power structure they oppose. Hence the tendency to present themselves to these audiences as locality development projects with an emphasis on co-operation rather than conflict.

Yet even allowing for this, the Rothman classification as it stood in 1970 cannot encompass the European Programme. It may have been adequate six years after the War on Poverty was launched but experience in Europe and America since then is difficult to fit into this framework.

There seem to be two major problems. One is that the Rothman models are all area-based, even though he insists on this only for the locality development model. But in every case we have the image of the project leader's office decorated with a wall-map outlining the target area with a heavy red line. The experience of the 1970s however, has increasingly been one of community work with 'communities' that have no territorial base, such as single-parent families, the disabled and so on. This has been linked with a partial disillusionment with the possibilities of achieving social change on a local basis, as evidenced in particular by several of the reports of the Community Development Project teams in Britain in the mid 1970s.[11] Our increased awareness of poverty has also brought home to us that most poor people do not live concentrated in ghetto areas.

The second problem is that the contrast between social development and social action presented by Rothman seems too stark, even though he admits to the existence of 'hybrid models'. While many community workers are ready to accept that their clientèle are victims of the social order, the 'war' that Alinsky speaks of is waged very much in the Clausewitz spirit of 'diplomacy by other means'.

Social action may indeed be a matter of fighting or bargaining for resources, but given that the power structure is seldom monolithic, that it has different segments with different interests, the possibilities for manoeuvre and coalition building may be considerable. The project often only exists because such a pluralist situation prevails, with some element in the power structure funding the project to achieve shifts in the balance of power which it favours.

This more diplomatic style of conflict has been identified by some commentators as a separate strategy. For instance, the Community Development Programme inter-project report in 1974[12] spoke of three strategies: consensus, pluralism and structural conflict (evidently social planning was not considered to be community work).

These three reappeared in 1975 as the traditional, liberal and radical strategies,[13] and in 1978 as the liberal democrat, libertarian and marxist strategies, with social planning coming back as the conservative strategy.[14] A paper presented to the conference of the Association of Community Workers in 1979 suggested that a further strategy may need to be defined, to embrace feminism in community work.[15]

We have preferred to attempt a slightly more sophisticated version of the Rothman analysis, first of all by allowing for each of his three models to apply to non-territorial communities. Rather than speak of 'locality development', we will call this 'area community development' and place alongside it 'sectional community development'. The word 'group' would sound more natural, but this would raise a confusion between group work (i.e. with small face-to-face groups) and community work. Sectional community development is based on the same collaborative principles, but it addresses itself to a non-territorial entity. The Gingerbread Clubs for single-parent families and the Women's Aid movement for battered women are examples of this so far as they are concerned with developing the potential of their members to co-operate for their mutual benefit. In both these organisations, there are some workers who would prefer a different orientation, but at the moment the community development strategy seems to be in ascendance.

'Social planning' remains a useful category for analysing the European Programme, and again we can distinguish, if not with fine precision, between those which deal with a complex of problems in a given locality and those which are addressed to the problems of particular groups which are considered to be similar in many localities. Obviously there is a spatial aspect to any plan and the plan for a special group will need to be carried out at particular locations, usually within the area of jurisdiction or of operations of the sponsoring agency.

The social action model we can elaborate to include the pluralist approach and the conflict approach as sub-categories. They are based on a common realist view of society, but the tactics are different, particularly in the readiness to form coalitions between the victim group and other groups in society. Again, social action can be area or sectional. To take the Irish Programme once again as an example, the North Centre City Community Action Project is an area-based project and the National Salmon and Inshore Fishermen's Association is a sectional group.

We prefer the term community action to social action, to try to minimise confusion with the French phrase *action sociale*, which covers all interventions in the social field (hence the European Community's Social Action Programme), although we recognise that in French *action communautaire* often applies to what the Anglophones call community development.[16]

The rest of this chapter considers the European Programme according to the principal strategies employed. In this way we hope to be able to compare like with like and avoid the bewilderment which followed several of the cross-project contacts, as in this brief confrontation between an Irish community action project and an Italian social planning scheme:

> One team member later went to Padua for eight days. She could see little basis for comparability. Padua was an experiment in Health Reorganisation at the higher administrative level. Its aim appeared to be more effective and rational use of existing local government resources. Our aims concern the mobilising of the resources of the people, and obtaining more resources from the State for the area as well as the defence of existing services.[17]

(12.2) SOCIAL PLANNING

(12.2.1) Social Surveys

Data collection is an important part of most social planning exercises, which are usually based on a detailed quantitative assessment of pre-selected target problems. A survey itself is only part of a true social planning exercise; the next stage is to communicate the results to the right quarters and then to mobilise the appropriate agencies and resources to tackle the situation which the survey has 'revealed'.

The *Areas of Special Social Need* (ASSN) project in Belfast is a very good example of survey data being put to use in this way. The first part of the project included in the European Programme concerned only the survey into the distribution of needs and services in the city, conducted by officials of the Northern Ireland Department. The action did not, however, end with the publication of the results. The department went on to convene a Belfast Areas of Need (BAN) Committee, with representatives of all the statutory services whose responsibilities seemed relevant to the problems uncovered by the research, from which flowed a host of further actions, including another action in the European Programme.

In the Republic, the Irish National Programme included a major survey into the operation of the Social Welfare Allowances Scheme introduced by the government in 1977. This involved a study of recipients of the previous scheme and interviews with officials responsible for carrying out the old and the new systems. Unfortunately, the results had still not been published at the time of writing.

An effective follow-up to this work might well have been to convene a meeting with the Department of Social Welfare to consider the shortcomings of the present scheme and to organise the appropriate responses, e.g. training courses for Superintendent Welfare Officers or better information services. This now seems unlikely to occur.

A major voluntary organisation, the Society of St Vincent de Paul, was assisted by the National Committee in conducting a survey both north and south of the border into the housing conditions and social relationships of old people living alone. This was expressly done as a basis for developing future actions by the Society. The survey was published in October 1980.

The ASSN-BAN project, embracing a wide range of problems in a given area, is a classic example of area social planning. In contrast, the SWA and the St Vincent de Paul projects present a nationwide approach focused on very specific issues.

(12.2.2)   **Area Social Planning**

By far the largest project in the European Programme was the area social planning exercise at Padua. This bold, imaginative and expensive project run by the local *comune* involved the reorganisation of the entire health and social services of a city of 250,000 inhabitants. The objective was to achieve an integrated but decentralised pattern of services open to all citizens on a non-categorical basis, with an emphasis on preventive care, aims which reappeared in different forms in all the other social planning projects in the European Programme. Like these others, Padua also had a strong bias against residential institutions and in favour of domiciliary care.

The inter-organisational linkages entailed by the project were manifold, including an extensive range of public services at city, provincial and national level and several voluntary social welfare organisations. Attempts to build in citizen participation through the neighbourhood councils were, however, largely unsuccessful. Although the project had participation as one of its aims, its failure to achieve this was regarded by the project workers and the authorities as of relatively minor importance, in comparison with its other achievements. This underlines the difference between social planning and the other strategies employed in the programme.

For all that the Padua project was all-embracing as regards the civic health and social services, it was very specific to its locality. The main impetus came from a reforming group of local councillors and senior officials who were only incidentally interested in setting up a model for the rest of Italy. They have indeed been happy to share their experiences, but Italy already has a variety of models for municipal reform and it is unlikely that a standard pattern will emerge.

(12.2.3)   Sectional Social Planning

The COPES project in the 14th Arrondissement of Paris, although more localised than the Padua project, was specifically intended as a model for the rest of the metropolis, as well as to inform government policy throughout France. COPES, the small research team which concluded the contract with the Commission, was only the consultant to the main experiment, the Secteur Unifié d'Enfance. For some time, the government had been attempting to secure greater co-ordination between the various agencies involved with the protection of children without adequate parental care. Prior to the experiment in the 14th Arrondissement, these efforts had all been at the *département* level. The COPES project experimented with a much more local level of co-ordination in a sector of Paris, as well as trying to exploit the more integrated pattern of service to develop a system of preventive care. The COPES team showed little interest in general community involvement in the SUE, but devoted the bulk of its energies to educating the professional workers, child minders and foster parents who were to work for it. This education was designed to put across certain technical concepts, although it used discussion groups rather than formal lectures as its main technique.

Alongside this social planning work, however, COPES included a small venture in community development, helping a tenants' association to set up its own part-time crèche and day nursery. Two different strategies were being employed in the same project, even if the second strategy was confined to a relatively minor sideline.

The project run by ARIM-PACT in central Brittany was a similar piece of multi-agency co-ordination to assist a particular problem group. The perceived problem here was that many elderly inhabitants of this thinly populated rural area were brought into residential care mainly because of inadequate housing. The answer proposed, based on two pieces of survey work, was to launch an integrated programme (*action programmée*) of sheltered housing, house improvements, home help and home nursing services, a collective laundry service and a network of old people's clubs. The latter, once established, were drawn into the planning of the rest of the exercise. Participation was a success in this project, and it made a significant contribution to the achievement of the project's other goals (e.g. it publicised the projects' schemes, identified potential beneficiaries and persuaded reluctant householders to accept home helps and house improvements), but it was still not crucial to the general success of the project, which was judged by the amount of finance it mobilised and the number and quality of its house improvements and grouped dwellings.

We can also number the PACT project in Orange as a social planning project, a plan which unfortunately did not get much beyond the paper stage by 1980. This again was concerned with the housing problems of deprived groups.

Germany presents two interesting examples of social planning projects which eventually moved on to other strategies. The Stuttgart-Tübingen project began as a consultancy arrangement between a university research team and a group of six residential institutions for vagrants at different localities in the Baden-Württemberg region. The work initially involved the application of theories of social development in small autonomous groups to the internal organisation of the institutions. From this the team became involved in organising preventive care (basically, flats for homeless men) and then to community development with a group of town tramps. This was more central to the team's work than the day nursery was to COPES, but the project remained fundamentally a social planning exercise. The fact that the team developed a trenchant critique of the economic and social system which was creating the increasing number of vagrants does not invalidate this. All the social planning projects in the European Programme have set out strong criticisms of those aspects of society they wish to change. Nor are they above criticising the socio-economic system at large, even though they depend upon powerful elements within it (e.g. ASSN squarely indicts unemployment as the main cause of social deprivation). The Cologne project made a far more radical move, turning in its last years principally to the community action strategy. The project began with a small independent research agency acting as consultants to the municipality on the improvement of its social assistance services, exploring their adequacy through social surveys in two contrasting areas. A move to a further stage of social planning, the provision of advice centres, was short-lived. In its place the team became heavily involved with the local welfare rights group and went on to help establish other groups throughout the North Rhine-Westphalia region. This is an example of a project which went through two distinct phases, using community work strategies at opposite ends of our spectrum.

(12.3)   COMMUNITY DEVELOPMENT

This is mainstream community work, once described by a senior government minister in Britain as a community pulling itself up by its own bootstraps. The phrase was used in relation to the Community Development Project 1968–78, several of whose twelve components were later to develop a marked community action stance. The drift towards community action was apparent in several of the European Programme's community development projects, although use of this strategy was sometimes only peripheral and transitory. At times, co-operation just does not seem to work.

Since community development was the preferred strategy of the majority of the projects of the European Programme, we cannot analyse each example in this section. Instead, we take some leading examples, looking in particular at the blending of strategies.

The five rural projects in western Ireland are the clearest examples in the European Programme of community development work of the traditional type, with its emphasis on economic co-operation and self-help, even though the National Committee baptised them the Community Action Research Project. Nonetheless, there was some recourse to community action, particularly with the dispute over fishing rights in Beara. This resulted in a specific community action project being launched with the National Salmon and Inshore Fishermen's Association.

Edinburgh was the home of two projects, one in name and fact a community development project and the other largely so. The Social and Community Development Project (later renamed the Urban Regeneration Programme – shortly before taking a rural component!) was run jointly by the regional and city councils. It was intended as a means by which the councils could relate to local communities as a whole, rather than as consumers of specific services, and work through community groups to resolve problems which the groups themselves identified. Since all the project workers were officials of the two councils, which were the dominant elements in the local power structure – being the major landlords as well as the political authority – they were not in a position to organise the people to contest the power structure. Their main purpose was to develop a constructive dialogue which could replace conflict. As one worker expressed it: 'We teach them to roll up their banners and sit down and talk'. But she went on to add, 'there are times when we have to say that we can't do any more for them and if they want to carry the matter further they will have to fetch their banners out and march'.

The Craigmillar Festival Society, having an indigenous leadership, even if paid from local authority grants, had no such scruples. It was none the less primarily a community development project. This was very much the image put across on a one-hour programme produced by CFS and shown on national television in September 1980. CFS exploited whatever government aid was available, adding it to the voluntary efforts of local residents to improve the cultural life, social services and economic well-being of its people. Hence an impressive array of old people's clubs, workshops, a family group home, a thrift shop, crafts centre, and so on. Despite this, CFS could not at times shirk pressure-group tactics. For instance, with the local authority as the major landlord, there are obvious conflicts of interest over repairs. Yet the fundamental reconcilability of interests is recognised in the CFS objective of 'shared government' to which the Craigmillar Comprehensive Plan was offered as a contribution.

The Marolles project in Brussels had obvious similarities with Craigmillar, an affinity which the project workers themselves sensed (they made brief cultural exchanges). Most of Craigmillar's activities had a parallel in the Marolles – cultural activities, although with a more cosmopolitan tinge, social service work and small-scale economic enterprises. Yet the Belgian organisation called itself the Marolles Action Committee and was born of a confrontation between the residents and the local authority over the redevelopment of their area. It started off with community action, which it never abandoned, and yet moved heavily into community development. There remained a strong sense in the project that their people were a victim group. Since a large proportion are immigrants, they are literally disenfranchised. Rothman would doubtless call this a project using hybrid strategies.

Having an organisational link between projects by no means entails common strategies, as the Irish Programme illustrates. The three Area Resource Centres in the UK were united in a common technique: the provision of seed-money, organising skills, technical advice and practical services to small local groups, but the strategy furthered by this technique varied according to the groups the centres encountered and which they chose to assist. The London ARC can perhaps be seen as the most developmental and the South Wales Poverty Action Committee as the most action-oriented.

The seven Family Day Centres were primarily community development enterprises, but they included the action-oriented ATD project. Two of the PACT projects were social planning exercises, but the third (Roubaix) was largely a community development project.

The Giugliano project near Naples is interesting for the contrast it presents with Padua. Both concerned a similar range of services, with a similar emphasis on decentralisation, integration, preventive work and community care. However, Giugliano took a developmental approach, working with the inhabitants to develop common priorities in health care. Participation was central to the project, which engaged in a variety of consciousness-raising activities through cultural events, work in schools, and so on.

The project also saw itself as a centre from which to spread a widening circle of community awareness and participation. For instance, its school social workers managed to move from individual counselling for 'problem' pupils to regular classroom teaching and organising field visits (e.g. to sweated labour workshops) and student projects (e.g. attitude surveys on equality between the sexes).

To end this section, it is worth citing one project among several where there were internal differences over the appropriate strategy. The Women's Aid movement in Britain has for some time been divided between those members who prefer to concentrate on bringing women together to set up and run refuges for the victims of family violence and those who press for it to be involved in wider campaigns for justice between the sexes. The rift was reflected in the Women's

Aid project in Dublin, where the two workers provided by the National Committee met with little success in their attempts to involve their fellow workers in wider concerns.

(12.4)   COMMUNITY ACTION

The essence of community action is a 'them and us' analysis of society as a contest for power, whether the 'them' and 'us' arises from a marxist class analysis, a feminist analysis, or any other analysis that opposes the interests of an under-privileged group against that of a power structure. As even the author of the Society of St Vincent de Paul survey of the elderly in Ireland observed:

> We are living in an era when most groups who share common interests and needs have banded together in their quest for rights, self-protection or self-advancement. It has become a measure of the deprivation of any group that it has no organisation or representatives to speak on its behalf. The old and alone have no organisation and no one to speak for them. Largely forgotten in a society where it has become essential for any group to make itself heard before it can attain even its most just demands, they contrive to make the best of what they have got.[18]

Several projects in the European Programme have identified strongly with the struggles of a particular group for a better place in society. In most cases they have preferred a pluralist approach, mixing war and diplomacy. Some have been more ready than others to engage in direct conflict but it is difficult to rank who is the most or least likely to do so – the approach varies with time and place and between workers. The distinguishing feature is the identification with a victim group and the focus on its relationships with the rest of society, rather than its betterment through mutual aid or public planning. As the Cork City project team phrased it:

> Our main objective is . . . to engage local people around certain key issues in an action research way, which leads them to increasing awareness of their rights and of the nature and operation of the social system and leads them to organisation for change.

(12.4.1)   Aide à Toute Détresse

The ATD movement, which ran six projects in the European Programme (four in France, one in the Netherlands and one in the UK) had the most elaborately articulated theory of a victim group, which it termed the Fourth World to symbolise its exclusion from the rest of affluent western society. The Fourth World is the sub-proletariat, the people who exist on the fringes of the labour market excluded from the main structures of economic, political and social life. While other projects tried to avoid 'stigmatising' the poor, ATD tried to teach its Fourth World a militant self-consciousness.

The Fourth World was 'discovered' in the bidonville of Noisy-le-Grand near Paris in the early 1950s. It was easy for workers and residents in the encampment to equate their situation with that in the other bidonvilles thrown up in the prolonged housing shortage in France in the 1950s and 1960s. ATD's theoreticians went beyond this to include in their concept of the Fourth World the groups from whom the bidonville residents were drawn and to postulate the existence of this 'layer' in all advanced industrial societies. While ATD's French projects still mainly deal with families living in housing complexes specially created for those who are unacceptable in any other accommodation, the Dutch project works with families in normal housing, as does the London project, although many of its clientèle were first known to ATD when they lived in temporary accommodation.

In one sense the Fourth World's leadership is indigenous, for the founder was a priest from a Fourth World background, but the personnel of the movement were drawn mainly from the middle classes, as were most of its 'allies' (a body of sympathisers who contributed voluntary help, subscribed to the movement's literature and attended Fourth World evenings). The movement was not, however, professionalised; not that it rejected professional expertise, but it did not offer a career structure with the usual professional rewards. Workers were expected to live among the Fourth World and share their standard of living. Some made this a lifetime commitment while others used it as an interlude in their outside careers. The movement always asserted the value of indigenous leadership, and put much energy into training a cadre of Fourth World militants, but the militants are still a long way from taking charge of the organisation.

Much of the projects' activity can be described as consciousness raising. Indeed, almost all the activity of the London project came under this heading. It provided no direct services (except incidentally, in that its meetings were a social event for the participants) but devoted itself to organising Fourth World evenings to discuss social, moral and economic issues.

The continental projects certainly did offer services. For instance, the pre-school programme in France was a well organised service of high professional calibre. Yet the Fourth World evenings remained important and, in the minds of the workers at least, all the services were devoted to the end of liberating their users. For instance, the pre-schools not only set children on the path to better school achievement and hence literacy and greater effectiveness in society, but were a means of contacting the parents, a focus around which to organise them, and a base from which parents could venture into other fields, for instance, joining the nursery school parents' association. The pre-school teachers were also a pressure group for making the nursery schools more responsive to Fourth World needs.

The outside observer cannot avoid sensing a contrast between the militant rhetoric of ATD's literature and its national and international rallies and the apparently non-contentious content of its services. The ATD pre-school programme draws heavily on the American Head Start experience (the author has sat in on classes in both programmes, which showed a marked similarity) which was the least controversial element in the War on Poverty. The Communist municipality in Reims, which saw ATD's ideology as a move to split the working class, was nevertheless able to support ATD financially for its 'social work'. It was a paradoxical revolutionary movement which found time to teach two-year olds to identify colours.

ATD's work at national level has already had some positive impact – Le Quart Monde is now a recognised term in France, and was used frequently at the Habitat et Vie Sociale conference in Paris in 1980. The HVS programme, which includes four projects in the European Programme, is a large-scale government inspired social planning scheme with a strong community development component. That many conference participants were concerned to take the Quart Monde into account is a tribute to ATD's propaganda.

(12.4.2)   **Other Action Projects**

More familiar types of protest-oriented community action groups could be found in north Dublin, Cork and South Wales. The NCCCAP project in north Dublin was the only project known to be involved in an infringement of the law. Several management committee members were fined for blocking a street during the rush hour and one was subsequently imprisoned for two days for refusing to undertake 'to keep the peace'. This was in connection with protests against the city corporation's redevelopment plan for the project area.

NCCCAP shared the distrust common to many social action groups for developmental activities such as playgroups, job creation schemes, advice centres or youth work, although it eventually undertook a number of pre-vocational training schemes for young people. The South Wales Poverty Action Committee (SWAPAC) was similarly disdainful of helping the poor 'administer their own poverty' and acting as the 'handmaiden of the state'. Its attitude to worker co-operatives vacillated, crystallising in feeling that they were mechanisms for the poor 'to exploit themselves', that is, they were just another way of organising low-paid labour to keep the capitalist system moving. What SWAPAC found more promising was to organise pressure groups, build liaisons with the trade unions and undertake welfare rights work.

The fear of being subverted into a community development project is characteristic of many community action enterprises. The experience of the European Programme is, however, that activities rejected on strategic grounds by some community action projects were quite congenial to others. Pre-school work, for instance, does not inherently belong with any particular strategy for social change; it depends on how the activity is conducted and for what wider purpose. Almost any activity can be a learning activity for the community.

(12.4.3) Welfare Rights

This is a tactic, not a strategy, and can be used by projects of all orientations. Padua instituted advice units in its local centres, several family day centres in England gave rights advice, the first director for the Irish Programme did not feel that welfare rights fitted in with community action programmes, and the Cologne team turned to rights groups when it entered its community action phase. Much of the problem that community activists have with rights work is that it involves specialist knowledge which is not the stock-in-trade of the usual community worker, nor is it readily available in the victim group — this is part of their victimisation. Community workers are also wary of work with individuals, which they feel is the social caseworker's province, though the Free Legal Aid Centre in Dublin and the Tribunal Representation Unit in Wolverhampton found it compatible with very community oriented projects. The Belfast

Welfare Rights Project was ostensibly a social planning exercise, with a precise pre-determined brief to collect data on the operation of the income maintenance system as a follow up to the ASSN–BAN project. It was to some degree also a cover for a community development project. The well-founded distrust of outsiders in the inner-city neighbourhoods of Belfast obliged the project to operate through local community groups, who used the information bureaux they were paid to set up as all-purpose community advice units. The arrangement worked to the satisfaction of all parties, although the local workers did not succeed in getting further funds to continue with their advice units.

In America this is sometimes called the 'Indians and blankets' approach – the American Indians wanted blankets and the missionaries to teach religion, so the result was a missionary trading post.

(12.5)   GROUPWORK

At least two of the projects did not profess community work aims. They were interested in helping individuals with personal difficulties, not through social casework, but by means of groupwork activities. The Copenhagen project was specifically directed at individuals who 'fall through the net' of the welfare state. It concentrated on nine men with chronic problems of unemployment and alcoholism, trying to re-establish them as adequately functioning citizens. Quite unexpectedly, the group evolved into an informal producers' co-operative, going on from refurbishing their own residential unit to conducting a city-wide business in renovating old doors and furniture, rather like the small production units in some of the community development projects. The social work team also made a film of their work which was shown on national television, which led them to see their project as helping to change the image of down-and-outs in society. Even such small exercises in group therapy tended to move in a community work direction.

The Camden Drop-In was another therapeutic exercise with a small face-to-face group. It was run by a social casework agency, the Family Service Unit, and most of the group's members also received traditional casework services. The group never got as far as setting up its own business, although it did cook its own meals.

Several other projects, for example the Liverpool Clubhouse and the Family Groups Unit (LVSC), mixed groupwork and casework along with community work activities. On the whole, however, projects in the European Programme were less concerned to provide better therapy for inadequate individuals than to change systems.

(12.6) CONCLUSIONS

The number and diversity of activities in the European Programme, while a major headache to the evaluators, provide a fascinating picture of the range of strategies in contemporary community work. The simple dichotomy which some observers still see between service strategies and 'influential' strategies does not hold in this programme,[19] almost all of whose components provided services.

The European Programme does not demonstrate the value of one strategy above others. Rather, the experience suggests there is no one best way in community work. Large-scale planning through bureaucratic structures will remain essential for social progress in Europe for the foreseeable future. We are unlikely to return to an exclusively communal neighbourhood basis for our social and economic lives. At the same time, there is a need to bring economic and social service structures closer to the people, not just by decentralising the large organisations, but by enabling people to participate directly in those structures which govern their lives. This would go some way to relieving the powerlessness of the poor. However, given that major decisions on the economy, the welfare system, and so on, will continue to be taken at city, national and international levels, there will always be a place for actions to secure that the interests of the poor are taken into account, if necessary by making life uncomfortable for the rest of us.

Notes

[1] By Edward James with grateful acknowledgements to the help and advice of his colleagues in ESPOIR and especially to the ESPOIR consultants, Brian Munday and Peter Ely of the Social Work course at the University of Kent at Canterbury.

[2] Definitions of community work (or community organisation as it is termed in America) are legion. For instance, E. B. Harper and A. Dunham in *Community Organisation in Action: Basic Literature and Critical Comments*, (New York, Associated Press, 1959), listed 13 definitions of

community organisation and indicated that 50 to 100 definitions had been put forward in the previous 35 years. The expansion of community work in the 1960s and '70s has added enormously to this wealth of definitions.

[3] O. Lewis, *Five Families: Mexican Case Studies in the Culture of Poverty*, New York, Basic Books, 1959. Lewis, whose work was based on recent migrants to Mexico City and New York, always denied that he put forward the culture of poverty as a universal phenonemon, but it was widely interpreted as such.

[4] E. James, *America Against Poverty*, Routledge and Kegan Paul, 1970.

[5] G. Hendriks, *Community Organisation*, Ministry for Social Work, The Hague, 1964. This is a collection of lectures given between 1959 and 1963, mainly to international audiences. It includes a paper given to an EEC seminar in 1960 proposing a programme of pilot schemes in community work.

[6] M. G. Ross, *Community Organisation, Theory and Principles*, Harper and Row, 1955.

[7] This terminology is confusing as American schools of social work never abandoned the term community organisation as a general term for all types of community work.

[8] United Nations, *Social Progress through Community Development*, New York, 1955.

[9] J. Rothman, *Three Models of Community Organisation Practice*, National Conference on Social Welfare, 1968, reproduced in *Strategies of Community Organisation*, edited by F. M. Cox, *et al.*, Illinois, Peacock Publishers, 1970.

[10] S. Alinsky, *Reveille for Radicals*, Chicago University Press, 1946. Alinsky's views, formulated as early as the 1930s, envisaged a form of trade union, or 'people's organisation' to confront the power structure in every poor district.

[11] The British Community Development Project (1968–78) is an example of an attempt to emulate the American locally based approach which was rejected after a few years by many of the programmes' own practitioners.

[12] Community Development Project, *The National Community Development Project Inter-Project Report*, CDP Information and Intelligence Unit, 1974.

[13] H. Rose, and J. Hanmer, 'Community Participation and Social Change' in D. Jones and M. Mayo (eds.), *Community Work Two*, Routledge and Kegan Paul, 1975.

[14] J. Smith, 'Possibilities for a Socialist Community Work Practice' in *Towards a Definition of Community Work*, Association of Community Workers, 1978.

[15] J. Hanmer, 'Theories and Ideologies in British Community Work', *Community Development Journal*, Vol. 14, No. 3, 1979.
See also three articles in *Community Development Journal*, Vol. 15, No. 2, 1980: M. Loney, 'Community Action and Anti-Poverty Strategies: Some Transatlantic Comparisons'; J. Higgins, 'Unlearnt Lessons from America'; and P. Shanahan, 'Negotiating the Definition of Community Work in Rural Ireland: A Descriptive Analysis of Three Interventions'.

[16] This fits in with the definition of Community Action accepted by the Boyle Committee in 1973 in its report on 'Current Issues in Community Work' which was the starting point for the Area Resource Centres project. The Committee quoted from a contemporary article in the *British Journal of Social Work* (R. Bryant, Vol. 2, No. 2, 1972):
'Community action may denote a particular approach to organising local groups and welfare publics; an approach in which the political impotence or powerlessness of these groups is defined as a central problem and strategies are employed which seek to mobilise them for the representation and promotion of their collective interests.'

[17] NCCCAP report to Irish National Committee, 1979.

[18] B. Power, *Old and Alone in Ireland*, Society of St Vincent de Paul, Dublin, 1980.

[19] For instance, S. Hatch, *Outside the State*, Croom Helm, 1980; and H. Butcher *et al.*, *Community Groups in Action*, Routledge and Kegan Paul, 1980.

13
The European Dimension[1]

(13.1) BORN EUROPEAN?

In the final analysis, the decision whether or not the European Programme, 1975–80, shall be a precedent for similar actions must rest not on the worthiness of the individual projects, which the Council of Ministers has never disputed, but on the gain in having a programme at European level. Most Member States have a history of supporting anti-poverty projects; why should this activity be passed to Brussels?

Many projects were included in the programme by chance. Member States passed to the Commission applications for government funding which were already at hand. The only selection criteria imposed by the Council Decision were the broad ones of innovation, participation and Community-wide relevance, cited repeatedly in this report. We know of no case of the Commission rejecting a project from a Member State, although the financial assistance requested was not always available in full. In a few cases, on the other hand, the Commission suggested projects to States slow in producing submissions.

The programme was not, therefore, European from birth, in the sense that there was an overall European design in the way that the Irish Programme attempted an overall national design. Certain European elements were, however, built into the 1975 structure:

(i)   The cross-national studies. Initially there were only two, both small and unrelated to the action-research projects. Not until after the December 1977 extension to the programme was this element strengthened.

(ii) The written reports from projects to the Commission. These were conceived mainly as a form of financial control, with instalments of money conditional on activity reports. The small projects — sometimes one-man teams — found the reporting requirement onerous.

(iii) The Commission report on the programme, required before the end of 1976. By this date, few projects had significant experience in the field, and the report could do little more than reproduce the 1975 planning reports.

(iv) The eighteen-member Advisory Group. This seems to have been envisaged by the Council mainly as a group for scrutinising Commission initiatives.[2] There was, however, a brief attempt to use the seven independent experts as an evaluation team in 1977.

If there was to be a European dimension, either the Commission had to create it from the random group of projects in its care, or it had to be brought about by some other agencies, or by the projects themselves.

(13.2)   THE FIRST PHASE, 1975–8

Not until December 1975 were the first contracts signed between the projects and the Commission and many projects did not start work until well into 1976. Not until 1977 did the Commission call the project representatives together to discuss progress. By then the date set by the Council in 1975 for the end of the programme (30 November 1977) was looming ahead, and naturally bulked large in everybody's thoughts.

The 1977 seminar at Chantilly near Paris was not only a social success. Even the dissatisfaction expressed by many participants about some plenary and group sessions was positive, in producing demands for new contacts. The result was three smaller meetings held during 1978 in Brussels. Unfortunately the participants did not seem to find this experience much more satisfactory, complaining of an overstructured schedule at Chantilly and structureless arrangements in Brussels. A major problem was the lack of Commission staff even to attend throughout the Brussels meetings.

In preparation for Chantilly, the independent members of the Advisory Group had been sent on a series of evaluation visits to the projects. The group decided in retrospect that this had not been an effective evaluation exercise, but had greatly increased the group's awareness of project activities.

The Commission's 1976 report was not followed up in 1977, for lack of manpower. The staff allocated to the programme by the Commission were barely enough to handle basic administrative arrangements and prepare proposals for extending the programme.

Nor was it possible to call in outside 'animators' or draw workers from the projects, since all programme funds were committed to project activities. As the Commission reported in 1979,[3] these first years were dominated by the imperatives of birth and survival.

Some spontaneous drawing together among the projects was, meanwhile, beginning to take place. A few had funds to spare for travel, notably the Irish Programme which sent workers to visit projects in Britain and Germany. The Padua team had applied to the UN Social Development Programme for a grant which eventually made possible their visit to Britain and Ireland.

The most significant move occurred in Germany, in response to the threat to end the programme. The projects at Duisburg, Cologne and Stuttgart made a joint approach to their government which undoubtedly influenced the Council Decision of 1977. It was also the beginning of a series of meetings in Frankfurt which the Amberg team later joined and which lasted to the end of the programme.

(13.3)   EXTENSION AND EXPANSION OF THE PROGRAMME

The Council Decision of December 1977 not only prolonged the Poverty Programme to November 1980 but also allowed a limited expansion and required an overall evaluation report. Four new cross-national studies were launched, on unemployment, subjective perceptions of poverty, persistent poverty and nomads. A comparative study of voluntary organisations was abortive. There was still little relation between the studies and the action-research, in spite of the Advisory Group's exhortations to the study leaders. Five new action-research projects were also approved: Belfast, Amberg, Giugliano, LVSC and HVS.

This time the Advisory Group was in being before the projects were presented for approval, giving it the chance of a role it had been formed too late to play in 1975. It met frequently during 1978, although none of the new projects was a group initiative. All resulted from private approaches to the Commission. The group did, however, modify some of the cross-national proposals, particularly those on unemployment and persistent poverty.

The extra finance was more than sufficient for the nine new ventures. A small part of the 'surplus' went to the evaluation exercise, but most went to a set of national studies of poverty and policies to combat it. This initiative came from the newly appointed Italian independent member of the Advisory Group, and was the group's major contribution to the programme. The team leaders met regularly, but again their contacts with the action-research projects were slight, except in France.[4]

The requirement for an evaluation report led to the creation of a new organisation with a Community-wide responsibility, the ESPOIR evaluation unit. Not only did the travels of the ESPOIR observers have a certain cross-fertilising effect, but the team held two European colloquia, at Luxembourg and at Bath, bringing together project workers and outside experts for a detailed discussion of specific activities. They also participated in several national gatherings of project workers. Both the two main colloquia were based on papers prepared by project workers, which had been an ingredient absent at the Chantilly seminar.

(13.4)   THE LAST PHASE, 1978–80

We have already gone ahead of ourselves in describing some of the ESPOIR activities for this period. The Commission remained as active as the small number of staff allotted to the work would permit and an extensive report was issued in October 1979, entitled 'Europe Against Poverty', prepared with the help of the ESPOIR unit.

A second seminar for project leaders was held in 1980 at Brussels, preceded by two smaller meetings to discuss the evaluation exercise and proposals for 1981–2. One effect of having a programme living from one short lease of existence to the next was that a large part of the Commission's energies were always absorbed in preparing proposals for the next renewal of the programme.

The most significant development in this period arose from the projects themselves, threatened by the imminent demise of the programme and inspired by the example of the German projects in lobbying their government in 1977. The deteriorating economic climate also played a part, for most projects were very uncertain of further funds should the programme end, so that a life or death intensity entered the debate. The British projects came together in late 1979 to discuss ways of encouraging their new government to support a continuation of the programme. Several Irish and Continental project workers attended this meeting in London, and from it ESCAP (European Social and Community Action Programme) was born.

ESCAP was principally a lobbying organisation, focusing on the European Parliament. An exhibition was held at the Parliament building in Strasbourg on the day the Commission's proposals for an 'interim programme' were debated. Several MEPs spoke in favour of the proposals, from briefs supplied by ESCAP, and Parliament approved the proposals unanimously. The Council was, however, unmoved by the Parliament's advice and rejected the proposals in June.

ESCAP was also the framework for many other inter-project contacts. For instance, the UK branch of ESCAP met twice in 1980, in the Midlands and Scotland; Craigmillar and Marolles made cultural exchanges; and the leader of the new Italian project at Giugliano was active in visiting his European counterparts to arouse their interest in the role of health services in combating poverty.

(13.5)   CONCLUSION

The programme was not born European, but its participants gradually became aware of themselves as Europeans engaged in a common endeavour. In this it achieved more than many other Commission programmes. It showed that projects whose workers were at the outset motivated principally by parochial concerns can develop an enthusiasm for collaborating with their European counterparts. If the European dimension was not satisfactory in 1975–80, it was a creative dissatisfaction – leading to appeals for a stronger dimension next time. The experience of the last five years indicates that such a strengthened European dimension would be possible, welcome and fruitful.

Notes

[1] Written by Philippa Watson and Edward James.

[2] The Advisory Group was based on a requirement in the 1975 Decision that the Commission should operate 'in close consultation with the Member States on all important matters'.

3 'Europe Against Poverty', Second Report on the Programme of Pilot Schemes and Studies to Combat Poverty, 1979.

4 France alone among the Member States insisted on submitting an official government report. The official allocated to this task was active in bringing together the French projects for a series of joint meetings, chaired by an official from the Ministry of Health.

14
Policy Implications[1]

(14.1) INTRODUCTION

The European Programme was not focused on particular areas of social policy. Instead, the sixty or so actions touch on almost every area of policy, if sometimes fleetingly. In summarising the policy implications one risks presenting either a long 'laundry list' of recommendations specific to different countries and localities, to different groups and services, or a set of observations at such a level of generality that they are rather obvious and not very useful.

Yet the programme does indicate some aspects of policy crucial to the problem of poverty which we feel are worth underlining. These could well be the foci for more systematic exploration in future programmes.

(14.2) POVERTY AND GROWTH

The most obvious and perhaps most important conclusion to be drawn from the European Programme is that each Member State has a poverty problem or, if one defines a problem as something which causes concern, it ought to have a poverty problem since poverty exists its territory. Even wealthy Denmark had more than enough clients for its modest project in Copenhagen, and affluent Germany had four projects of medium size, dealing with vagrants, the homeless, immigrants and social assistance recipients.

The projects in declining areas (Belfast, Govan and Roubaix) suggest that the vital issue is to revive economic growth. With an increasingly large cake to share, the problems of redistribution would clearly be less intractable, but there are two cautions to this formula for eliminating poverty.

First, the lesson of twenty-five years of economic growth is that it creates disparities between regions and groups which public policies have not been very effective in countering. Some regions suffer positively for the sake of prosperity elsewhere. Growth is not an automatic solution to all problems, as the preamble to the ill-fated Social Action Programme pointed out, before the growth slowed up.[2]

Secondly, in most of the Community the economy has continued to expand since 1973, even if slowly and erratically. Most of us are still better off than we have ever been. Unlike the Third World, the European nations could eliminate poverty now through an internal redistribution of resources. The real problem is that redistribution is politically more difficult in a slow-growing economy.

On the other hand, although we look forward to an end to the current recession, we cannot reasonably expect a return to the growth rates of the 1960s. We cannot wait for future wealth to solve our present problems, but must devise solutions within the context of our present resources.

(14.3)   AREA DISCRIMINATION

Apart from the Leiden university survey on subjective poverty, the European Programme says little about the regional distribution of poverty except for the relatively detailed studies in both parts of Ireland. Some of the poorest parts of the Community were not represented at all among the action-research projects, notably the rural Mezzogiorno, western France (apart from Brittany), the Meuse valley and the rural areas of Wales and Scotland.

All that we possess from the under-developed rural periphery of the Community are a few vivid illustrations of life in parts of western Ireland and Brittany. They show us that these are not just areas left behind by the economic growth of other regions; they have directly suffered to contribute to the growth of these regions. Emigration has limited the areas' own potential for growth and created severe welfare problems with the unbalanced demographic structure. A similar picture emerges from the declining industrial regions of central Scotland, Merseyside and South Wales. Industrialisation is not a once and for all catching up. Regions which once led the world in industrial development now present problems similar to the rural areas they once bled for manpower.

These vivid if fragmentary illustrations plead for a reinforced regional policy at national and European levels and for a careful look at the impact of Community agriculture and fishing policies on poverty. At least in parts of Ireland the latter policies seem to be working at odds with regional policy. More attention might also be given to linking community development with economic development, with particular attention to the possibilities of producer co-operatives. The importance of pre-vocational training as a pre-requisite for more specialised training facilities is underlined by several different projects.

The European Programme also documents the distribution of poverty within urban areas. This is done in great statistical detail in Belfast, which also produces some of the most disturbing case studies of urban poverty. We have other examples from Dublin, London, Brussels, Paris, Cologne, Naples and other cities. Besides illustrating the problems of the worn-out hearts of older cities, the programme provides numerous illustrations of poverty in suburban environments. The four Habitat et Vie Sociale projects in France dealt with post-war housing developments on the edges of cities, the Giugliano project operated in an area of new housing near Naples and several other projects (e.g. Cologne and Belfast Welfare Rights) contrasted inner-city and peripheral areas. The large-scale interventions which all Member State governments have made in the housing market since the war have probably spared the poor the worst impact of the shortages which existed, at least locally, in every country. Nonetheless, we have ample evidence that many poor people do not escape housing and environmental deprivation, even in modern subsidised dwellings. The relative isolation of these areas often imposes further costs on the residents in terms of travel to work, commercial and social facilities and the disruption of community and kinship networks.

At least half the projects in the programme were exercises in 'positive discrimination' on an area basis. There has been strong criticism of this approach,[3] but the evidence from the programme is that the spatial allocation of resources within urban areas should be an important focus of policy. At present, there are indications of severe negative discrimination. For instance, the Areas of Special Social Need study in Belfast shows a distribution of many important social facilities that was negatively related to need. The survey did not cover facilities such as transport and shopping, but we have no reason to doubt that a similar relationship exists.

This is an example of the multiplier effect of low income, reducing access not only to goods and services provided through the market, but also to public provision, such as good quality education and recreational facilities. This effect is most evident in poor areas, even if most of the poor do not live in poor areas.

The ASSN survey bears out this last point. Even in Belfast, where the concentration of poverty in particular neighbourhoods is especially marked, a large proportion of the most severely deprived do not live in 'areas of special social need'. Although the action projects rarely show examples of poverty where the poor are a minority, we do get occasional glimpses (e.g. Kilkenny). The answer to 'where are the poor?' is 'almost everywhere', as Booth found in London a century ago, but there are more of them in some places than others.

Area discrimination cannot therefore substitute for national income maintenance services, minimum wage legislation, and the like. Local action to limit the multiplier effects of concentrations of poverty is necessary and urgent, but it cannot eradicate poverty.

(14.4)   GROUP SELECTIVITY

Even before the concern with the geography of poverty, researchers were busy listing groups in the population likely to be poor. The 'rediscovery' of poverty in the 1960s began with marginal groups, such as nomads and the sub-proletariat, leading on to larger and rather less deviant groups, such as ethnic minorities, single-parent families and the elderly. The working poor, that is low wage earners, were a relatively late discovery.

Several projects in the European Programme highlight the poverty of marginal groups: vagrants (Stuttgart), nomads (Ireland and France), 'problem families' (London), 'down and outs' (Copenhagen) and the 'Fourth World' (France, London and the Netherlands). Numerically these may not be a major problem, but they are a test of society's humanity and justice.

The elderly are probably the largest group among the poor. Only two projects in the programme were primarily concerned with old people, both in peripheral areas: the Breton project and the St Vincent de Paul study in Ireland. Both illustrate the deplorable housing conditions of old people in some rural areas. The Cologne project also included a look at the elderly in a central area of a large, rich city and observed that even Germany's generous state pension scheme does not prevent an appreciable number of them living in poverty.

In Cologne researchers linked poverty among the elderly with the weak position of women in the labour market. In earnings-related pensions schemes, low earnings attract low pensions, so that few women could earn substantial pension rights, even with uninterrupted careers. Coupled with the poor provision for widows in the German social security scheme, this meant that the elderly poor were mostly female. On the peripheral housing estate surveyed by the same researchers, there was a similar association between women and poverty, this time with single-parent families (usually mother-headed households, as the Americans term them) as the main poverty group. A woman who is not linked with a male breadwinner runs a severe risk of poverty. No anti-poverty policies can ignore the inequality between the sexes, in pay, social security, family law and other fields. The majority of the poor are either women or children dependent on unsupported mothers.

In general unemployment is still not a major cause of poverty, as Professor Willmott's survey notes. However, it has grown recently to become a dominant cause in many localities (e.g. Belfast). Also, it is the dominant cause among certain groups such as young people, who otherwise are not poverty-prone. Two other aspects of unemployment are brought out in several projects. Apart from young people, unemployment naturally tends to strike at people who already have financial difficulties, such as single-parent families, and the link between unemployment and poverty is growing stronger as the unemployed tend to spend longer out of work and exhaust their social security entitlements. Only Belgium offers an unlimited duration of unemployment benefit.

This points to policies which discriminate in favour of certain categories, or at least reduce the discriminations exercised against them. However, social ills do not strike at random. The poverty categories tend to be recruited unequally from different strata of society. For instance, a stable job not only, by definition, has a low risk of unemployment, but it generates a history of social security contributions sufficient to qualify for the maximum level of benefit should the contingency arise, plus redundancy payments and perhaps other compensation from public or private sources. Another way of looking at the groups in poverty is not to see them as separate groups but as people from a vulnerable stratum of society who for different reasons are going through a phase of their lives in poverty. Likewise poverty neighbourhoods can be seen as concentrations, sometimes temporary, of a low-income population which is part of the fabric of society throughout the country. While we have this vulnerable stratum, we will continue to have 'outbreaks' of poverty among certain groups and in certain areas.

In general social security systems reinforce differences between social strata in their vulnerability to poverty. They improve each income level's capacity to 'look after its own', through earnings-related pensions and other benefits, but the stratum which lacks the resources to look after its less fortunate members gets little help from the others.

The most difficult policy to implement, but the only one which can finally eliminate poverty, is to reduce the inequalities in society which leaves the lower level so vulnerable. As a beginning a minimum wage policy that keeps pace with inflation seems essential provided it is backed by a strong family policy.

(14.5)   SOCIAL MOBILITY

Several projects, as well as the Luxembourg-based study of Professor Schaber, were concerned with the mechanism which keeps people in poverty and transmits it between generations. Some projects indicate a strong inter-generational linkage (ATD France), others a weak one (Cologne). Yet even ATD's research, for instance the follow-up study of ex-residents of the 'Maroc' bidonville at Reims, shows an appreciable amount of social mobility.

In a fast-growing economy, which recruits individuals from lower social groups into expanding skilled technical and managerial occupations, barriers to upward social mobility handicap growth and so prevent poverty being reduced. In a slow-growing economy where the relative number of well-rewarded jobs is not increasing, one person's upward mobility is at the price of another's downward mobility which is no great social gain. Reshuffling the pack does not reduce poverty or make it more acceptable.

(14.6)   POVERTY AND THE SOCIAL SERVICES

Several projects point to the inadequacy of the income maintenance system. The principal criticism is of means-tested benefits (i.e. social assistance). Irish, British and German projects all comment on the widespread ignorance of entitlements and barriers of stigma and administrative complexity. ATD also cites the complex procedures for paying family allowances and their means-tested supplements in France. No expansion of social insurance benefits is likely to avoid the need for means-tested supplements in the foreseeable future, so the effectiveness of the social assistance system must continue to be an area of concern.

In the personal social services, the movement to transform the character of residential care and reduce dependency upon it in favour of community facilities and preventive intervention has by no means exhausted its mission. Projects in France, Germany and Italy present models for such reforms with different groups. All point to the need for greater inter-professional co-operation, particularly between health and social services, and the importance of decentralisation.

Several projects (Brittany, Paris, Stuttgart, Roubaix) emphasise the link between social services and housing. COPES in Paris recognised that most of its deprived children come from sub-standard housing, while PACT in Brittany found it impossible to institute an effective home help scheme in advance of its housing renovation programme (the home helps found the unimproved dwellings impossible to clean). The increasing population in post-war Europe and the big internal migration in many countries made inadequate housing one of the commonest characteristics of poverty. This was particularly true of France. The slow-down in population growth is still too recent to have much impact on the number of new households being formed (the new households currently seeking accommodation are the product of relatively high birth rates in the early 1960s), but we should soon reach a breathing space which must be put to good use. It is possible to break the association between poor housing and low income, as the first Willmott study shows.

The European Programme had few projects which dealt primarily with education. These included the ATD pre-school projects in France and various pre-vocational training schemes for teenagers. The lack of emphasis is partly because of the existence of alternative Commission schemes, under the Social Fund and the Community Action 'School to Work' programme. Several anti-poverty projects have, however, underlined the importance of literacy not only for occupational progress, but for effective citizenship.

The traditional social services are not the only public services which redistribute resources. Town planning redistributes rewards and penalities, not always in favour of the under-privileged (e.g. North

Dublin and Brussels). Recreational facilities and public services are often geared to middle-class needs. All aspects of government need to be sensitive to their effect on the poor.

(14.7) POVERTY AND PARTICIPATION

A large section of the European Programme was devoted to community development activities. For some this may hold out the promise that poor people can overcome their own poverty, if not by individual effort at least by co-operative endeavour. In practice, few poor communities can pull themselves up by their own bootstraps — the bootstraps are not strong enough. Some outside injection of money and skills is necessary if local people are to be expected to contribute their own time and energies. This was the purpose of the Area Resource Centres in the UK and the lesson of the Urban Resource Scheme in Ireland. Community development offers not so much money-saving ideas for the social services, but models of social service and economic activity which do not regulate poor people from outside but give them some control over their own destinies.

Certain projects showed a trend from community development to a community action approach, rather like the nineteenth-century evolution of mutual aid clubs into trade unions, from self-help to collective bargaining. The rediscovery of poverty in the 1960s owed little to militant activity by the poor, although fear of violence among racial minorities may have played a part. For the momentum to be maintained, however, it cannot rely on policies initiated from above. Poor people need to be brought into the pluralistic bargaining system which is western democracy. But it takes resources to bargain for resources (e.g. the difficulty experienced by some projects in getting professional advice to contest town-planning decisions), which is how the poor came to be outside the bargaining system.

The European Programme indicates that both community development and community action projects warrant support from governments and other agencies seriously concerned with fighting poverty. It also shows that sponsors of such projects must be prepared for an uncomfortable ride. At times, projects are certain to press for changes which, for the moment at least, are politically difficult to accept.

It is unlikely that the European Community will eliminate poverty in the foreseeable future, but programmes such as the European Programme of Pilot Schemes to Combat Poverty can alert policy-makers, officials, professional workers, poor people themselves and the general public to the processes which create poverty and, at the very least, help counteract policies which might intensify the problem.

Notes

[1] Written by Edward James.

[2] Social Action Programme — Bulletin of the European Communities, Supplement 2/74.

[3] For instance, at the workshop 'Anti-Poverty Policies in Europe' held at Baden, Austria in September 1977 supported by the European Centre for Social Welfare Training and Research and the UN Division of Social Affairs. See Eurosocial report no. 14 and E Thom, 'Strategies Against Poverty: A Policy Analysis', *International Social Work*, Spring 1980.

PART IV

Conclusions

15
A Mandate Fulfilled?[1]

Columbus set sail for Japan, not America, reminding us that the significance of an enterprise is not only to be measured against its declared aims. However, an evaluation cannot avoid comparing achievements with declared aims, even if it tries to go beyond this. The Council of Ministers laid down certain broad objectives when it charged the Commission to carry out the Programme of Pilot Schemes to Combat Poverty in its decision of 22 July 1975. Our first task therefore will be to examine how far the Commission fulfilled its mandate.

First, how successful were the Commission, the Member States and the other agencies involved in translating the authority to spend money contained in the Council Decision (Article 1) into a set of activities on the ground? Did these activities represent a real increase in the level of study and action-research in this field or merely a transfer of support from one source of funds to another? Were these activities a distinctive addition to the range of activities already supported by the Community? We have considered these three related issues under the heading 'an effective programme?'

The Council Decision required the programme 'to test and develop new methods of helping persons beset with or threatened by poverty' (Article 1a). In consequence, our next two sections examine whether this was truly an anti-poverty programme and whether it was innovative.

The Decision also required the participation of the target population (Article 1a). The fourth section of this chapter considers this issue and the fifth section considers whether there was a sufficient research element to justify the requirement for studies to improve the understanding of poverty (Article 1b). Finally, in response to the requirement that projects should address themselves to issues of concern to more than one Member State (Article 1a), we have asked whether this was a European Programme in any sense other than being part financed by the Community.

(15.1) AN EFFECTIVE PROGRAMME?

It is implicit in every Council Decision involving a financial intervention that the money set aside shall result in contracts being made, money spent and relevant activities taking place within the time limits laid down. For those inexperienced with financial intervention programmes at Community or national levels, this achievement may seem to go without saying. In practice new programmes often fail to commit all the allocated funds within the initial time limit and contractants often fail to spend all their money on activities in the field. This has been the case many times with the Social and Regional funds and Overseas Development Aid.[2]

The record of the anti-poverty programme compares favourably with that of other Community interventions, considering it was a novel programme, speedily mounted and with very short time limits for the adoption of new schemes. Longer time limits for adopting new schemes and pluriannual contracts, enabling 'underspending' at one stage to be set against 'over-spending' later on, would have avoided most of the under-spending which did occur.

All Member States except Luxembourg co-sponsored projects either through their national, regional or local administrations. The Luxembourg government withdrew support for its two action-research projects in June 1976, after the date limit set by the Council for accepting further projects. This was the cause of some of the money allocated to the programme being unspent. Only one project, in Copenhagen, ended prematurely, in this case because its leaders failed to find alternative funding after a private bequest had been exhausted. A plan to make good the deficit by the commercial activities of the poor themselves had to be abandoned.

A few projects had delays in getting started, notably the project at Govan near Glasgow. A very few did not get under way with their main activities during the life of the programme, as was the case with the PACT project at Orange in France and the Habitat et Vie Sociale projects. The contracts for the latter were, however, only signed in September 1979. It is easy to under-estimate the starting-up time necessary to launch a new project particularly if, as the Council recommended, the population concerned participates in the planning as well as the execution. This is even more true when, as with PACT and HVS, the project activity has to be co-ordinated with that of several other agencies, each with its own potential for delay.

Some very successful projects took over two years to develop the full rhythm of their activities. The project in Brittany was held up for almost two years, mobilising the finance for its house improvement programme with which the Commission-funded 'social component' was linked. The Irish projects also got off to a very slow start. But for the extension of the programme in 1977 there would have been little to show for these projects. Other projects also entered their most fruitful phase after 1977. The Cologne project, for instance, only started its welfare rights activities throughout North Rhine-Westphalia in 1978, while the Stuttgart project moved from its concern with vagrants in hostels to developing non-residential alternatives and preventive work.

As for the cross-national studies and the national reports, difficulties were encountered and time lost in launching the comparative study of voluntary welfare agencies and the study on Gypsies originally entrusted to the Romany Congress. These two contracts broke down before the main research started due to unforeseeable events. The Commission eventually found alternative researchers, after considerable modifications to the research design.

In short, the programme successfully promoted a great deal of activity. Its effectiveness would have been far less had the programme been terminated in 1977 as envisaged in the 1975 Council Decision and it would have been greater had the programme been offered a five-year guarantee at the outset and had the financial arrangements been more flexible than the system of annual contracts in use for most of the programme.

Did the activities which were promoted, represent a real increase in the amount of study and action-research carried out or did the Commission finance activities which would have taken place in any event with other funds? Hypothetical questions can rarely be given conclusive answers. Since public authorities provided half the cost of almost every action-research project it would have been surprising if none had been willing to take full charge of at least some of them had the European Programme not existed, particularly since the governments had been free to propose almost any type of anti-poverty project they wished. We estimate that just over half the action-research projects outside Ireland might well have been funded in 1975 without Community support, but none of the cross-national studies is likely to have taken place without it. The Irish programme was set up in the expectation of Community funds, although the government guaranteed it if the European Programme failed to get Council approval. The changing economic and political situation in Ireland after 1975, evidenced by the Combat Poverty budget cuts in early 1980, makes it improbable that, had the Irish programme gone ahead on government money alone, it would have been sustained at the level at which it operated as part of the European Programme. Instead, the programme might have closed down in the seventies and most of the twenty-six eventual projects would never have been started.

Similarly Craigmillar and the Marolles might well have been funded without Community support in 1975, although whether they would have obtained so much money from elsewhere is doubtful. Both these projects had severe problems in keeping open their other sources of finance during the period 1975–80. Without Community funds some curtailment of activities would probably have been inevitable.

The Padua project, which employed almost a fifth of the European Programme's funds, possibly had sufficient political backing to have operated without Community support. Certainly, the Italian government and the municipality seemed intent on carrying it forward after 1980. On the other hand, the municipality had to make difficult sacrifices to maintain the project, particularly during the freeze on hiring extra local government staff in 1976.

The fact that funding for anti-poverty projects became much more difficult to obtain and retain over the period 1975–80 enhanced the importance of the programme. In a small way it cushioned the general cut-back in research support. A successor programme is likely to be born in a climate of austerity. For cross-national projects with the possibility of 100 per cent Community support this will enhance the significance of the programme. On the other hand, for 50 per cent funded projects there may be an increased tendency to use Community funds to cover expenditure to which the national government is already committed. This is an argument for the Commission (not necessarily the Council) to impose stricter criteria on the selection of projects (see Section 15.6).

This speculation on 'might have beens' has practical implications. If the field operations would have taken place in any event the most effective use for Community funds might well have been to have concentrated them on co-ordinating, animating, recording and evaluating the programme, leaving the rest to be paid for from national sources. This is a tempting argument which recognises that the over-riding value of the programme was its European dimension and seeks to achieve this as economically as possible. There are precedents for this division of responsibility between the Commission and the Member States,[3] but in the case of the Poverty Programme where not all Member States have a tradition of this type of research, it would probably not have been possible to involve them all without direct Community support for field operations. Without such support there would also have been a strong risk of the programme being cut back during the course of the 1970s. Funding of field operations was also a gesture of commitment by the Community and created a direct link between it and the project workers. We feel that funding of field operations was essential even if in some cases it substituted for rather than augmented national spending.

The likelihood of finding alternative funds was usually higher with projects run by government agencies than by non-government bodies, while the resources available from the Commission were much more significant in relation to the total resources of non-government bodies. The programme was therefore justified on grounds of effectiveness in devoting a large part of its funds to the non-government sector.

Might not the Commission have funded these or similar projects under some other part of its budget, had there been no anti-poverty programme? Other programmes run by the Commission have included pre-vocational training schemes for teenagers (education), producers' co-operatives, inner-city employment initiatives and training schemes for alcoholics and drop-outs (Social Fund) and other projects similar to some in the anti-poverty programme. However, it is unlikely that any extra funds would have gone to these programmes had the anti-poverty initiative not been launched. The Poverty Programme provided additional funds for this type of activity, and even though some projects were similar to those run by other services of the Commission, there were others which would have found difficulty in fitting into any other programme. Also, poverty is not an operational concept in any other Commission programme: the label was important in giving recognition to the problem.

(15.2) AN ANTI-POVERTY PROGRAMME?

The Council expressly included in the target group those 'threatened' as well as those 'beset' by poverty and they defined poverty in broad relative terms. The Commission accordingly did not oblige projects to impose a poverty test on the users of their services, but let each project justify its relevance to poverty in its own way. This is in contrast to the American War on Poverty in which there were strict income limits on the users of projects such as Head Start.

In our view all the European projects were directly relevant to the needs of poor people. An income test on the users of project services would have militated against the projects which were most successful in fighting poverty. For instance, it would have excluded the Ginger-bread project in Croydon because it succeeded in keeping single parents out of poverty.

Other projects would have rejected the 'means test' approach on philosophical grounds. The Padua project in particular was anxious to universalise its socio-medical services, believing that services reserved for poor people inevitably become second-rate and stigmatising.

Not all projects, on their own admission, served the very poorest people in their localities. Community development and action projects tend to work with the more active and articulate members of the community; to ignore these would be to forgo the opportunity to raise the economic and social level of many poor areas. At the same time, ventures such as the ATD projects and some of the Family Day Centres discriminated in favour of the most deprived. The programme served the poor without neglecting the poorest of the poor.

Anti-poverty projects have sometimes been criticised as employment schemes for social workers and researchers. Professional salaries were the principal expense of most projects in the European Programme but increasingly many of them recruited workers from the local population, besides involving numerous volunteers. A major thrust of the programme was to develop alternatives to professional social work services.

(15.3)   AN INNOVATIVE PROGRAMME?

The Council Decision required projects to 'test out new methods' of combating poverty. But how new is 'new'? None of the projects developed methods which were completely novel to the ESPOIR team or its consultants. This is understandable since a project is unlikely to attract public funds until professional opinion has been sensitised to a particular issue or approach over several years. Pilot schemes are a further stage in the sensitisation process, building on each other's experience until their techniques and approaches drop out of favour or become part of the conventional wisdom.

We cannot therefore demand total originality from any project proposed by its government for inclusion in the European Programme. Rather, we must expect ideas that may have been current for some time but are not yet conventional. The main claim to originality in most projects was the application of an established idea in new settings or the introduction into a Member State of approaches and techniques pioneered beyond its borders.

Some project workers tended to be defensive on the point of originality (as was evident at the 1980 'Action Against Poverty' seminar), fearful perhaps that they might be asked to produce some radical new discoveries. Some workers from the smaller British projects went so far as to reject innovation as a relevant criterion – their first responsibility was to serve their chosen group to the best of their ability by either traditional or innovative means.

In fact there was an identifiable element of originality in every project, as we have pointed out in our commentaries on individual schemes. We recall as examples:

> New forms of residential care for vulnerable groups (children, vagrants, old people, psychiatric patients) and the development of non-residential alternatives and preventive care (Paris, Stuttgart, Guéméné, Naples, Padua).
> Ways of making services more accessible to poor people, through decentralisation, information services etc. (Padua, Paris, Edinburgh, Cologne, Naples).
> Educating poor people to an awareness of the rights and opportunities available to them and helping them to claim them (Wolverhampton, Cologne, Dublin, S. Wales, Belfast).
> Stimulating self-help ventures in recreational facilities, child care and employment, notably producer co-operatives (rural Ireland, S. Wales, Glasgow, Brussels, London).
> Educational and training activities for children of all ages and teenagers, particularly from marginal groups (London, Paris, Reims, Roubaix, Brussels, Dublin. W. Ireland, Duisburg).
> Articulating the needs of poor people to the wider society and developing structures through which they can participate in decision-making (Ireland, London, Brussels, Cologne, Breda, Reims).

Somewhere in the European Programme there may have been the germ of a new idea, which in time may transform our entire approach to poverty, but that we can only know in the light of history. All we can safely affirm is that there have been incremental advances, building up our experience of various techniques in different circumstances and in different combinations, and some diffusionist gains in spreading ideas across frontiers.

(15.4)   A PARTICIPATORY PROGRAMME?

In 1964 President Johnson had spoken of 'maximum feasible participation'; the Council of Ministers spoke of projects which were 'planned and carried out, as far as possible, with the participation of those concerned'. Unlike the Americans,[4] neither the Council nor the Commission attempted to lay down a formula for participation. Each project was left to justify its participatory nature in its own fashion, just as it was left to justify its own relevance to poverty.

The 'reform from above' type of project had the greatest practical difficulties in securing participation. The Padua workers recognised this as their main shortcoming, having had little success in interesting the neighbourhood councils in social and medical services. The four Habitat et Vie Sociale projects were part of a nationwide reform from above programme which followed the American and European examples with a general requirement for participation. The discussions at the 1980 HVS seminar in Paris demonstrated the difficulties of carrying this into practice. Participation ranged from active collaboration with local groups to in-depth interviews with a representative sample of consumers. Accusations that the latter was mere 'consultation' were met with a challenge to the representativity of self-selected citizens' groups.

At the other end of the scale, the local grass-roots groups had few worries about participation; in general they were service-oriented groups with participation inherent in their organisation. Self-conscious anxieties about participation were strongest among projects where participation was an objective but was not inherent in the structure, the workers being mostly professionals, employed by outside public or semi-public agencies. In the evocative French phrase, they are 'parachuted' into the local community.

Our chapter on the strategies employed by projects deals with the ways they achieved participation. The only ones to achieve mass participation were Marolles and Craigmillar, both of which had been in operation for nearly twenty years. However, nearly all projects succeeded in mobilising groups of local people around particular issues, as co-operatives, claimants' unions, tenants' associations and the like. Most of the parachutists succeeded in 'going native', recruiting local staff and organising locally approinted management committees. In at least one case (Downtown Family Day Centre), the original workers withdrew completely to leave the enterprise to indigenous workers.

In summary, the many forms of participation and self-help developed in the European Programme not only fulfil the Council criteria but are one of the programme's most important achievements.

(15.5) A RESEARCH PROGRAMME?

The Commission was required to conduct studies 'to improve understanding of the nature, causes, scope and mechanics of poverty'. The 1975 Decision did not require schemes (i.e. action-research) and studies to be mutually exclusive. In practice all the action-research projects contributed in some way to our understanding of poverty, as witnessed by our chapter on that theme. Some action projects included specific long-term research components as with the Irish study of social welfare allowances and the ATD Reims study on the income of poor families.

The 1975 Council Decision made separate provision for cross-national studies which the Commission could fund 100 per cent. In the initial programme there were only two short-term social surveys, but after 1977 the cross-national element expanded sharply, rising to six studies plus the set of eight national reports on poverty and the ESPOIR exercise, in all 20 per cent of the programme budget. As noted earlier, the study on voluntary social welfare agencies had to merge with the eight national reports while the second Gypsy study was eventually confined to four Member States.

In its last years the European Programme thus included a considerable cross-national research element. However, a large part of this was taken up with the national reports which the Commission expressly excluded from the evaluation exercise. Although certain pairs of studies were closely related, as with the first and second three-nation surveys by Professor Willmott and the two Gypsy studies, overall they had little relation to each other or to the action-research projects.

We feel that the Council was right to emphasise the research role of the programme, and that cross-national studies were an important feature which should be developed in any future programme. Not that there should necessarily be more cross-national studies, but they should be linked with some of the themes explored by the action-research projects, perhaps helping to link groups of projects around common themes.

(15.6)   A EUROPEAN PROGRAMME?

The Council required each action-research project to 'deal with problems common to more than one Member State'. The programme certainly demonstrated that poverty is endemic in the Community. Thus it could be argued that all anti-poverty projects have been shown to have a Community-wide relevance. One would imagine, however, that the Council had in mind that projects should address themselves to particular aspects of poverty known to exist in more than one state. The lack of much cross-national research before 1975 made the existence of such aspects often speculative, so that a useful role for the first phase of the programme might have been to establish what common aspects there were.

This has been achieved to only a very limited degree, largely because the action-research projects in different countries were not designed to complement each other (except perhaps with the ATD projects). The cross-national studies were valuable, but initially there were only two, and they never had more than accidental relevance to the work of the action-research enterprises.

The lack of planned relevance to common problems might have been offset by a relevance discovered or developed during the life of the programme, through contacts between project workers in different countries. Our chapter on the European dimension outlines the history of these contacts, concluding that awareness of common problems and objectives was beginning to emerge by the end of 1980.

The developments were hampered by lack of staff and funds to promote international contacts, but it would have been extremely optimistic to have imagined that such a heterogeneous collection of schemes could ever have been knitted into a coherent research enter-

prise. The Commission would be well advised, in any future programme, to draw up a set of priorities in consultation with the Member
States and, more importantly, insist that all projects accepted for
Commission support should be compatible with these priorities. This
would have to be reconciled with the political necessity of spreading
projects among all Member States, if necessary by providing Commission advice on the setting up of suitable projects.

(15.7) SUMMARY OF ACHIEVEMENTS

Judged by the criteria of the Council Decision the verdict on the
European Programme can be expressed concisely:

1. The programme was effective in running a large range of activities
   of direct relevance to the needs of the poor, at least half of which
   would probably not have been run without Commission support.
2. All the action-research projects were to varying degrees innovative
   in their regional and national contexts and all of them developed
   structures for the participation of the people they served. The
   development of these structures was indeed the principal purpose
   of several projects.
3. Very limited resources were put into exploring the mutual relevance of experiences across frontiers and the programme was not
   structured to facilitate this. Very little has therefore been achieved
   in this respect. The beginnings of more intensive contacts between projects in the last stages of the programme may help
   develop ways of achieving this in the future.

Notes

[1] Written by Edward James.

[2] See the Court of Auditors' report on the Commission budget for 1978.
    Official Journal of the European Communities, special issue, Volume 22, C236,
    1979.

[3] For instance, in sharing the experience of local authorities on sewage
    disposal and other environmental topics through STCELA (Standing
    Technological Conference of European Local Authorities).

[4] The American formula (1967) was that each local community action
    programme should have a board of management, a third of whose members

were representatives of the poor, either as residents of poor areas or persons with a close association with the poor, e.g. pastors of poor parishes or leaders of trade unions in low-paid occupations. In the event, most board members were poor by association. Several CAPs (e.g. Philadelphia) organised elections in poor areas, with generally disappointingly low turnouts.

For an analysis of participation levels in five Californian CAPs, see R. M. Kramer, *Participation of the Poor: Comparative Community Case Histories in the War on Poverty*, Prentice Hall, 1979.

16
Conclusions and Prospects[1]

(16.1) POVERTY AND THE EUROPEAN COMMUNITY

The European Poverty Programme ended in 1980. There is now a hiatus, while the Council of Ministers and the European Parliament consider the Commission's report on the programme, which was presented in December 1981. At first sight, the prospects for a further poverty programme or, better still, a full-blooded Community anti-poverty policy, are not good.

The first Poverty Programme was born in the early 1970s at a time of continuing economic growth. It was part of an attempt to create a 'human face' for the European Community; to create a social Europe alongside the Europe of industrialists and farmers; to celebrate the economic successes of the European Community with a flourish of social concern. Over the subsequent five years, the energy crisis and the deepening recession have seen economic growth come to a virtual standstill; inflation and unemployment are now the pressing issues of public debate and political concern; and the Community's budget is close to its ceiling and in a state of crisis.

Nevertheless, the need for a co-ordinated Community-wide attack on poverty is, if anything, even more pressing in 1981 than it was in the early 1970s. The Poverty Programme has demonstrated, first, that poverty has worsened during the 1970s as a concomitant of the deepening recession. Secondly, the programme reveals that poverty is by no means confined to marginal groups of Europe's population; rather, the poor are those who suffer most severely the economic and social disruption to which the citizens of the European Community are much more generally subject. Thirdly, the programme suggests that in the 1980s new forms of deprivation and poverty are likely to be the fate of increasing numbers of people, as a result of rapid technological change coupled with a continuing high level of unemployment. Finally, the programme has demonstrated that poverty is a *European* problem in at least two senses: poverty takes similar forms in the different Member States, and it is linked to wider social, economic and political changes which transcend national boundaries and which include many of the traditional areas of activity of the European Commission.[2]

1981 saw the beginning of a major debate within the European Community over its expenditure priorities. It seems likely that social and regional policies will in the future be given greater weight. The entry of Greece and, in due course, of Spain and Portugal will add further to the pressures for more energetic social policies at the Community level, including measures to combat poverty in its various forms. The European Poverty Programme demonstrates the potential value of co-ordinated action to combat poverty throughout the Community: whether or not the various participants in these debates will attend to its lessons remains to be seen.

A co-ordinated Community attack on poverty would not of course be limited to activities by the Directorate-General for Employment, Social Affairs and Education; rather, it would range across all of the Community's policies which have an impact on the creation, persistence or alleviation of poverty. Or, at the very least, procedures would be established for monitoring this impact.[3]

(16.2)   THE FUTURE OF PILOT PROGRAMMES

Whether or not the Community embarks upon such a broad anti-poverty policy, an important place will remain for the sort of pilot programme which has just ended. As seen in earlier chapters, the first Poverty Programme has involved four distinct elements, none of which has realised its full potential, but each of which has demonstrated its value. All four elements would need to be combined in a more integrated strategy in future pilot programmes.

(i)   In each the Member States a national report has been commissioned on the extent and patterns of poverty and on the success of existing social policies in combating poverty. In some countries, this research has had more of a pioneering character than in others, and here these reports may serve to sensitise public opinion to the persistence and dimensions of poverty in the midst of relative affluence. Nevertheless, the various research teams have to some extent gone their own way and only to a limited extent are the reports comparable with each other.

(ii) The cross-national studies have taken a much narrower and more specific focus than the national reports, but they have been more successful in achieving cross-national consistency of approach and comparable results. However, as argued in Chapter 10 above, not all of them succeed in relating their findings to the broader national contexts of the various Member States, nor do they all succeed in generating specific policy proposals.

(iii) The action projects have been practical experiments in social change which have enlisted the participation of the poor themselves, in ways which demonstrate how social welfare measures more generally might be made more effective. The projects have also, however, made their own distinctive contribution to our understanding of poverty, through a process of *action-research*. Although the conventional academic researcher can include large numbers of respondents in his examples, he often provides only a 'snapshot' of a single moment in time; in contrast, the action-researchers in the European Programme have engaged in a continuing dialogue with the poor and have monitored a continuing process of social action. The conventional academic researcher tends often to reify the formal institutions of society and to portray people as merely adjusting to those institutions; in contrast, the action-researchers have been able to explore how the poor can contest and challenge existing social arrangements and creatively experiment in alternatives. This action-research also, however, exposes the barriers and obstacles to this creative action and, therefore, the distribution of power in the wider society that perpetuates poverty.

There have, however, been two obstacles limiting what these action projects could achieve. The rushed start to the European Programme and the uncertainties and delays over funding have denied many projects the stable and assured planning horizon which they need, if they are to build up a relationship of mutual trust with the disadvantaged, and if the innovatory activities are to become self-sustaining. Secondly, they have worked in relative isolation from each other, and there has been insufficient opportunity for the strategies which they have individually developed to be tested by other projects in a variety of different contexts. In future programmes, therefore, there should be multinational teams of projects tackling similar problems and engaged in the collaborative adaptation of the strategies which they individually develop. In addition, there must be more explicit provision for the dissemination of their work, so that future European programmes can be an effective vehicle for a cross-national exchange of innovations which can benefit a much wider audience also. It is by this new form of cross-national action-research that practical skills and knowledge which can be used for combating poverty can best be tested out, exchanged and diffused.[4]

(iv) The evaluation exercise in which we ourselves were engaged has suffered from certain limitations, but it also provides lessons for future programmes, as seen in Chapter 2. In brief, any future evaluation exercise should (a) extend over at least the period of the programme as a whole; (b) be co-ordinated at the outset with the various other evaluation systems existing within particular portions of the programme; (c) be accompanied by a process of more intensive *animation* than has obtained in the present programme.

(16.3) CONCLUSIONS

Whether or not the Community engages in further measures designed specifically to combat poverty will depend ultimately – as also will their scale – upon the governments of the Member States. It remains to be seen, if these governments decide against such measures, whether it will nevertheless be possible for the Commission and Parliament to keep poverty as an issue on the political agenda of the European Community. At the very least, even if there is no continuing Poverty Programme, it might be possible for the Commission to provide a communications system among action workers, researchers and policy-makers dealing with problems of deprivation and poverty in the different Member States. Out of this process of communication would then come a continuing flow of ideas and proposals for possible initiatives at national and European levels, based upon their pooled experiences. Poverty would remain an issue on the European policy agenda; and a European dimension would be injected into the national poverty debates in the different Member States.

Notes

[1] Written by Graham Room.

[2] See especially Chapter 11 above on *Understanding Poverty*.

[3] A precedent for such an exercise may be found in the Fourth Annual Report of the Regional Development Fund (1978) (COM) (79) (349), paras. 98–107.

[4] See also Section (2.6) above.

Appendix 1

Key Commission Documents

All of these documents are available from the Directorate General for Employment and Social Affairs, Commission of the European Communities, 200 rue de la Loi, B 1049 Brussels, Belgium.

Working Paper on Pilot Schemes, 1974 (V/650/74-E)

'Council Decision of 22 July 1975 concerning a programme of pilot schemes and studies to combat poverty' (75/458/EEC), *Official Journal of the European Communities*, 30 July 1975 (No. L 199/34).

'Council Decision of 12 December 1977' (77/779/EEC), *Official Journal of The European Communities* 17 December 1977 (No. L 322/28).

Report from the Commission to the Council (First Report), (COM(76)718), 13 January 1977.

Second Report of the European Programme of Pilot Schemes and Studies to Combat Poverty (COM(79)537), 17 October 1979.

Interim Evaluation Report on the Programme to Combat Poverty (COM(80)666), 4 November 1980.

Europe Against Poverty: Evaluation Report of the European Programme of Pilot Schemes and Studies to Combat Poverty (ESPOIR Report), 5 volumes, November 1980.

Final Report from the Commission to the Council on the First Programme of Pilot Schemes and Studies to Combat Poverty (COM(81)769), November 1981.

Appendix 2

Addresses of Participants

The addresses of the various participants in the Programme are given below, in case readers wish to seek further information about the work of particular projects and studies. However, many of the projects no longer exist and many of the research teams have turned their attention to new fields of investigation. We cannot guarantee, therefore, that readers who try to make contact with them will in every instance be successful.

The numbering indicates the section of the book which deals with the project or study concerned.

M. R. Draperie
EUROPEAN COMMISSION
Directorate General for Employment and Social Affairs
200, rue de la Loi
B 1049 Brussels
Belgium

Action Projects

BELGIUM
3.2   Pere J. van der Biest
          Comité général d'Action des Marolles,
          3 rue de la Prevoyance,
          1000 Bruxelles

DENMARK
3.4   Hr G. Mortag
          Kofoeds Skole,
          Nyrnberggade 1
          2300 Kobenhavn S

FRANCE

4.2   Dr M. Soule
       Centre d'Orientation Psychologique et Social
       COPES,
       23 rue Lalande,
       75014 Paris

4.3   M. B. Couder
       Mouvement ATD – Science et Service,
       57 rue de Venise,
       51100 Reims

4.3   Mme G. Duche
       ATD – Science et Service,
       122 Avenue de Général Leclerc,
       95480 Pierrelaye

4.4   M. C. Chigot
       Fédération Nationale des Centres PACT,
       4 Place de Vénétie,
       75643 Paris

4.5   M. A. Trintignac
       Habitat et Vie Sociale
       14, Rue Saint-Benoit,
       75006 Paris

GERMANY

5.2   Dr W. Breuer
       Institut für Sozialforschung und
       Gesellschaftspolitik,
       29–31 Sachsenring,
       5 Köln 1

5.3   Frau U. Becher
       c/o Institut für Sozialarbeit und Socialpädagogik,
       Am Stockborn 5–7,
       6000 Frankfurt 50

5.4 Dr A. von Keyserlingk
Verein für Soziale Heimstätten (Stuttgart)
und Psychologisches Institut der
Universität Tübingen
29 Falkertstrasse,
7 Stuttgart 1

5.5 Herr. W. Würstendörfer
Sozialwissenschaftliches Forschungszentrum (SFZ)
der Universität Erlangen-Nürnberg,
Findelgasse 7–9,
8500 Nuernberg

IRELAND

6 Father M. Mernagh
Irish National Committee on Pilot Schemes
to Combat Poverty,
8 Charlemont Street,
Dublin 2

ITALY

7.1 Prof O. Terranova
Amministrazione comunale di Padova
Palazzo Moroni,
Padova

7.2 Dr L. Carrino
Comune di Giugliano,
Centro di medicina sociale
Via Colonna 43
80014 Giugliano (Napoli)

NETHERLANDS

3.3 Mevr A. Howeler
Stichting ATD – Nederland,
Habbemastraat 125,
Den Haag

UNITED KINGDOM

8.2.2   Dr J. Graham
        Northern Ireland Dept. of Health and Social Services, Dept.
        of Finance, Statistics and Economics Unit, Stormont,
        Belfast BT4 3SW

8.2.3   Dr E Evason
        (Welfare Rights)
        Dept. of Social Administration,
        The New University of Ulster
        Coleraine BT22 1SA

8.3   Mr M. Stock
        National Association of Citizens Advice Bureaux
        West Midland Area Tribunal Representation Unit,
        63 Waterloo Road,
        Wolverhampton WV1 4QU

8.4   Mrs P. Willmott
        Institute of Community Studies
        18 Victoria Park Square
        Bethnal Green
        London E2 9PF

8.4.1   Miss M. Rabagliati
        ATD Fourth World
        48 Addington Square
        London SE 5

8.4.2   Ms R. Gallagher
        Camden Family Service Unit
        62 Camden Street
        London NW 1

8.4.3   Ms D. Corner
        Croydon Gingerbread Group
        c/o 28 Bishopscourt
        Radcliffe Road
        Croydon
        Surrey

8.4.4   Ms J. Cameron
         Defoe Day Care Centre
         Hackney College
         Ayrsome Road
         London N16

8.4.5   Mrs M. Willis
         COPE
         London Voluntary Service Council
         68 Chalton Street
         London NW1 1JR

8.4.6   Mr C. Rochester
         Downtown Family Centre,
         c/o Cambridge House and Talbot
         131 Camberwell Road
         London SE5 OHF

8.4.7   Mr T. Heavey
         Liverpool Personal Services Society
         34 Stanley Street
         Liverpool L1 6AN

8.5   Mr A. Simpson
         Govan Area Resource Centre
         121 Langlands Road
         Glasgow G51

8.5   Mr M. Fleetwood
         South Wales Anti-Poverty Action Committee
         55 Pontcanna Street
         Cardiff
         Wales

8.5   Mr L. Donnelly
         Community Work Service,
         London Voluntary Service Council
         68 Chalton Street
         London NW1 1JR

8.5   Professor R. Lees and Mrs M. Mayo
         Polytechnic of Central London
         76–78 Mortimer Street
         London W1

8.6   Mrs D. Dalton
        Social and Community Development Project
        Urban Regeneration Programme
        Lothian Regional Council
        George VI Bridge
        Edinburgh EH49

8.7   Mrs H. Crummy
        Craigmillar Festival Society
        108 Mountcastle Drive South,
        Edinburgh EH15 3LL

CROSS-NATIONAL STUDIES

9.2.2   Prof B. van Praag
        Economisch Instituut
        Hugo de Grootstraat 32
        2311 XK Leiden
        Netherlands

9.2.3–
9.2.4   Prof P. Willmott
        Institute of Community Studies
        18 Victoria Park
        London E2 9PF

9.2.5   Prof G. Schaber
        Institut Pédagogique
        Walferdange
        Grand-Duche de Luxembourg

9.2.6   Mme David
        Les Etudes Tsiganes,
        2 rue d'Hautpoul
        75019 Paris
        France

9.2.6   Prof M. Chaumont and M. P. Grell
        CACS
        Université Catholique de Louvain,
        B1348 Louvain-la-Neuve
        Belgium

Index

This index is limited to the principal participants in the European Programme. In the case of the individual projects and studies, bold type indicates where the principal discussion of their work may be found.